T0383147

"What Phil Kirby has done for Bostik's business in the Americas has been transformational and this insightful book covers all the reasons why process thinking is so critical. *The Process Mind* business model opens capacity, reduces cycle times, improves quality, improves customer service and enhances the safety environment. Incredibly, we spent almost zero capital and employees have never been more engaged."

Bob Marquette, CEO
Bostik, USA

"I have worked with Phil Kirby in several companies over the years and with his help we have delivered consistent year-over-year financial growth while improving our work place. If you're serious about organizational change, you have to change the way you think! This book tells you how to do it."

Eric Sejourne, Group VP
Assa Abloy, USA

"If you want to dominate your competition and double your productivity then Philip Kirby's business process model and *The Process Mind* is for you!"

Peter Psichogios, President, CSI International
Founder, Blanchard Solutions Group, part of the Ken Blanchard Companies (The One Minute Manager *and* Situational Leadership II—*the world's most widely taught leadership development system*)

"This book is chock-full of what process thinking is all about. By adopting the principles and methods of *The Process Mind*, we have never been better at meeting customers' needs with more efficient and flexible processes, and all at lower costs."

Gary Haley, CEO
Vantage Foods, Canada

"I have worked with Phil Kirby on identifying improvements to a recruitment process. The results were immediate. The time required to fill a role fell by 25%, the number of steps in the hiring process were halved, turnover rates fell, with more recruits making it past the crucial first 90 days on the job. Cost per hire dropped 34%. Read *The Process Mind*, you owe it to those who work for you."

Liza Provenzano, Human Resources Executive and Founder
SparkHR Inc.

"Phil Kirby is a master in the art of implementing continuous improvement. He combines his passion for eliminating process waste with his deep experience for engaging employees and changing behaviors. At three different companies, Phil helped me create and then implement plans and structure, which transformed our operations and delivered real business results. Now he has documented his powerful methodology in *The Process Mind*."

Chris Mosby—Vice President Operations
A.W. Chesterton Company

"In *The Process Mind*, Kirby teaches us how to truly understand the collective thought of our organizations—the thoughtware—and then how to change it strategically, effectively and in a fact—based manner. This is a must read for anyone looking to change how they make change in their organization."

Mary-Kay Lippert, VP Operations
Fluidigm Canada Inc.

PHILIP KIRBY

THE PROCESS

MIND

NEW THOUGHTWARE® FOR DESIGNING YOUR BUSINESS ON PURPOSE

CRC Press
Taylor & Francis Group
Boca Raton   London   New York

CRC Press is an imprint of the
Taylor & Francis Group, an **informa** business

A PRODUCTIVITY PRESS BOOK

Thoughtware® is a registered trademark of Organization Thoughtware International Inc.

CRC Press
Taylor & Francis Group
6000 Broken Sound Parkway NW, Suite 300
Boca Raton, FL 33487-2742

© 2015 by Taylor & Francis Group, LLC
CRC Press is an imprint of Taylor & Francis Group, an Informa business

No claim to original U.S. Government works

Printed on acid-free paper
Version Date: 20140917

International Standard Book Number-13: 978-1-4822-2895-3 (Hardback)

Library of Congress Cataloging-in-Publication Data

Kirby, J. Philip.
    The process mind : new thoughtware for designing your business on purpose / Philip Kirby.
        pages cm
    Includes bibliographical references and index.
    ISBN 978-1-4822-2895-3 (hardback)
    1. Organizational change. 2. Organizational behavior. I. Title.

HD58.8.K51789 2015
658.4'013--dc23   2014013460

Visit the Taylor & Francis Web site at
http://www.taylorandfrancis.com

and the CRC Press Web site at
http://www.crcpress.com

In memory of Stefanie

Contents

Foreword

In August of 2011, Bostik was facing a crisis. In one sector of the business, our ability to properly service customers had reached a critical level. On-time / in-full delivery rates had reached a low of 10%, inventories were climbing, lead times had increased to 21 days from an industry standard of 5 days, and people were losing confidence in our ability to fix the problems. We were on the verge of losing the entire business, not just a few orders. After a frustrating day at one of our major plants, I returned to my hotel and called the one person I knew could help, Phil Kirby.

I had a long-standing relationship with Phil, dating back to 1994 when he helped us launch an initiative to reengineer the organization. At the time, we were a traditional, functionally structured organization with zero knowledge of horizontal workflow and process thinking. Our business was strong and the outlook was promising. However, we wanted to improve our competitive position, so we brought Phil in to lead a major overhaul of the organization and enhance our ability to compete in multiple segments. Under Phil's direction, we gained significant ground and achieved much of what we set out to do. But, then, as with most initiatives, we coasted for a few years. In 2001, the slowdown in the U.S. economy led us to turn, once again, to Phil. We needed to jump-start another transformation, realizing that continuous improvement really does have to be continuous. There is no letting up. Again, we made great progress. Phil catalyzed new thinking, helped us regenerate our processes, kick-started new performance improvements, and we moved forward. As in the past, Phil left us in good shape. Until our 2011 dark period hit. I knew this time that a few months of incremental improvement were not going to be enough; we needed both an immediate fix and a long-term transformation. Something disruptive.

At Bostik, we call Phil the "master disruptor." He is not your usual change agent with a bag of tools trying to help tweak the organization; he gets inside the processes, gets everyone exposing problems, and literally changes the thinking—on the run. His thinking is disruptive because it has to be. And it works. Our most recent road to recovery required Phil's methodology and business model, which is designed around "experimenting, learning, and adapting"—immediately and continuously. We mapped out the most critical work processes and engaged the people who understood the problems best and who could create the best solutions—our frontline people. I had learned that success comes from understanding and applying several of the key learnings that Phil engenders. First, respect your people; they are the key to reducing the waste that destroys value. Second, trust your people to expose problems. Third, understand that process thinking must run throughout the organization in order to create sustainable, performance improvement. Everything else is just a short-term reprieve.

Within weeks of that initial telephone call, our work processes were generating output beyond any known standard and, by December 2011, the local team had developed new key indicators, utilizing visual management tools, and they were calling our sales force, pushing for additional orders. This time, we didn't let up and over the past two plus years, Phil has remained a trusted advisor to Bostik's business in the Americas, and our transformation has moved beyond a single production line at a single plant. With Phil's oversight, support, and coaching, we are breaking down functional silos and continuing to improve business results. The journey is far from complete; in fact, in many ways, it is just beginning. And, as we change our thinking and engage employees across our organization, the possibilities are endless and the organization is truly changing itself. Thanks, in no small part, to Phil Kirby, his business model, and his transformative thinking—his brilliant process mind, which he openly shares in this insightful, hands-on, rich-in-detail book. It's a must-read.

Bob Marquette
President and Chief Executive Officer
Bostik, Inc.

Prologue

Faced with the choice between changing one's mind and proving that there is no need to do so, almost everyone gets busy on the proof.

John Kenneth Galbraith (1908–2006)

A FUNDAMENTAL MISUNDERSTANDING

In 1990, two seminal, bestselling books were published, widely read, somewhat understood, and gradually forgotten. Unfortunately, in many cases, the thinking was never adopted, while in others it was embraced, but not sustained. In *The Fifth Discipline*, Peter Senge introduced the theory of the learning organization, which focused on group problem solving by using the systems thinking method to convert companies into learning organizations. Senge observed, "Business and human endeavors are systems ... we tend to focus on snapshots of isolated parts of the system, and wonder why our deepest problems are never solved."[1] Also in 1990, the term *Lean production* was coined in the book *The Machine that Changed the World*, which is a reference to the Toyota Production System (TPS). TPS introduced a new paradigm in manufacturing—a new way of thinking— one that the authors proposed would "change the world ... the adoption of Lean production, as it inevitably spreads beyond the auto industry, will change everything in almost every industry—choices for consumers, the nature of work, the fortune of companies, and, ultimately, the fate of nations."[2] Ever since, Lean has been touted as a blueprint for remaking organizations and, as a business operating system, it has moved beyond the automobile industry to all types of industries and organizations, from chemical processing and pharmaceuticals supply chains to defense bases and banking, insurance, hospitals, and more. And yet, 25 years later the overarching theory in these remarkable books—the primacy of the business as a process—remains the exception, not the rule. *IndustryWeek* magazine, reporting on a large survey, found that only 2% of companies that have a Lean program have achieved their results.[3] More and more material has been published to help with the practical application of systems thinking. A follow-up book by Senge, *The Fifth Discipline Field Book* (Crown Business) was published in 1994, as a how-to guide. It attempted to answer the practical question: What does the learning organization do on Monday morning? And, in 2006, Jeffery Liker and David Meier published *The Toyota Way Handbook* (McGraw-Hill) in response to demand to "codify" Lean production. During this same period, in 1997, David Hughes and I wrote *Thoughtware: Change the Thinking and the Organization Will Change Itself* (Productivity Press). We addressed the same concern and provided an operating concept that stated: If an organization can change its collective thinking, the organization will change itself. We posited that there is a need to replace the old framework of organizational thinking with a new framework and offered the Thoughtware® theory, a new context for organizational design rising from a different understanding about how we work together and how to unleash the power of organized, human effort. We put forward that the failure of Lean efforts to stick (and many related concepts, such as Six Sigma, Total Quality Management, Just-in-Time, Quality Circles, and other business improvement programs) pointed to a fundamental misunderstanding of the process revolution initiated by the Toyota Production System. We submitted that the sustained success of any continuous improvement initiative came from its focus on process thinking and cross-functionalization, and that the success of tools and techniques alone was negligible in the long term.

ORGANIZATIONS HAVE LOST GROUND

Thoughtware offered an integrated model to help organizations shift their thinking patterns from the contemporary paradigms based on division of labor, departmentalization, span of control, and concentrated authority to the powerful systems of a process-focused organization. It required a new context based on knowledge, measurement, time-to-action and allowment.[4] In short, it urged organizations to think and act horizontally, not vertically. In addition to the theory, we presented an eight-step installation model grounded in applications across industries and around the world. Where installed, the results, as measured by performance, productivity, and financial improvement, have been remarkable. And yet, to this day, little attention has been paid to the insights afforded by a process approach to performance improvement and the majority of organizations continue to ignore the systems thinking underlying TPS, Lean, and Thoughtware. There are many success stories through the adaptation of continuous improvement techniques and tools with at least temporary yields in performance; however, there is little evidence of a change in the human thoughtware and core processes that underlie these practices.

In 1988, the Shingo Prize for Operational Excellence[5] was established at Utah State University to annually recognize companies around the globe that "achieve world-class operational excellence status" in any industry or geography at any time. Referred to as the "Nobel Prize of Manufacturing" by *BusinessWeek*,[6] the Shingo Prize is recognized as the premier award for the application of universally accepted principles of operational excellence, alignment of management systems, and the wise application of improvement techniques. Robert Millar, executive director of the Shingo Prize, in commenting on a significant study of organizations that have received the award, said:

> We were quite surprised, even disappointed that a large percentage of those organizations that had been recognized had lost ground ... we studied these companies and found that a very large percentage of those evaluated were experts at implementing tools of Lean, but had not deeply embedded them into their culture.[7]

It seems that the core lessons—to embed new thinking—have fallen on deaf ears, which raises the bigger question: Why are so many organizations stone deaf? This book, *The Process Mind: New Thoughtware for Designing Your Business on Purpose,* sets out to answer that question and provide the thinking, navigational instruments, and practical approaches needed to finally (hopefully) build more and more organizations based on a process-focused model.

In *The Process Mind*, I extend the original thoughtware thesis, borrowing heavily from the twin concepts of systems and Lean thinking and address the organization's web of interdependence as business processes. It is about a causal operating capability to drive the enterprise's business model based on designing process-focused organizations. Underlying this model and theory of systems thinking is the principle of process thinking as it applies to all business processes, end-to-end. Essentially, no system's issue is ever resolved and no sustainable performance improvement is ever achieved without addressing the entire workflow—the process. Working on any resource subset or discrete point in the workflow will always lead to poorer performance of the process; therefore, only by concentrating efforts on the entire flow of value are sustainable improvements possible.

The book provides evidence and learning in what it takes to create a process-focused organization and the practical techniques for deployment, including *treasure hunting* and *experimentation*. However, while offering some leverage and insight as to what we might do differently, I have stopped short of being prescriptive because the process thinking mind is about tacit knowledge, not explicit procedural knowledge, and the resulting implied gain is from experience and reflection, not from a recipe.

SHAREHOLDER VALUE IS A MORAL HAZARD

At the core of the thesis is the premise that continuous performance improvement is all about learning by doing, experimenting, and adapting, and this book is all about adding value to customers through a focus on process, people, and the organization's collective intelligence. This is the new thoughtware that so many have had so much trouble adopting. There is no shortage of procedures and methods for continuous process improvement (i.e., how-to kits on *kanban*, quick changeover, mistake proofing, Heijunka, 5S, variance analysis, etc.) and they are but a click away, but they do not get at the causal malaise. The "how-to" toolkits provide ways to implement visible tools; however, the process mind sees the tools only as a navigational milestone, a brief overnight camp on the continuous improvement journey. The tools are not solutions, they are aids to develop solutions (i.e., kanban is a visible way of regulating production between processes, but to the process mind it is a way to expose problems in the process, to provide a basis from which to problem solve).

Process thinking requires a fundamental change in the organization's operating thoughtware. It starts with a change in deeply rooted doctrine of making major decisions based on short-term financial goals instead of long-term philosophy and the ultimate purpose of the organization, which is to grow and sustain itself and its offspring organisms. This requires moral courage by leadership, demanding that senior management and the organization take on the consequences and responsibilities of its actions, including short-term setbacks (e.g., missing month-end results). I consider the current thinking of maximizing shareholder value as a moral hazard, a situation where leaders have a tendency to unreasonably risk the long-term health of the organization, with no consequence to their own well-being, in exchange for short-term profit. It is embedded in management DNA, as well as in its reward structure, overtly or otherwise. No drum beats louder than the street's mantra of month end or quarterly results; consequently, when faced with competitive cost pressures, management gets on with the easy work of employee downsizing rather than the tough slogging to identify and remove waste. Not only is moral hazard embedded in the shareholder value model, it provides an intractable excuse not to address and develop a process mind. It is hard work.

CUSTOMER VALUE VERSUS SHAREHOLDER VALUE

The process mind thinks—and knows—that the purpose of any and all processes is, first and foremost, to generate value for the customer, not the shareholder. And, that value can only increase if the organization *sees* the flow of value to the customer and continuously takes countermeasures to eliminate any disruption to that flow (i.e., problems). The paradox of the process mind is perhaps most clearly exemplified in the practice of exposing problems versus concealing them. It's about the manager's dilemma of encouraging the uncovering of the things that disrupt the flow of value versus creating and maintaining policies, practices, and processes that hide problems; bury them, never to be seen or solved. There are many competing dynamics, such as customer value versus shareholder value, that challenge the development of a process mind and everyone in an organization faces these contradictions and paradoxes when new thoughtware begins to replace the old. The paradox of short-term financial success versus long-term growth is overarching, but there are many more, all rooted in the fundamental need to expose problems versus hide them. For example, the need to control versus the need to be flexible; the need to direct versus the need to adapt; the balance between employees taking responsibility versus telling them what to do; and the need to experiment and fail versus do it the same way and make no mistakes. Changing the thinking requires addressing the paradoxes and the difficulty in doing that underscores the reason why so few organizations are process-focused.

In Chapter 1, I exemplify this inherent contradiction in what I call the Chennai Paradox, a term I coined after doing some work in Chennai, India. The Chennai Paradox represents the essential conflict confronting management; exposing versus hiding of problems, in all their rawness. And, once exposed, the root cause needs to be determined, eliminated, and prevented from recurring. For the contemporary manager who is under pressure to perform, to create results now, this problem solving is a time-consuming, expensive, resource-draining activity. Allocating assets to permanently prevent recurrences requires redirecting scarce resources from today's put-out-the-fire priorities. What I found in Chennai was a wrenching contradiction between the old, poverty-stricken life and the new, emerging prosperity and, yet, they exist side-by-side and are changing and improving in incremental steps. The old is exposed, and problems are being solved. For me, it was the glaring exposure of the problems juxtaposed against the gleaming growth that drove home the struggle—albeit, much less severe—that organizations have in dealing with change. They don't see and don't deal with the problems because it is their natural tendency to work around problems and contain them—ignore them—rather than expose and celebrate them and get on with preventing their reoccurrence. In Chennai, the problems cannot be ignored. So, too, the process-focused organization cannot ignore the exposed problems.

TWO PILLARS

The process mind focuses on two pillars. The first is reducing waste: what gets in the way of work and detracts from creating value from the perspective of the customer. Second, it has an inherent commitment to the full utilization of human talent, a high respect for people. Done right, these two mainstays deliver unmatched, long-term sustained value. And, the value is in leveraging the knowledge, experience, and creativity of the people who work in the process. It is straightforward but not easy. It requires a major change in thinking, which I develop throughout the book. For example, the process mind deeply understands that employees have the right to be successful every time they do their job, and the art of doing their job is finding problems and making improvements. If management wants people to be successful and make improvements, they have an obligation to provide them the means to do so. They must make it easier to see problems, solve problems, and learn from mistakes. This is the essence of respect for people. The fact that this thoughtware is missing from today's management mind is at the heart of the paradox and this is a cornerstone of the process mind: designing processes to expose problems and creating people who are willing and able to solve those problems as they occur.

THE PROCESS AHEAD

Chapter 2 offers an example of how the paradox might be overcome. It starts with understanding the problem and there is no better way to see that than to look at an extraordinary success story, Apple®. One of the primary reasons for Apple's success is what I call, its little secret: process thinking. It comes from the deep understanding inherent in Steve Jobs' and Tim Cooks' process minds.

Chapter 3 delves into history—from Machiavelli and Ford to Deming and Hammer—because it is essential to know how we got to where we are today. Like the title of an earlier book I wrote, *The Future. You Can't Get There From Here*, I believe the old thoughtware can't get us there. Chapter 4 discusses the root causes that are so ingrained in our conventional organizations and the clash of two titans: vertical thinking versus horizontal thinking. Chapter 5 addresses the imperative of respect for people, and it's not about the so-called "empowerment" of people that we have been preaching for decades; it's much more fundamental (and necessary) than that. Without it, there is no performance improvement, no change. Chapter 6 talks about the critical link between strategy and process thinking and how one without the other is, well, somewhere between underachievement and ineptitude, and it demonstrates how the primacy of purpose and financial performance are inextricable.

The second half of the book is dedicated to how it all gets done. In Chapters 7, 8, and 9, I describe the model that drives the transformation from old to new thoughtware. I have named the model Purpose–Measure–Action, and it sets out in detail how to define and achieve the purpose of the process, and, through a measurement system, provide constant feed-back on the capability of the process to achieve that purpose. And, in so doing, incite action on the process to move closer to achieving the pur-pose. From there, we jump into the hands-on way of doing it all. I have conducted over 1,600 "treasure hunts" in organizations around the world, and Chapter 10 takes you on one of those hunts, which uncovers some of the most amazing buried treasure (i.e., problems) that, in turn, provides opportunities for as-yet unimaginable, performance improvement. The seeing is the believing. I finish with two getting-started principles: Chapter 11 sets out eight steps to creating a processed-focused organization and Chapter 12 describes the Carrot Diet, which tells you what it takes to lose all that waste and become a Lean, healthy, continuously improving, outstanding performing organization.

The Process Mind: New Thoughtware for Designing Your Business on Purpose focuses on the primacy of process and its purpose, which is to deliver customer value. The critical starting point is always value, value that can only be defined by the customer and is created by the producer, from the customer's perspective. The problem is that it is difficult for the producer to define and see value because he/she lacks the ability to see the flow of value to the customer—a process perspective. The charge of the process mind is to assure that every person in the organization can see the flow of value to the customer and fix it when it breaks before it reaches the customer.

ENDNOTES

1. Peter M. Senge. *The Fifth Discipline, the Art and Practice of the Learning Organization* (New York: Doubleday, 1990), 19.
2. James P. Womack, Daniel T. Jones, and Daniel Roos. *The Machine that Changed the World* (New York: Harper Collins, 1990), 12.
3. Rick Pay. "Everybody's Jumping on the Lean Bandwagon, but Many Are Being Taken for a Ride," *IndustryWeek* (March 1, 2008).
4. Kirby J. Philip and David Hughes. *Thoughtware: Change the Thinking and the Organization Will Change Itself* (Portland, OR: Productivity Press, 1997).
5. The Shingo Institute is a not-for-profit organization housed at Utah State University and named after Japanese industrial engineer Shigeo Shingo. Dr. Shingo distinguished himself as one of the world's thought leaders in concepts, management systems, and improvement techniques that have become known as the Toyota Business System. Dr. Shingo received his honorary Doctorate of Management from Utah State University in 1988, the year the Shingo Prize was initiated.
6. "And the Shingo Goes to …," *BusinessWeek* 38b (May 15, 2000).
7. Robert Miller, executive director of the Shingo Prize, interviewed on radiolean. com, July 2010. Lean Enterprise Institute: http://www.lean.org/search/default. aspx?sc=radiolean.

Acknowledgments

Bringing change to organizations requires an immense effort from many people, along with a combination of considerable talents and an unfailing commitment to purpose. Although writing and creating a book do not compare to changing an organization, I have done both and have learned that neither can be accomplished without a great deal of help from others.

As in all worthwhile endeavors, one must surround him/herself with those who can encourage, assist, and collaborate. The creation of this book was possible because I had so much encouragement from my wife Karen and invaluable advice from my colleague David Hughes. Karen reassured me when my extensive rewrites cast doubts, inspired me when my energy waned, and let me be when I was fit to be left alone. David helped me structure the flow of the book, organize scattered paragraphs, and refine the articulation of my thinking into the overarching theme and core points.

I also thank the author of the Foreword, Bob Marquette, who is president and chief executive officer of Bostik, a global leader in the design, manufacture and marketing of technologically advanced adhesives and sealants. Bostik collaborates closely with its customers to provide high-performance solutions, creating stronger bonds for a better life.

Of course, at the end of the day, I must thank my many customers who adopted the new thoughtware of the process mind, turning their facilities over for treasure hunting, experimentation, and learning, which, in turn, led to much success. Of course, customers have taught me as much as I have taught them, and that is the way it should be. Now, because of them, I have this opportunity to share all that learning in this book.

Also, I want to thank Michael Sinocchi, executive editor, and all the staff at Productivity Press and Taylor & Francis Group for their guidance and commitment to this project.

About the Author

Phil Kirby is a recognized, international expert in continuous process improvement, Lean, and overall business performance. Known as "The Process Guy," Kirby has, for over thirty years, helped hundreds of organizations around the globe achieve extraordinary performance improvement—from airlines, banks, and government agencies to manufacturing, supply chains, customer service centers and pharmaceutical laboratories. Kirby believes that a company's competitive advantage and customer value come primarily from its business processes, not its products and services. He has helped organizations adopt revolutionary process thinking in almost every type of business and proven, many times over, that an organization can be not only fast, but flexible *and* low cost, if the focus is on process.

Phil Kirby is founder and CEO of Organization Thoughtware International, Inc. based in Guelph, Ontario, outside Toronto, Canada. He is a sought-after executive coach and award-winning speaker, addressing audiences around the world. He is the author of: *Thoughtware: Change the Thinking and the Organization Will Change Itself* (Productivity Press, 1997); *The Future: You Can't Get There from Here* (OTI Inc., 2004); and now, *The Process Mind*.

To learn more, visit the OTI website http://thoughtware.ca/. And for more information about booking Phil, email info@thoughtware.ca

1

The Chennai Paradox

The problems are hiding in plain sight.

SEE THE PROCESS, SEE THE PROBLEM

In 2008, I found myself in Chennai, India, gazing out the window of a gleaming office tower, amazed by the juxtaposition of life in this "Cultural Capital of South India." Chennai has been called the most livable city in India by the Institute of Competitiveness[1] and yet, I could see edging off the banks of the Adyar River below a haphazard row of wooden planks that looked like toothpicks extending from rickety cardboard huts from which the homeless emerged to begin another day in abject poverty. The contrast was raw. The conditions of poverty, squalor, and deprivation were in stark contrast to the modern, prospering city skyline with its eclectic mix of steeples, minarets, temples, four-star hotels, and gleaming office towers. It was emotionally conflicting. Simultaneously, I could see the promise of a new and better future existing side by side with the exposed problems of the old way of life. It was a visceral paradox.

Seeing poverty—the problem—"living" in the streets, while the new solutions were being hatched in distant glistening office towers set me to thinking. As shocking as the deprivation was, as wrenching the contrast between old and new, my process mind saw the real advantage of *seeing* the problem. It could not be ignored as long as I was willing to learn to look and directly observe the place where the problem occurred, where it manifested itself. Later, when I walked the streets of Chennai, I saw the depth and extent of the city's situation and learned, first-hand, the magnitude of the problems. Obviously, a picture of Chennai is not Chennai, statistics of Chennai are not Chennai, and a map of Chennai is not Chennai; they are simply representations. The truth is in the streets.

Similarly, in an organization, an organizational chart is not the organization, a financial statement is not the organization, and a value stream map of the process is not the process. It is not until one gets "into the streets" of the organization—its processes—and directly observes those processes operating in real time that the reality can been seen. Only then are the true problems exposed. For me, in that moment, the Chennai Paradox crystallized the challenge I have faced over the past 25 years when organizations have tried to improve performance. At first, they have been very uncomfortable at exposing problems because it is always a shock to their operating systems and beliefs. They don't like staring at reality, so consequently, they avoid it, often meeting with abject failure. Improvement does not happen in the comfort of the conference room. It happens on the street, in the process where the wasteful truth is revealed. Organizations more often than not fail to meet performance improvement expectations because they do not design their businesses to expose problems, they design them to hide problems, the very problems that when solved deliver performance improvements. However, they don't solve them because they don't see them and they do not see the problems because they are not looking out the windows of the shiny office towers, they are looking inward, sitting in conference rooms, looking at spreadsheets, data-based financial reports, performance measurement scorecards, and other extrapolations contained in management information factories. The conference room interprets the problem; it is an abstract assumption, but it is not the problem. The problem is in the street. The problem is embedded in the organization's business processes, only visible through direct observation, by going to the place where the value is created. We cannot expect to achieve dramatic performance improvement from our continuous improvement initiatives from the conference room; it is only available to us if we wander deep into the streets of our process and look and listen with profound respect to the employees living and working in those streets. At least in Chennai, the problems are there for all to see. In Chennai, the paradox is illuminated; in most organizations it is hidden.

EXTREME IMMERSION

Continuous process improvement can only come from extreme emersion "in the streets" of the process, not from analysis of abstract data and discrete departments, each with their functional specialists, which are well removed from the workplace. Because sustainable performance improvement happens in the actual place of work, in the core processes where the value is created, it cannot be done in the abstraction of an engineering, human resource, or financial department; or even the management suite. It must be done in the process where the work takes place, not from a rinsed and sterilized view through data collection, spreadsheets, and "maps" of what is going on. Performance improvement comes from a dogmatic adherence to the underlying business processes, or operating system of the enterprise. It has no regard for functions, departments, and management structures that damn up the flow of those processes. The process mind can dramatically improve the performance of the business because it has a deep reverence for process and listening to the people living in it who can help identify and eliminate disruptions in the flow of value to the customer. The process mind demands that employees have a right to be successful every time they do their job, and the art of doing their job is to find problems and make improvements. Organizations have an obligation to provide them the means to do so. They require a process-focused operating system.

Let me be clear, I do not pretend to distill India's economic and cultural disparities down to an operating system, but there was, in that moment, an inherent lesson for me. This city, and its diametrically opposed realities were on display—the promise of the "new" and the intransigence of the "old"—along with clear evidence of continuous improvement. Even though there is a long way to go, there is, step-by-step, a new economic model emerging. The Chennai Paradox reflects, in part, the contradictions organizations face when trying to integrate a new business operating system into an old culture. The new flies in the face of the old and replacing the old is a daily struggle. In my work, the process-focused business model is foreign to the established orthodoxy entrenched in an organization's vertical structure, which consists of many departments and discrete parts. This mindset is steeped in more than 100 years of history and it focuses on optimizing isolated parts with people thinking and acting as functional specialists. This no longer fits the reality of the twenty-first century, which is all about speed, agility, variety, and constant change. Instead, to achieve the magnitude of performance improvement required, I believe organizations must move to a processed-focused model that recognizes the whole system as one natural, horizontal flow of value. This dictates that we stop with the obsessive focus on shareholder value and trying to improve an old, outdated organizational hierarchy and move to a new model that focuses on customer value and a horizontal view of the process that delivers that value.

PARADOXES ABOUND

Like many cities in India, Chennai lives the paradox as it strives to improve. It's a city of 4.7 million people and an urban agglomeration of suburbs that is home to 8.9 million. It is the fourth most populous metropolitan area in the country and 31st largest urban area in the world.[2] It's a major commercial, cultural, economic, and educational center and has a rich history of commercial endeavors that began in colonial times when the British East India Company established Fort St. George in 1644.[3] Today, Chennai's economy has a broad industrial base in the automobile, computer, technology, manufacturing, and healthcare sectors. The largest business sector is electronics manufacturing with telecommunications giants like NOKIA, Flextronics, Motorola, Sony, Ericsson, Samsung, Cisco, and Dell selecting Chennai as their South Asian manufacturing hub. The city is India's second largest exporter of business process outsourcing (BPO). That's why I was there. BPO entails the contracting of specific business processes to third-party service providers like those in Chennai. Typically, they are categorized into either back office outsourcing, which includes internal business functions, such as human resources, finance, and accounting, or front office outsourcing, which usually relates to customer services like call centers. The BPO business caters mainly to Western multinational corporations and offers educated, English-speaking, youthfully demographic, low-wage locations like India. In India, around 2.8 million people work in the outsourcing sector. Annual revenues are around $11 billion, which is about 1% of India's GDP (gross domestic product). According to International Data Corporation, the global outsourcing market was approximately $164 billion in 2009 and is expected to grow at a 5% compound annual growth rate to $208 billion in 2014. Nearly 75% of U.S. and European multinational companies now use outsourcing or shared services to support their financial functions and 29% of U.S. and European companies expect to increase their use of outsourcing of financial functions, with spending expected to be nearly 16% higher than current levels.[4] The BPO that I was working with, processes more than 18 million medical claims annually for health benefit providers and has 50% of the Fortune 500 as clients. One of its clients is a large healthcare company managing healthcare benefits for large employers, each with a minimum of 3,000 employees. They service 70 million Americans, 72,000 physicians, and 80,000 dentists including 65,600 hospitals and drug plans (for 13 million people). In addition to significant investments in research and development, they invest heavily in technology—nearly $3 billion in the past five years. Numbers like these represent the new, which is in stark contrast to the old.

If we look closely at conventional business organizations and compare them to the process-focused model, the differences also are stark. And, what is obvious is the fact that it is impossible to install a new business model, based on horizontal process, in an old, vertically structured organization.

Process thinking creates paradoxes, from the overarching contradiction of the old and new model to the smallest elements, which I cover in the ensuing chapters. But, to give you an idea of the endless contradictions in thinking, here's a partial list of some new and old thoughtware paradoxes:

- Go slow to go fast.
- Economies of flow versus economies of scale.
- Processing one piece at a time is more profitable than the economics of quantity (i.e., batch and queue).
- Measuring process variation is better than measuring results.
- Finding problems is better than ignoring them.
- Pulling a string is more effective than pushing a string.
- Focus on cash flow instead of gross profit.
- Focus on experimentation and learning instead of control and reliability.
- Use information that comes from, and is integrated with, the process, not separate from it.
- Managing discrete resources causes costs to go up, always, while managing the entire workflow causes costs to go down, always.
- Concentrate on the capability of the process as opposed to performance targets (usually financial).

- A target has no value if you don't have a process that is capable of achieving the target (hello, stock analysts).
- Focus on customer value that increases shareholder value rather than focus on shareholder value that does not increase customer value.

Batch thinking is the root of all evil.

IDLE TIME IS 95% OF THE PROCESS

I was in Chennai on a small wager, of sorts, with an old client, and what we addressed there was one of the mothers of paradoxes: batch and queue thinking versus processing thinking. Batch and queue thinking emanates from the contemporary organizational structure where isolated departments are optimized at the expense of the whole, and large batches of information or materials are processed by one specialist function and moved on to the next specialist function, regardless of whether they are needed or not—and then they wait in a "queue." Process thinking produces and moves one piece of information or material at a time—or a small and consistent batch—through the functions or departments as continuously as possible, with each function providing just what is requested by the next function. I had done process and performance improvement work for the same BPO in seven large medical claims processing centers in the U.S. and the Caribbean. This BPO collaborates with large companies, helping them deliver efficient healthcare benefits to employees and future retirees. I was brought in by the CEO, let's call him Tom, who I had done work for in the aerospace industry. In that case, we had dramatically reduced the time it took to get components and assemblies to the original equipment manufacturer (OEM), using customer-focused thoughtware. Tom had witnessed the power of process thinking in the manufacturing world and understood that process is process regardless of what he is delivering—widgets or services. Wherever there is an exchange of information there is a process and that process invariably has more activities that get in the way of work, than the work itself (Figure 1.1). From Tom's personal experience, that ratio in aerospace was about 10 to 1 (i.e., in Lean language, waste to added value).

Across the spectrum of businesses, the amount of time required to execute a service or an order or manufacture and deliver a product is far less than the actual time the service or product spends in the value delivery system.

FIGURE 1.1
Work Ratio—waste versus added value.

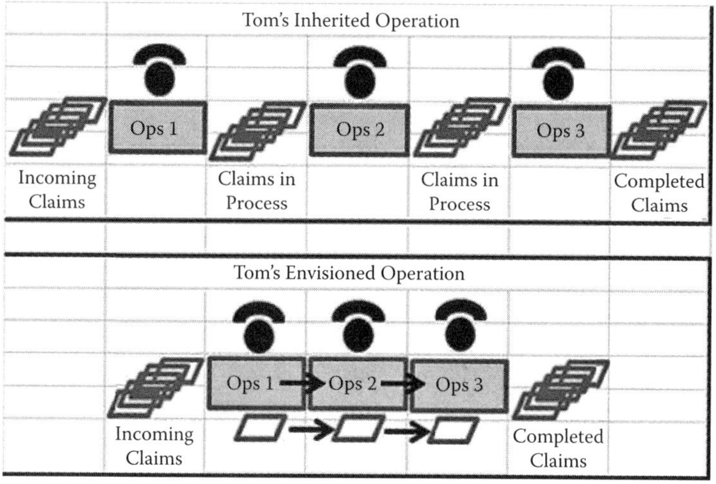

![Tom's Inherited Operation and Tom's Envisioned Operation diagram]

Tom's Inherited Operation

Ops 1   Ops 2   Ops 3

Incoming Claims   Claims in Process   Claims in Process   Completed Claims

Tom's Envisioned Operation

Ops 1 → Ops 2 → Ops 3

Incoming Claims   □→□→□   Completed Claims

FIGURE 1.2
Batch versus flow.

In fact, the product or service is only receiving value (work) 0.05% to 5% of the time that it is in the value delivery system. During the other 95 to 99.95%[5] of the time, the product or service is waiting (dealing with that which gets in the way of work). Unfortunately, the functional organization does not have a department called waiting, therefore, this massive amount of idle time is not visible and, by not being visible, it is not addressed or resolved. The waiting is usually caused by the time required to finish a batch and then move it to the next process, regardless of whether it is actually needed yet. There it usually waits in another queue.

Tom had learned that improved performance depends on changing the fundamentals within the process (i.e., ratio of work to getting-in-the-way-of-work), whether it was aerospace or healthcare. The process-focused model was the basis of his success in aerospace and he knew it could do the same in healthcare services. As he said, "It's a healthcare services factory." The specific task was to define the activities that get in the way of work (i.e., waste) by exposing them through a gradual reduction in batch size, which moves toward continuous flow processing (Figure 1.2).

Think of his company as the operations arm of a large healthcare firm and the goal is to run the operation as cost-effectively as possible. This is common in the industry, where everyone is out to win contracts for supplying health-care plans to Fortune 500 companies. The way they win is by competing on two main criteria. The first is turnaround time. How fast can they get the reimbursement back to the customer's employee? After a person goes to the dentist, they are waiting for the money from their healthcare provider. The wait starts after the dentist's work is finished. Forms are filled out and submitted and then they go through a protracted process. Sometime later, a check arrives in the mail. It takes time. The second factor is cost; specifically, cost per transaction, which is the standard metric. What Tom's company does is contract that processing business out to the BPO industry. In Chennai, they were processing medical claims, but it could have been almost anything. In the BPO business, the value proposition is that they can get more claims through faster with less cost. BPOs are scattered across the globe and typically pay the operators who process claims at unskilled labor rates, usually minimum wage. Tom's BPOs are in India because the labor rates are much lower than in the United States (70–90% lower). However, this view of cost is part of the paradox motivated by the false promise of functional thinking in which labor cost difference, as opposed to total cost difference, is seen as the primary opportunity. The big opportunity is to significantly improve the overall process, thus, the overall cost, by removing the things that get in the way of the work. Once relocated to India, the BPO's direct wages only account for about 35% of the total outsourced costs and, when focusing only on wage arbitrage, the BPO saved 25%. Moving an inefficient process to a low-cost country not only leaves it with the transferred inefficiencies, but also adds other difficulties, such as infrastructure. So, while labor rates can be 70 to 90% lower in offshore locations such as India, most firms save only 25 to 50% on their global sourcing initiatives. Tom wanted more. He wanted the 200% productivity improvement results we achieved in his domestic operations (i.e., about 210% more claims processed per man-hour paid) (Figure 1.3).

THE WAGER

In Tom's American operations, we had applied process thinking and a methodology to deploy it and delivered significant results (Figure 1.3). Note the three overall measures: throughput, time, and cost (productivity).

Results for Tom's BPO Claims Processing Operation (U.S.)*		
Resultant Measure of Success	Definition of Measure	% Improvement
Throughput	Claims processed per day	200%
	Ave. Hourly throughput	190%
Time	% claims processed within 24 hours	91%
Cost	Claims processed per Capital employed	235%
	Claims processed per man hour paid	210%
Quality	Errors per 1000 claims	from 8.3% to 2.4%
*6 Processing Centers between 2003–2006		

FIGURE 1.3

Tom's BPO Claims Processing Results (U.S.).

In a process-focused organization, these three resultant measures namely throughput, time, and cost (productivity) assure a focus on the process and customer value and can be seen on the bottom line, thus, assuring an increase in financial performance. I go into these in more depth later.

I asked him, "Why don't you go after the same magnitude of improvement in India?" This is where an increasing percentage of claims were being handled. He thought it was a good idea, until I quoted him a price. Obviously, it was more than what we work for in the United States. He wasn't sure if we could get the same results in such a different country and culture. I told him that process is process regardless of industry or country.

To make my point, I suggested a wager. If we were able to hit a 50% improvement target (beyond the labor advantage) based on our regular metrics, then he would pay my quoted price. If we didn't, he would pay the U.S.-based price. He went for it. And we got the results. And he paid, happily. Also, we demonstrated that the fundamentals of process and performance improvement apply, whether working in the foreign waters of Chennai or the sophistication of urban America.

Even though I won the wager, Tom's business won the big prize—results (Figure 1.4). We achieved these by applying one of the paradoxes of process thinking, less is more. This is based on the principle that processing one claim at a time is better than processing a batch of 50 because the economy of flow beats the economy of scale (Figure 1.5 and Figure 1.6). We essentially address the work ratio, attacking not the individual resource efficiency, but the economies of flow by mitigating the waiting time through batch size reduction. Simply put, it is faster to process one claim at a time through the workflow than 50 at a time.

Results for Tom's BPO Claims Processing Operation (Chennai)*		
Resultant Measure of Success	**Definition of Measure**	**% Improvement**
Throughput	Claims processed per day	160%
	Ave. Hourly throughput	148%
Time	% claims processed within 24 hours	90%
Cost	Claims processed per Capital employed	137%
	Claims processed per man hour paid	171%
Quality	Errors per 1000 claims	from 10.0% to 3.3%
*2 Processing Centers 2008		

FIGURE 1.4
Tom's BPO Claims Processing Results (Chennai).

Results for Tom's BPO Claims Processing Operation (Chennai)*			
Measure	**Batch of 50**	**One at a time**	**Difference**
First Claim Complete	3 hrs & 2mins	4 mins &12 secs	2 hrs & 57 mins
			97% faster
100th Claim Complete	4 hrs & 58 mins	2 hrs & 52 mins	2hrs & 6 mins
			42% faster
Hands-on Labor Time (Processing Time)	6 hrs & 5 mins	6 hrs & 56 mins	51 minutes
			14% more time
*2 Processing Centers 2008–3 operators per center			
Note the Paradox: One at a time, the claims were completed 42% faster, but the actual hands-on processing time (labor cost) was 14% more, because each operator uploaded each claim individually. Since labor was the basis of performance decisions the batch of 50 looked 14% more cost effective.			

FIGURE 1.5
Batch versus Flow (i.e., one at a time) Results (Chennai).

Although the time to get 100 claims processed, one at a time (i.e., batches of one) took 2 hours and 52 minutes (the first claim was completed 4 minutes and 12 seconds after first initiated), there were 6 hours and 56 minutes of labor cost. When doing two batches of 50, it took 4 hours and 58 minutes to complete (the first claim only came through with the initial batch of 50 after 3 hours and 2 minutes). However, there were only 6 hours and 5 minutes of labor costs—a labor cost reduction of 14%.

The traditional "batch and queue" business model focuses on the principle of keeping all discrete elements of the process (the operator or machine) busy. I call it "the labor-cost-is-everything-model," where the emphasis is on the all-important utilization factor, focusing on doing

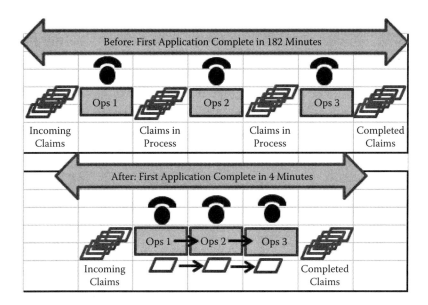

FIGURE 1.6
Before and After Processing Times (Chennai).

Marshal	Upload to Key	Key-1	Key-2	Upload to Compare	Compare	Export to File	Total Time
5 secs	9 secs	99 secs	102 secs	13 secs	18 secs	4 secs	250 secs

FIGURE 1.7
Steps to process one claim.

50 claims at a time versus doing one and waiting nine seconds to upload the next one. This is the utilization of a discrete resource instead of a focus on the workflow, thus, ignoring the time in between. Processing one claim (Figure 1.7), takes 5 seconds to marshal (collect data), 9 seconds to upload to key, 13 seconds to upload to compare, and 4 seconds to export to file. Done in a batch of 50 saves 31 seconds 49 times (25 minutes of labor) and done in a batch of 250 saves 2 hours and 24 minutes of labor. The paradox is that by increasing the batch size to decrease the apparent cost (average unit cost)—old thoughtware we degrade the work-to-waiting ratio, or the truc total cost. If we focus on time, or flow to the next workstation (think availability of capacity as opposed to utilization of capacity)—new thoughtware—we improve performance. This kind of process thinking is paradoxical since the shaded activities are done once in a batch of 50 versus 50 times in a batch of one.

In Figure 1.7, each shaded box is required for *each* group of claims, regardless of the number of claims in each batch. In other words, I need to marshal, upload to key, upload to compare, and export to file once for each batch, regardless of the batch size of 1 or 250. Traditional thinking in a vertical organization is to try and do as many as possible, let's say 50, so you only have to do the shaded boxes twice, once for each batch of 50. If I do it one at a time, I have to do each of the shaded box activities 100 times; one for each time I pull up one claim. I, therefore, am adding 14 minutes of labor costs when I do a one-piece flow, which I wouldn't have to do if I did 2 batches of 50. However, what's interesting is that the first claim is completed when done one at a time in 4 minutes and 12 seconds. Therefore, I have completed the operation of the first claim in 4 minutes as opposed to 3 hours and 2 minutes. That is 97% faster. This illustrates the paradox in that the concept of economies of scale would say, "do batches of 50," but the economies of flow say, "do a batch of 1." And, because the functional organization measures utilization at each discrete point, thus, emphasizing "utilization" or "labor efficiency" at each function (regardless of the impact to the whole process workflow), the traditional vertical organization gets trapped in the paradox of doing 50 at a time rather than 1 at a time. This paradox stems from the contemporary organization's accounting architecture, which focuses on "average unit cost" (AUC). However, this is an abstraction—producing excess at each discrete location in the process— that actually drives up total cost. Total cost is real. Producing more and more output to reduce AUC is a time-honored pathway to excessive delays and abnormal variation, the very drivers that increase total cost.

Looking at Figure 1.5, we can see AUC in action. In the batch of 50, it took 4 hours and 58 minutes to complete the 100th claim, but only 2 hours and 52 minutes to achieve the 100th claim when we did it in a "one-at-a-time" fashion. That's a 42% improvement in flow. However, the traditional "optimize the function" organization would not look at this; they would look at labor consumption or total processing time. In this case, the 6 hours and 5 minutes that it takes to do the consignment as a batch of 50 is less (by 14%) than the 6 hours and 56 minutes required to do it one at a time. Although we have improved the utilization of the employee or resource, we have not improved the workflow. The costs go down when focusing on flow, but not when focusing on the discreet resource, again the paradox.

In Chennai, I saw a real-life analogy that helped me explain more clearly the corporate cultural problems that we all wrestle with when trying to understand and implement process and performance improvement. It exemplified the type of shock you get when confronted by two very different cultural phenomena, particularly when one is so different to your current way of thinking. Traditional thinking focuses on the work we do, but process thinking focuses on the things that get in the way of the work we do (Figure 1.8). Empiricism shows that in any organization there is 10 times as much stuff that gets in the way of the work we do versus the work itself. Mostly this nonwork consumes resources and costs without producing value or revenue and can best be defined as "waiting" or delays in the flow of the process. Generally, there are three types of waiting, which are divided equally among the nine-tenths of the things that get in the way of work:[6] (1) waiting for the completion of a full batch that a particular product or service is a part of, (2) waiting for the physical or intellectual rework to be completed, and (3) waiting for management to get around to making and executing the decision to send the batch to the next step of the process. Only process thinking and the process mind can get at these three major impediments.

Improvement and cultural change go hand-in-hand; one without the other cannot prevail, whether it's a foreign country trying to change its economy or an organization attempting to change its business model. Major shifts in a culture come gradually, as the "old" must live side-by-side with the "new" for some time. That's the Chennai Paradox. Improvement is slow, not fast. But it comes, if the leadership understands, believes, and commits. The culture must change and, if the culture is to change, the thinking must change. As I said in my earlier book, *Thoughtware*

The Chennai Paradox

...a focus on the workflow reveals 95–99% of the process is not work, but stuff that gets in the way of work...eliminating the 95–99% requires the ability to see the process, which can only be done processing one claim at a time, not 50 claims at a time.

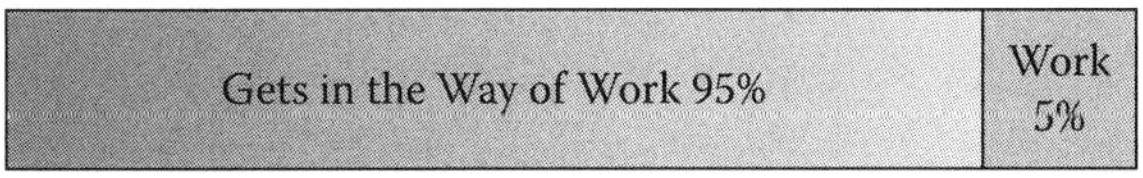

Gets in the Way of Work 95%	Work 5%

FIGURE 1.8
Application of the "Work" to "Gets in the Way of Work" Ratio.

(Productivity Press, 1997), if you "change the thinking, the organization will change itself." And the foundation on which we have constructed the new thoughtware business model is process thinking.

> No great improvements in the lot of mankind are possible, until a great change takes place in the fundamental constitution of their modes of thought.
>
> **John Stuart Mill**

THE NEW THOUGHTWARE

I want to emphasize that I am referring to the underlying thoughtware system that drives the business model, not a business tool or technique. In the past, we have seen and applied many tools, such as reengineering, TQM (Total Quality Management), and Six Sigma. These are changes in practice, which are relatively easy to implement even though they are difficult to sustain. But, and it's an important but, moving from one business model to another is a whole different undertaking and requires a fundamental change in the underlying thoughtware and operating system. In the case of the process mind, it requires moving from the ubiquitous and long-standing, vertically integrated business model to a horizontal, process-focused model. That's a paradigm shift that has to deal with the Chennai Paradox. Until organizations change their structure—ignore their vertical structure—and adopt process thinking, none of the management practices of the day (i.e., reengineering, Six Sigma, continuous improvement) will be effective or sustainable. Once the organization is process-focused, then management tools become more effective and sustainable.

Around the globe, many companies have made significant disruptions to the traditional, vertically integrated business model, including Toyota, UPS, Southwest, Apple, Amazon, and Danaher, to name a few. However, the vast majority of corporations remain mired in a century-old model and have yet to construct the scaffolding that will allow them to change to the new model. In Chapter 3, I go into the vertically integrated model and its history in some detail to show the folly of trying to improve performance by running each and every part (i.e., department, function, role) as efficiently as possible. The problem is that it never deals, in any depth, with the interconnections between the parts—the process.

A HUNDRED-YEAR OBSESSION

This conventional model and the thinking behind it has evolved from Adam Smith's "pin factory" and the eighteenth-century concept of the division of labor. In the late nineteenth century, it was refined by Frederick Taylor as "scientific management" and applied at Bethlehem Steel, and with much tinkering and tweaking, it remains the go-to operational model today. This operating, thoughtware system has not fundamentally changed over the past 100 years.

This scientific management was based on observing how the most effective workers went about their job, standardizing what was noted and applying it across the board. Success was based on a high level of managerial control over employee work practices, which, in turn, necessitated a higher ratio of managerial workers to laborers than had been required in previous management methods. (e.g., craft production). Thus, we have the current obsession with labor and headcount as the main measure of cost and its attendant problem of interpersonal friction between workers and managers. The consequence of Taylor's method was the excessive, functional complexity even though the benefits of this division of functions into their simplest components was indeed a dramatic increase in operational efficiency and apparent financial success, as measured by lower unit cost and higher output; apparent because lower unit cost does not mean lower total cost. The vertical integration is classically manifested in Henry Ford's development of "mass production." Ford pushed Taylorism to its limits, seeking more and more vertical integration and divided activities into smaller and smaller pieces, but did so by limiting variety as captured in his famous statement, "Pick any color, as long as it's black." This is not to say Ford and Taylor were right or wrong, rather they were building operating systems to support business models appropriate for the challenges of the day. The "break it down into its most discrete functional parts" was an operating system built for the times, a time when volume growth was king and labor was the highest component of cost. However, today, variety, not volume, is the new sovereign; not mass production but mass customization, not batches, but individualized design. And, the highest component of cost is time, as manifested in nonvalue-adding activities or waste. I am referring here not to what is a necessary activity (necessary under today's organization), rather I am referring to activities that do not add value to the purpose of the process—fulfilling customer demand. The basic vertical integration was perceived to be successful because it increased the amount produced, thereby, allowing for significant average unit cost reductions. And, low cost was the way to win because, generally, costs go down by about 15% when volume doubles.[7] However, we are now living in a twenty-first-century world where variety rules; there are an estimated 10 billion product offerings in the world and speed is everything. Now, the equation has changed; although costs may go down when volume grows, costs go up by 20 to 35% when variety doubles.[8] Therefore, we need a business model to accommodate both the cost effectiveness of standardization and the agility of product variety. We need a process-focused organization.

THERE IS A PRICE TO PAY

Focusing on the end-to-end process, rather than optimizing every discrete piece or part, is the only way to effectively manage variety. It's about reducing development time-to-market or fulfillment time-to-consumer while maintaining competitive costs and premium quality. This is different than the efficiency of the vertical integration, which assumes growth in volume, not variety. The vertical integration model comes at a cost, a trade-off in variety, and those trade-offs include accepting the cost of poor quality (i.e., batches, instead of one at a time); the cost of employee skills development (i.e., narrow skills replaced the highly skilled craftsman, and employees became a variable expense, not a human capital asset); and the cost of expensive, inflexible, single-purpose machines and equipment (i.e., instead of simple, flexible tools that afforded agility). Of all of these, the biggest cost is the intolerance to individual variety (i.e., customization).

For illustrative purposes, consider a transactional process with two distinct activities. Activity one is to "fill out the document" and the second is to "get the document signed off." Assume the person filling out the document is at the far end of the room from the person signing the document. The tendency would be to do a batch of documents, let's say a day's worth, and then take them to the person signing the documents because this would *justify* (read hide) the long walk through the room between the two operations. In a vertical business model, this disruption to flow is hidden and called "walking distance." The process-focused thinker would see this walking distance as a disruption to flow (i.e., document #1 is done in the morning, but sits idle all day waiting for the last document of the day). Process thoughtware exposes this waste and would consider moving one document at a time; however, this would be cost and time prohibitive, *unless* the walking distance (waste) could be eliminated. The countermeasure becomes obvious: Move the two operators side-by-side at one end of the room so they can complete each document one at a time and move it to the customer. Eliminate what gets in the way of work (walking distance), don't justify it.

Process thinking is the new thoughtware and it creates a process-focused structure that generates a capacity for performance improvement. It requires an understanding of what process means, why it's difficult to embrace, and what it takes to make it happen. It's well worth the learning curve because the organization's capacity to improve customer value and financial performance increases by order of magnitude. And that's what this book is about.

A PRÉCIS ON HOW THE MODEL WORKS

Process thinking is rooted in the relationships that connect three distinct requisites of all work: *Purpose–Measure–Action*. These are the foundation of the model and it begins with this understanding:

A business process is a set of activities that produce an outcome, a specific service, or product for customers. Value is always the result of some process.

First, we define the purpose of a process, then the measure tells us how far from the purpose we are (i.e., a variance). And, the measure incites action on the process to improve it (i.e., an experiment). In turn, the measure validates the experiment by telling us if it got us closer to the purpose (i.e., Did the experiment provide a countermeasure to the variance?). Figure 1.9 depicts the process.

Purpose: To fulfill customer demand. The purpose becomes an external focus on customer value, at every point of the process, rather than an internal, top-down focus on shareholder value and its sub-elements, such as meet the budget or make the month end. The primacy of purpose, throughout the organization, concentrates

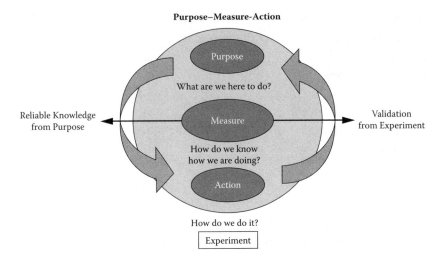

FIGURE 1.9
Process-focused model.

on meeting customer demand and delivering customer value, not shareholder value. The latter is a result of the former. Too often, the "contrived" purpose of an organization is seen as shareholder value, which is valued by the capital markets, not the customer. Of course, ultimate performance lives or dies by dollar signs, as it is the language everyone understands, but is not the purpose of the process. For the process mind, shareholder value, or for that matter, profit, are not the purpose. They are, like quality, a process specification.

Measure: To measure and improve the process as defined by its purpose (based on reliable knowledge from the purpose). Measure becomes a preoccupation with the capability of, and variation in, the process rather than an obsession with targets. The measure is embedded in the work itself and comes from real, concrete, in-the-moment observation, not from remote, abstract, after-the-fact information systems that are separate from the work. New measures incite action *on* the process, *on* the flow of work, in real time. And, they divert action away from efforts to control resources. In the new model, the only true value of a measure is whether it helps the organization understand and improve process. If it improves process, it will improve performance.

Action: To apply experimentation, based on the measure, so as to incite an action on the process. Actions are experiments that validate, through the measure, how to get closer to achieving the purpose. The actions are taken on the process, on the workflow, not on things that control discrete resources and manage people. Actions are designed to learn, not impose controls.

To change the business model, we need to adopt the new thoughtware of Purpose–Measure–Action.

Despite the litany of organizations that have not achieved expected levels of improvement, there is a growing number who have, and I tell many of their stories throughout the book. They are, perhaps, like the gleaming towers of Chennai, a beacon to the many organizations that remain stuck on the wrong side of the performance paradox and have not yet found their way to sustainable process and performance improvement. It is my hope that this book will be a starting point for many. It can be done—is being done—and my visit to Chennai certainly reinforced my resolve to help more companies develop what I think is an imperative operating system and the requisite thoughtware for a twenty-first-century enterprise.

REFERENCES

1. Institute for Competiveness: Livability Index. 2012. Online at: http://competitiveness.in/2012/12/26/liveability-index-2012/ (accessed December 26, 2012).
2. Muthiah, S. 2004. *Madras rediscovered*. Madras, India: East West Books Pvt. Ltd., 6.
3. Roberts, J. M., and O. S. Westad. 2013. *History of the world*. Oxford, U.K.: Oxford University Press, 300.
4. The Evolution of the BPO Industry in India. 2005. Survey by PricewaterhouseCoopers Pvt. Ltd. Online at: http://www.pwc.in/en_IN/in/assets/pdfs/evolution-of-bpo-in-india.pdf
5. Stalk, G., Jr., and T. E. Hout. 1990. *Competing against time: How time-based competition is reshaping global markets*. New York: Free Press Macmillan, 76–77.
6. Ibid., pp. 76–77.
7. Ibid., p. 50–51.
8. Ibid., p. 46.

2

Apple's Little Secret

Stop trying to build a better mousetrap.

DUMBEST IDEA IN THE WORLD

Many say that Steve Jobs was a genius. He went where few have gone before, creating products and markets where none existed and where only he imagined. That genius is evident throughout the Apple® kingdom and, for many organizations, it is difficult to duplicate because cloning Steve Jobs is impossible, and consistently generating innovative products and improving performance is, at best, demanding—tried by many, achieved by few. At the core of Apple, there is a not-so-evident principle that is part of its genius and something that other organizations *can* duplicate. It is the principle that is at the heart of this book and at the core of many successful companies. Its essence is captured in this axiom: *Stop trying to build a better mousetrap and start building a mousetrap better.* Steve Jobs and Tim Cook did exactly this. It's what I call Apple's little secret.[1]

Before I delve into that secret, let me comment on the vagaries of Apple's stock. The decline in the stock price from 2012 to 2013 has little-to-no relationship to the principle I am addressing—performance improvement. Jack Welch (chemical engineer, author, and former chairman and CEO of General Electric), named by Forbes magazine, "CEO of the twentieth century," has called maximizing shareholder value the "dumbest idea in the world."* He understands that it is the wrong driver of performance and success. There is no real leverage in shareholder value because it is an outcome,

---

* (Interview with Francesco Guerrera of *Financial Times* on March 12, 2009).

not a driver. The Apple stock may be down based on market "expectations," but it is still a very profitable company and a significantly superior performer.

Apple has done what millions of companies should do. And *can do.* And, it doesn't require a Steve Jobs. In fact, what I am talking about can be attributed, in large part, to Tim Cook, an industrial engineer. He's a warehouse and distribution guy. Part of Job's brilliance was hiring Cook in 1998. Jobs and Cook both knew that one of the cornerstones of competitive advantage was anchored in the capacity to create better products faster and get them in the hands of customers faster than anyone else—from idea to sold. They understood that in addition to making a better mousetrap (i.e., iPhones, iPads, iPods), they would have a significant advantage if they focused on building a mousetrap better using a process to generate demand (e.g., Apple stores), a process to fulfill demand (e.g., supply chains), and a process to innovate (e.g., series of new products in rapid succession). Cook and Jobs understood *the primacy of process* and fundamentally changed the core process of generating and converting a customer request into customer satisfaction.

The process is the most innovative product you can build.

Building a mousetrap better might sound like a simple turn of phrase but, in fact, it is a dramatic turn of thinking. It is new thoughtware rooted in process. The original phrase, "Build a better mousetrap and they will beat a path to your door," was coined by Ralph Waldo Emerson (1809–1888) and ever since it has been an inspiring metaphor for innovation. And, as Nike CEO, Mark Parker, says, "Innovate or die."[2] But in the twenty-first, speed-is-everything century, product innovation alone is not enough, process innovation is more critical. Process innovation is about delivering more customer value. Apple's customer value exceeds everything its competitors have done (so far) and its time-to-market and time-to-fulfillment is unprecedented. It's about being a process thinker, not just a product thinker. If you spill milk and then try and save it, you are a product thinker, but if you focus on changing the process so there's less spilled milk, you are a process thinker. Innovation only happens in process thinking organizations and the process is the most innovative "product" you can build. If you become amazing at process, you have a chance of being like Apple. If not, you might be more like Microsoft®, or even BlackBerry®. In 2010, Microsoft, one of the best product innovators over the past two decades, launched a social phone called "Kin." It was a disaster and, within six weeks of launch, the entire product group was shut down and the company took at least a $240 million write-off. One of the reasons? They never really recognized process innovation as a critical prerequisite to product innovation and integrated them.[3] BlackBerry's near $1 billion write-down on hardware inventory in the second quarter of 2013 is sufficient information to recognize their intergalactic distance from being a process thinker.[4]

INNOVATION IS AN UNDEPENDABLE PROCESS

An article on the *Management Innovation eXchange* blog (Why Most Innovative Companies Aren't) states that: "What makes innovative companies unique is, well, that they are unique."[5] Essentially, what the authors say is that most companies have few innovative competencies or practices in common, with the exception of their brand, that distinguish them as unique. They don't have distinct strategies, special financing, or unique recruiting practices. They are unique because they are highly adapted to their specific situation and they are highly adaptive because they are process-oriented organizations. Corporations spend billions of dollars on innovation training every year and innovative programs, such as stage gating, and other creative methods, but they fundamentally miss one thing. They are limited in coordinating and integrating innovation across their businesses because of the conventional organization design: compartmentalized, segmented, and disconnected functions and associated policy set up under the illusion of optimal efficiency, performance reliability, and predictability. Innovation has nothing to do with departments or functions nor is it a reliable process. Innovation is, in fact, an undependable process.

Consider the 2010 *BusinessWeek* Innovation Survey[6] of thousands of senior managers in dozens of countries. It identified the following as the greatest challenges to make innovation happen in their companies:

1. Lengthy development times
2. Lack of coordination
3. A risk-adverse culture
4. Limited customer insight

Ironically, during the worst recession in nearly a century, money was not among the top barriers, nor was strategy nor technology nor competencies, which are usually the excuses. According to these executives, the biggest challenge they faced was connecting the dots between departments, regions, and other companies. The main limitation is control-based rules and vertical organizational structures. Innovation requires not prescriptive rulebooks, but instructions on experimentation and discovery; not functions called "research and development" or "marketing" or "information technology" or "product development," but new value delivery processes that collect knowledge, provide an experimental method that creates valid results, and an entire end-to-end process flow that connects the dots. This change may not be sufficient by itself, but it is fundamental to innovation. Apple knows it.

Apple has great products and brilliant people, but Jobs and Cook knew that, in the technology industry, competitors like Samsung, BlackBerry, and Microsoft could, and would, compete on product innovation, services, and people, but to compete on process innovation and time-and-cost-to-market was a much higher barrier. Tim Cook came in and dismantled and rebuilt Apple's supply chain as a make-to-order business not as a make-to-stock one. He knew that all processes consisted of two types of time: the time that the work facilitates flow (we call that the work itself) and the time that something disrupts flow, gets in the way of the work, which is referred to by Lean apostles as *waste*. Cook brought a process mind, process thinking, and waste removal to every facet of Apple's business.

According to Walter Isaacson in his book on Steve Jobs:

> Cook reduced the number of Apple's key suppliers from a 100 to 24, forced them to cut better deals to keep the business, convinced many to locate near Apple's plants, and closed 10 of the company's 19 warehouses. By reducing places where inventory could pile up, he reduced inventory. Jobs had cut inventory from two months' worth of product down to one by early 1998. By September of that year, Cook had gotten it down to six days. By the following September, it was down to an amazing two days' worth. In addition he cut the production process for making Apple computers from four months to two. All of this not only saved money, it also allowed each new computer to have the very latest components available.[7]

Today, Apple has a major competitive advantage because not only are they better at building new products, but they have a process that is bringing them to the customer faster and more cost-effectively. The lesson-learned is that it is not the complex business environment that is the issue (i.e., globalization, technology, financial markets), it is the appropriateness of the business process used to respond to that environment that dictates success, just as it is not the weather that matters, but how one dresses for the weather. Today, businesspeople are confronted with more of everything and the future is more and more uncertain and decisions have to be made faster. Approximately 60% of Apple's revenues are generated by products that are less than four years old.[8] Harvard Business School's William Sahlman warns today's businesses about the "big eraser in the sky" that can come down at any moment and "wipe out all their cleverness and effort."[9] This is forcing the replacement of sluggish command-and-control management and associated discrete functional-focused organizations with more agile self-organizing networks, optimizing, not the parts, but the entire flow of value to the customer. In this world, it is the health of the process that prescribes success, not the well-being of any particular function.

PROCESS DEFINED

Wherever there's an exchange of information or material, there's a process.

Understanding the primacy of process is straightforward when we recognize that w*herever there's an exchange of information or material there's a process*. A process is a set of interrelated tasks that transform inputs to outputs. Organizations have hundreds of processes, however there are really only four major types:

1. Logistics processes (i.e., make a widget, ship a widget, as in manufacturers and distributors)
2. Transactional processes (i.e., converting data into decision-making information, as in back-office processing, e.g., from the time a credit card application is made to the moment the customer spends on the card)
3. Relationship processes (i.e., where production and consumption are simultaneous, as in call centers, or almost simultaneous, as in storefronts and restaurants)
4. Knowledge transfer processes (i.e., seeking to ratify answers to new questions, as in the conversion of concepts to applications, e.g., the creation of architectural drawings in engineering offices, new chemical formulas in laboratories, or new product development in research centers or ideation teams)

Although not a universal rule, the first two types of processes (logistics and transactional) can be made more effective by becoming continuously more reliable, like an automated teller machine (ATM) that works the same 99.9% of the time. The more reliable the process, the more predictable the desired outcome (i.e., customer fulfillment). In these cases, the enterprise should be making, selling, shipping, and servicing an existing customer base with the highest degree of reliability possible. The goal of such a process is to remove any variance that would impede a consistent outcome. For example, it is critical in providing customer value with ATMs that the machines are stocked with cash and read your PIN number every time. Its outcome is contingent on the binary nature of the process and if the ATM is out of order, it is not reliable. The more reliable it is, the more customer value. However, the other two types of processes (relationship and knowledge) don't necessarily have permanent, continuous activities and often don't know what the outcomes of their activities will be, regardless of the reliability of the process. There is not a direct correlation between the reliability of the process and the predictability of the outcome. These processes, in fact, are, for the most part, nonlinear, and like innovation, do poorly in a "linearized" process. Inevitably, the specifics of these types of processes are somewhat unique each time. It is difficult, for example, to give the same set of inventoried answers to every caller into a customer call center, despite the specificity of the inquiry. Instead, these processes can be effective, not through reliability, but through ongoing confirmation of the degree to which the outcome of the process meets the objective of fulfilling the customer's demand. Did the caller get the right answer (inquiry resolved) the first time? These are cogent processes, as opposed to reliable processes, in that they need to convince or persuade the result each time, as opposed to creating unfailing trust in the predictability of the process.

These processes are what I call "belly button dependent," they rely on the trained judgment of the individual to react to the situations. The reliable process of the ATM machine is not the best process for an individual's mortgage request. It would be better to use a relationship process, where the particulars can be customized for the individual applicant's circumstances. Trying to build an algorithm into the ATM to accept all types of mortgage permutations would not only be costly, it would reduce the reliability of the multiple daily, mundane transactions for which the ATM is so exceptional. In addition, the relationship process allows an up-sell opportunity for such products as investment certificates and credit cards. The mortgage process is effective to the degree the outcome ratifies the objective of customer fulfillment (i.e., an aligned mortgage meets the customer's needs, and they are so pleased they buy the investment certificate and apply for a credit card). All four types of processes can actually represent a mix of reliability and cogency. It is important to acknowledge that nothing is static; ongoing developments in technology and ever-evolving market demand require a continual reassessment of the process categorization and, as such, all four types of processes can represent a mix of reliability and cogency. For example, the customer service center may not know what type of call will come in or when, therefore, it needs to create a relationship process. However, it also can increase the likelihood of the outcome meeting the customer value objective by predicting, from history, the "flavor" of calls it will most likely receive, thereby, creating elements of a reliable process (i.e., scripts on operators' computer screens to respond to 8-of-10 of the predicted call flavors, staffing at peak hours accordingly, etc.). The restaurant relationship process cannot predict with certainty who will show up when, and order what, but they can create some reliable processes, such as assuring the servers know the specials by memory, reciting the beer selection in order of most expensive to cheapest, arriving at the table within 60 seconds of the customer being seated. Process is critical in every business, from manufacturing and logistics to finance and retail, and the opportunities to improve process are extensive throughout every organization. However, the process taxonomy is getting more and more complex and it is critical that the process be properly classified. For example, a relationship process, like the creation of a will, now looks more like an online transaction of ordering a magazine subscription and the simple logistics of buying a smartphone looks more like an elongated relationship process in order to understand the ever-increasing proliferation of packages, offerings, and options.

RELIABLE VS. COGENT (VALID) PROCESSES

In his brilliant book, *The Design of Business*, Roger Martin articulates the fundamental differences between a reliable process and a valid (i.e., cogent) process, why the distinction is at the heart of the "*innovation dilemma,*" and why organizational success requires a balance of the two. Martin says the goal of reliability is to produce consistent, predictable outcomes. The goal of the valid process is to produce outcomes that meet a desired objective (i.e., in the context of the process-focused organization discussion, that objective is accomplishing the specific outcome the customer required).

Martin suggests reliability and validity are inherently incompatible[10] and they are incompatible because they require different measures. However, for a variety of reasons, organizations have a strong bias to reliability; driven by how they set short-term goals (i.e., immediate financials, debt schedules, and quarterly analysts' reports); therefore, the proliferation of the current measurement and monitoring systems. For example, granting executives share options has prompted them to focus on short-term performance rather than the long-term health of the business, because a firm's share price can suffer a big fall if it misses its quarterly earnings target. Conversely, spending money on research and development (R&D) may hit profits in the short term, but it is vital for the firm's ultimate survival. Employee development and advertising fall into a similar vein. Roger Martin writes:

> Validity is very difficult to achieve with only quantitative measures, because those measures strip away context and nuance. Typically, to achieve a valid outcome, one must incorporate some aspects of the subjectivity and judgment, but they are eschewed in the quest for a reliable outcome.[11]

On the chart (Figure 2.1), the diagonal across the four types of processes illustrates how much reliability is in that process, how close to an ATM machine it is, and how much dependency on "belly button" operating is necessary, as far away from an ATM machine as possible. A logistics process tends to be predominately designed for reliability, while a knowledge transfer process has a high degree of customization and variability. The point being, it is necessary for the executive to balance the mix of each process and, yet, without the power of process-focused organizational structure, without a process mind, it is difficult to manage with, and across, these variations. That is the challenge and, yet, all the continuous improvement and productivity enhancement initiatives (TQM, Six Sigma) tend to reinforce reliability in seeking to make processes more reliable. To move across core business processes from logistics to knowledge transfer, there is a need for less reliability and more personal bias, more discovering from experimentation, and constant midcourse adjustments as the process learns and adapts to achieve the desired (valid) outcome. Therefore, they are cogent processes, requiring ongoing influence and persuasion from the "belly buttons" in the process. However, it is difficult to move to creating healthy processes in the expanding world of knowledge transfer,

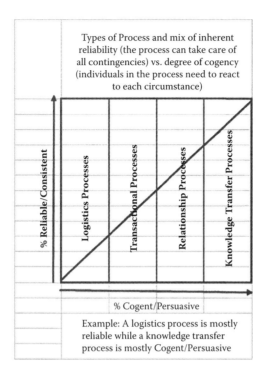

FIGURE 2.1
Process types: Reliability vs. Cogency.

relationship dependent and transactional processes that look more and more cogent as they inject more and more variety into these processes. Again to quote Martin:

> … today's complex, elaborate, firmware, software … Enterprise Resource Planning (ERP), … Customer Relationship Management (CRM) …, Six Sigma and Total Quality Management (TQM)… and Knowledge Management (KM) to organize all the knowledge of the corporation … enable the modern corporation to crunch data objectively and extrapolate from the past to make scientific predictions about the future. …[12]

THE APPLE DOESN'T FALL FAR FROM THE PROCESS

Apple is just one example, albeit, an excellent one, of the performance value of process. Jobs knew he had to build lean, healthy, vibrant, fast processes. That was his not-so-secret ingredient and his secret weapon was

Tim Cook. Most good business practitioners know that they have to be good at reducing inventory, wait times, transactional time, rework, hand-offs, etc., but what they don't realize is how inextricably linked all of these are to the health of their processes. Too often this "stuff" is seen as the mundane, the details, the in-the-trenches stuff, and so it becomes some-one else's job to understand and fix.

Tim Cook and leaders like him know the incredible hidden costs buried in the trenches and they roll up their sleeves and dig into it. It's about understanding that the purpose of the process is to deliver customer value and in a marketplace that seeks more variety, more individualized products and services, success means a process capable of fulfilling that customer demand and doing so inside the window of time, where the clock only starts after the confirmed request is made (i.e., make to actual demand, not schedule to a forecast). Your process must be faster to market than the demand time, faster than the competition. Steve understood it; Tim knew how to do it.

We are well aware of Apple's financial success. In August 2012, the shares hit $708 and had a market capitalization over $600 billion. And, although the stock price dropped significantly in 2013, Apple remains a great performer. Not bad considering Steve Jobs didn't begin to resurrect the company until 1997. The real story begins back in 1980 when Apple was three years old. They went to New York, got publicly listed, and opened at $14 a share. It sold something like 4.8 million shares in a matter of hours and created about 300 millionaires.[13] It was the highest market cap or IPO since Ford in 1956. It traded in the $21 to $29 range and was worth about $1.8 billion. It had a good run … but by 1985, the stock was down to about $7 a share. That downslide was, in part, after John Sculley, ex-president of PepsiCo, had joined Apple in 1983. At first, he was considered a great addi-tion, but it became apparent that his views were very different from those of Steve Jobs. Ironically, when Jobs had pressed Sculley to come over from PepsiCo and join him, he ostensibly said, "Do you want to sell sugared water for the rest of your life or do you want to come with me and change the world?" Sculley's strategy was to go toe-to-toe with IBM in the hard-ware market, so he built up the necessary supply chain infrastructure. It turned out to be a bad decision. Worse, in 1985, he forced Jobs out. After the precipitous decline of Apple, Sculley left in 1993.

In 1996, Apple stock was $7. But then, in late 1996, Apple bought Jobs' company, NeXT, for $427 million.[14] The NeXT operating system would evolve into the Mac OS X. In 1997, Jobs was officially back. Initially, they called him an "advisor," but by late 1997, he was the de facto chief and, in 2000, he became the CEO. Jobs made two brilliant decisions. First, he changed the business model. Whether explicit or implicit, every organization has a business model and the more explicit, the more successful. A business model describes the manner in which value is delivered to the customer—in most cases for a profit. It is set up to respond to three key questions: What do customers want? How do they want it? And, how do we best optimize the organization to do it? But most importantly, and often lacking in a good business model, is a fourth question: How does the business model provide the opportunity for the organization to continually innovate for future customer wants? The fourth question is most important and most often the least thought through, because it provides the underlying operating thoughtware system for long-term innovation, growth, and, ultimately, survival. Apple's business model was to make downloading digital music easy and convenient. It was the opposite of the Gillette model that gave away the razors to sell the blades. It reversed it by giving away low-margin iTunes music in order to sell high-margin iPods. However, the Apple model could only be deployed with effective and appropriate operating thoughtware. In Apple, as in all businesses, the operating thoughtware is powered by business processes. The business process can be thought of as the organization's circulatory system, where smart processes continually oxygenate and enrich the blood, while lousy processes yield bad blood and sluggish enterprises. I define "smart processes" as ones where every employee can see the flow of value to the customer and can fix any variance (i.e., disruption to that flow) before it reaches the customer.

END-TO-END PROCESS VALUE

Then came the second big decision—Jobs introduced the Apple stores, which delivered the most critical stage of customer value in the end-to-end process. Jobs saw the bigger picture and knew that there would be a real competitive advantage in being both fast-to-market and managing the entire process from customer back upstream to product development. He did not want Apple products caught up in someone else's distribution channel or retail system. So, he went retail and, by January 2014, there were 432 stores in 14 countries with global sales of $16 billion (2011) and

Apple leads the U.S. retail market in terms of sales per unit area.[15] However, this was about more than simply being in the retail business; he wanted to add value through the entire process. He didn't just design a store, he created an experience, a market, a theater, and a process that ended in a place where customer satisfaction met customer expectations, and delivered better than anyone else. Apple stores redesigned the retail process. Like an army general, he understood that no matter how capable, if you can't control your supply chain, you are operating at high risk and low competitive advantage. And, if you are to be really fast, you must have the very best internal processes. Jobs and Cook decided they would build product on a make-to-order basis and, to achieve that, the lead time had to be inside demand. That was a tall order, an order that could only be achieved with a focus on process innovation that complemented product innovation.

Steve Jobs was a good manager. Apple board chair, Ed Woodward, said, "He became a good manager, which is different from being an executive or visionary, and that pleasantly surprised me."[16] Even today, this aspect of Jobs' brilliance is little recognized. Why? Because many leaders still do not see what he saw or understand what he understood. His success is usually seen in his design of innovative products and in his passion, focus, and "right or nuts" character. However, his focus mantra led to the search for, and elimination of, inefficiencies and waste in the process—anything that disrupted flow. Perhaps his intuitive understanding of the power of flow stemmed from his lifelong following of Eastern, mystic beliefs like *Prajna* (i.e., wisdom) and the dynamic action and human involvement that is essential to Zen practice. This is the less understood factor in Apple's achievement and its capacity to deliver an endless stream of great products to satisfy extraordinary demand better, faster, and more efficiently than the competition.

It's simple. It's brilliant. It's process thinking. Thinking that reaches from the process mind to being installed in the guts of the company. Jobs and Cook designed their processes and instilled an understanding, in a macro sense, that *the purpose of their process* was to fill demand; meet and exceed customers' expectations. That's it. And, everything works toward that purpose. In Jobs' words, process design is not "how it looks, it's how it works."

The purpose of the process is to deliver customer value.

Tim Cook is not a tech genius or a nerdy guru or a John Sculley. He graduated from Auburn University in industrial engineering and got a business degree from Duke. He came to Apple from Compaq, where he was running the procurement operation and he had been at IBM overseeing distribution. At Apple, Cook dismantled Sculley's infrastructure. By 2012, Apple was carrying four days of inventory and turning it 74 times a year.[17] That's extraordinary. Samsung was at 17 times a year. To put some perspective on it, in 2013, RIM (developer of the BlackBerry), at the height of their struggles and the low point of their value, had to write down almost a billion dollars or two years' worth of inventory.[18] That represents about half a turn, which starkly illustrates the correlation between process thinking and dollars. In the retail electronics market, compare Apple carrying four days of inventory to people like Circuit City (we know what happened to them) who carried 60 days, or Best Buy at 50 days, Walmart at 40 days, Amazon at 30 days, and you see the difference—competitively and financially. Every day a product sits on a shelf, due to the inefficiency of the process, its value erodes by 1 to 2%.[19]

Of all the lessons from Apple, I believe the correlation between process design and success is the most important. So, why can Apple do it while so many others can't? Was Steve Jobs that prescient? Is Tim Cook the only industrial engineer who understands that the guys with the better process win, every time?

Apple's designing of the best products and the best processes is anchored in time: time-to-market, time-to-fulfillment, and time to solve problems. As noted, one place where time manifests itself, and can be measured, is in inventory, which can be a gauge of the health of your overall process. Inventory is a measure of how quickly material and information flows through the customer value delivery process. Inventory is easily seen and touched, but it is best described as "a representation of time," it's a measure of time. In the logistics process, inventory is concrete and visible, but, to the process mind, all processes can dramatically improve, like Apple's, by recognizing the "inventory of time." In a transactional process or a relationship process or a knowledge process, we have time stacked up, or information in queue. Although it's not called *inventory*, it serves the same purpose of creating a buffer, which is a disruption in the process. It is waste and all it does is disrupt flow. You may think you don't have inventory and assume that building a better process does not apply. However, all processes have an inventory of time called waiting. For example, the business process outsourcing (BPO) in Chennai had applications waiting to be processed, or in process, or finished, but waiting for the completion of their batch. It was all inventory-in-process. The inventory of time is a huge hidden cost. Huge. For example, if you could have a perfectly linear process, you wouldn't need inventory, but inventory is carried because you need more time to get to market and you have to protect yourself against demand exceeding supply. So, the buffers are built into processes along with their intrinsic costs, which are buried in plain view when you begin to use process thinking. The great opportunity is the reduction of time. I call it "buried treasure" and I elaborate on how to turn all that waste into treasure in Chapter 10, How to Conduct a Treasure Hunt.

SMART PROCESSES: APPLE IS NOT ALONE

Many organizations are doing what Apple is doing and all is not in disarray in the not-well-understood world of process design, but the doers are certainly in the minority. I have seen incredible performance improvement in companies around the globe, from underground mines to big banks, and from two degrees south of the Arctic Circle (Finland) to two degrees north of the equator (Indonesia). What do these companies have in common? Two things: a business model built on smart processes, and an aligned and effective thoughtware system that drives them. Discount retailing (championed by Walmart and Target) now accounts for 75% of the retail sector (America's Top Stores Consumer Report, June 2012). They've broken the conventional model by building better processes, moving from a retail mindset to a distribution mindset and understanding that accelerating the supply chain process was the critical element of their success. A discount pricing business model is enabled by the low costs derived from the volumes (throughput) and the lead times (time) that a smart logistics process provides.

Today, the vast majority of everything we buy comes from retail discounters.[20] Low-cost airlines broke the hub-and-spoke model with the discount, quick-turnaround model, and now represent a major segment of all flights people take. Others like Bank Corp, although only sixth in assets (behind the likes of JP Morgan Chase, Citigroup, and Bank of America), exemplify the success of a process business model based on creating a brilliant circulatory system of process thinking in the mundane world of accepting deposits, making loans, issuing cards, and providing wealth management advice. Danaher is a poster child even though hardly anyone has heard of them. They are a very successful, diversified $18-billion corporation owning more than 60 companies. I have seen what they have done first-hand, having managed a project for a company that was bought by Danaher. Interestingly, their website says, "The origin of the name Danaher goes back to the root 'Dana,' a Celtic word dating from before 700 BCE and meaning *swift flowing*." For me, if you think swift flow, you are thinking process. In their own words, they state, "Danaher became one of the first North American companies to utilize the principles of *Kaizen*, the Japanese word for continuous improvement and utilize process thinking at '*every location, function, and level to shape strategy, focus execution, and create value for customers and shareholders alike*.'" They get it, from the origins of their name to their current, everyday thoughtware, they get it.

It's not just what you sell, it's how you sell it.

Of course, new models become old models and competitors change the landscape with yet another model; thus, my emphasis is on the often overlooked and critical fourth key question of the business model. How does the business model allow the opportunity for the organization to continually adapt and innovate for future customer wants? In retail, the classic example is Amazon. The September 2013 issue of *Fast Company* noted that Amazon beat out Apple in a Harris poll of the most trusted companies in the world. They said, "Amazon disrupted and defined the global marketplace" and, in 2012, had $61 billion in sales and, for the first time, ecommerce sales cracked $1 trillion and Amazon has a 5% share. They have grown to 210 million customers in 20 years.[21] What is important is not what Amazon sells, but how they sell it. It's about their process. They have built the mousetrap better with process improvements like the "iclick" ordering app tailored to impulse buying and "subscribe and save" for regular replenishment of essentials. They are process-oriented and all about speed and convenience for the customer. Amazon Prime, for $99 a year, guarantees second-day delivery on any and all purchases for that year. Two years ago, Amazon Prime had 5 million subscribers, and by 2013 it was 10 million, and by 2017 it is projected to be 25 million. Each prime subscriber spends an average of $1,224 a year compared to non-Prime subscribers at about $700 a year.[22] One of the reasons they can compete at this level is because they have 89 fulfillment centers around the world where they fulfill an order in two and a half hours and, worldwide, they fulfill 309 items per second. They also have full-time process improvement teams at these centers who are continually trying to reduce the two and a half-hour process. Even more illuminating is the fact that Amazon, despite $61 billion in sales, only had $82 million in profit in the first quarter of 2013,[23] which tangibly makes the point that they focus on customer value, not shareholder value.

THE PROCESS MIND AT SOUTHWEST AIRLINES

There are other business models driven by process-focused operating systems that have been quite successful. Going back to the mid-1990s, we can learn a lot about process thoughtware from Southwest Airlines. Southwest Airlines' business model gave birth to hundreds of discount airlines around the globe and today there are well over a hundred, self-claimed discount airlines, and, with that proliferation and the continued subsidization of legacy operators (i.e., through bankruptcy protection and government handouts), the industry continues to get more competitive. Even though Southwest is currently struggling to move to the next level of performance while managing with razor-thin margins (about 3%), it's a great story about what the process mind can achieve. Herb Keller, founder of the airline, was one of the first to recognize the power of process. Southwest's dominance of the low-cost carrier segment of the industry has been attributed to the application of operational efficiency techniques rooted in process thinking. In two years (1992–1993), it increased market share in California from 26% to 45%. It achieved a flying cost of 7.1 cents per mile versus over 10 cents for other major airlines. It used 81 employees per aircraft versus 150 needed by competitors. It also handles 2,443 passengers per employee compared to 850 by competitors. Southwest's tarmac turnaround time is a good illustration of how a culture of process thinking gave it a key competitive advantage.[24]

A discount or low-cost airline is one that offers low fares in exchange for elimination of many traditional passenger services. It is an industry within an industry. However, Southwest pioneered the idea and, in the 1990s, it was revolutionary thinking. Since then, they have been copied by WestJet, JetBlue, Ryanair, and many others. However, not everyone got it right. Some of the early adapters crashed miserably (pun intended) because they didn't understand the critical role process played in gaining and sustaining cost efficiencies. Remember People's Express airline? They failed for several reasons, primarily because they tried to run a discount airline without changing fundamental pieces of the business model. For example, they tried to get landing rights in places where the big guys could keep them out instead of flying into smaller hubs. That meant that customers who wanted to fly from Buffalo to Washington, ended up in Baltimore. More importantly, they didn't think of changing essential processes like tarmac turnaround time that had significant inherent costs. Instead of thinking differently, they just stripped costs. They thought they could simply buy secondhand planes, pay staff less, eliminate reservations, serve cheap food, and cram in more seats. They thought they could just build a better mousetrap and the people would come. But, stripping out easy-to-get-at costs didn't get them there because many more costs were buried in the processes. People's Express became known as "People's Distress." To compete they would have had to change the underlying operating system of the discount business model. They didn't. It was a hard landing. Ultimately, they were financially stretched and became part of Continental Airlines.[25]

At Southwest, Bill Franklin, former vice president of ground operations, knew airplanes only made money in the air, so he and others calculated that three airplanes could do the work of four if the planes were in and out of a gate in 10 minutes. And, back then, at $50 million a plane, that was a huge cost savings. It was about putting more passengers on fewer planes. The birth of the "10-minute turnaround" meant passengers and baggage were unloaded, the plane was cleaned and restocked, and passengers boarding in 10 minutes. At the time, most airlines took over an hour for that process.

Southwest's thinking started with a disregard for the traditional airline business model built around functions and departments and a high regard for the people in the organization. Soon employees figured out how to work together to get the flight airborne in such a short time. Operations agents performed numerous tasks, including loading and unloading baggage, emptying waste, and helping passengers—a lot of multitasking. Even flight attendants and pilots chipped in by cleaning and the pilots volunteered to work the ramps to better understand what ramp workers did. Someone characterized it: "It's like there's nobody anywhere and then all of a sudden everybody comes in like a beehive, going zoom, zoom, zoom … they all just swarm in, and then the next thing you know you're boarding the aircraft."[26] There were other benefits as well. By having one type of plane, they could train pilots, crew, and mechanics at lower costs by reducing training time and improving on-the-job performance. The same was true for suppliers who installed galleys and seats, which saved millions in bills for material changes. Here, as in all these models, the high respect for people is paramount, as is providing a horizontal process in which people can move around and do what delivers customer value versus being restricted by rigid rules and stupid policies. Interestingly, a recent study by Boeing, *Role of Computer Simulation in Reducing Airplane Turn Times*, showed that the pace at which passengers board a plane has slowed by 50% since 1970.[27] Reasons might include a longer list of priority boarders and more carry-on baggage blocking the aisles; nevertheless, quicker boarding time means airlines save money—approximately $30 for every minute saved, according to CNN *Business Traveler.*[28]

Your business processes more than your products and services will best predict your ability to compete, generate profit, and outperform your competition.

PROCESS THINKING AND THE PROCESS MIND

Like most things, a focus on process begins in our heads, it starts with a process mind. It's not that we don't think about these things, we do, a lot. Rather it's that our minds are not good at changing the way we think. We believe what we believe, we know what we know, and we can't know what we don't know. So, if something is not obvious or not understood, then we are more comfortable with what we already think. Ergo, we don't open up to new thinking despite evidence that appears to oppose what we know. We stay in our comfort zone. Roger Martin, dean at the Rotman School of Management at the University of Toronto, has another book, *The Opposable Mind*, that illustrates that leaders who do break out of this pattern " ... have the capacity to hold two diametrically opposed ideas in their heads and ... are able to produce a synthesis that is superior to either opposing idea."[29] He calls this *integrative thinking*, the process of consideration and synthesis. This is part of process thinking. For example, when we think of speed, we usually tend to think of it as mutually exclusive from quality, but new thoughtware sees speed and quality as one and the same. In the same way, respect for people and productivity are the same, as are safety and superior performance. One of the opposing, classical limitations to process thinking is the preconceived notion that speed (flow) and efficiency (low cost) are mutually exclusive. As such, the traditional organization tries to optimize the parts (functions) for productivity and, yet, we know if we optimized flow (less efficient at nonconstraint parts) we will get better productivity (i.e., the Chennai BPO project).

Applied process thinking fills customer demand faster.

Have two teams of four people sit in a line, with four blank cards in front of the first person on each team. Team A is a "vertical, batch-thinking" team. Team A's first person writes their full name on each of the four cards, then passes them, in a batch, to the second person. The second person will likewise complete all four cards before passing them to the third person, etc. Team B is a "horizontal, process-thinking" team. Team B's first person writes their name on one card and passes it to the next person, then repeats the process with the next card. Meanwhile, the second person writes their name on the first card and passes it to the third person, etc. As you can surmise, Team B will complete the exercise (i.e. fulfill customer demand) an order of magnitude sooner than Team A. What's the difference? Applied process thinking.

THINK ABOUT IT

It's far better to have the wrong answer to the right question than it is to have the right answer to the wrong question.

A ball and a bat cost $1.10 in total. The bat costs a $1 more than the ball. How much does the ball cost? The initial reaction of most people is "10 cents." Don't feel bad, more than half of a group of students at Princeton and the University of Michigan gave that wrong answer.[30] Why? Because the $1.10 neatly separates into a $1 and 10 cents and our brain defaults to the easiest, to the most familiar. The same is true about our familiar vertical organizational structures that neatly separate thinking and doing between functions and departments and between experts and workers. It's often called silo thinking and it has the tendency to optimize the parts at the expense of the whole. A survey by AtTask, a Utah-based software firm, determined more than 50% of respondents said departmentally siloed information is their top challenge in managing data.[31] Our traditional response to this silo mentality is meetings, often called the prison of the working dead. The survey determined that 74% believed meetings were a waste of time and that they do other work during meetings. Meetings, spreadsheet proliferation, memos, reports, etc. are all efforts to overcome the dysfunction of functionality-siloed organizations. Silos not only hide the right answer, but deceive us into believing the wrong answer is right. The right answer in this case is, of course, five cents.

The right answer is hard to see; we have to work at it. We go to the wrong answer because it's simplistic, easier, and quicker to rationalize. Professor Daniel Kahneman of Woodrow Wilson School of Public and International Affairs at Princeton University and author of a groundbreaking book, *Thinking Fast and Slow* (Farrar, Straus, and Giroux, 2011), warns us not to look at this baseball query as a trick question. He says, "People are not accustomed to thinking hard and are often content to trust plausible judgment that comes quickly to mind." His Nobel Memorial Prize in Economics resulted from research that "reveals these logical inconsistencies in managers' decision-making represent the rule rather than the exception." It is "the pathological mistakes and persistent miscalculations" managers make that are at the heart of his research. And it supports my premise that the process mind and process thinking requires *thinking hard*. That's why most organizations don't do it. Creating process structure is fairly straightforward, but using process thinking is tough work. It requires the ability to reach beyond the traditional department walls where managers influence with authority, to the "white space" between functions where one must now influence without authority. The latter is a much more difficult and rarer skill. The leadership approach for the Process Mind is to lead as if you have no power.

―――――――――

OLD THOUGHTWARE STICKS LIKE GLUE

ABC Adhesives (name changed) achieved a dramatic shift in thinking. ABC is a manufacturer in a suburb of a large U.S. city with plants across the country. They were at a stage where the CEO, let's call him Alan, said, "People can now do 85% of what we have learned about process. We understand it. But that's not good enough; I need 100%." I continued to work with them and Alan said my role was "to continually provide disruptive new thoughtware and help them uncover that last 15%." Essentially, I made sure that the primacy of process was front and center, all of the time, and kept them true to the principle that their most important job is to improve the process.

When I first went to the main plant, I found what I find everywhere I go—a lot of old thoughtware. They were taking the traditional inward-focused top-down, productivity-financial perspective rather than an outward, customer perspective. ABC makes adhesives and sealants like caulking (glue) and it is mainly a chemical process that mixes big vats of a variety of recipes. This is then fed into lines to fill tubes, tubs, and pails. We started with a $20 million product process (i.e., model or demonstration line) and looked at it horizontally instead of the conventional vertical view. The first step was to change the thinking about the purpose of what they were doing. Instead of making vats of glue, they began to see they were creating products for customers who were not buying what was mixed in the vats, rather they were buying tubes, pails, or tubs of products that helped them in renovating and building homes. Then we looked at the performance measure. Their key performance metric was labor-cost-per-pound, so I pointed out the disconnect between such a measurement and what customers were buying. Customers weren't buying pounds of chemical mix, so why measure the labor component that way? Instead of measuring the labor component, we started measuring the number of products we were satisfying the customer with, which meant measuring the number of tubes, tubs, and pails produced. They set up a visual management process and a new measurement: the number of pallets filled. The reason we did pallets was because they were all the same configuration and provided a consistent unit of measure, whereas, the size of tubes, tubs, and pails varied. Every time a pallet went out, they counted it. At first, this new process made Alan nervous because labor cost was the historical measurement on which he depended. But, he decided to experiment. This was a big breakthrough—experiment, and learn.

Initially, they set an objective of 60 pallets per shift. First run, they did 30. Then 39, then 40, then 50. At 50, they analyzed the variances (i.e., problems) and why they were happening, and fixed them. Within eight weeks, they were consistently hitting 60. At this level, they were fulfilling demand and could hit that demand in four days. So, the question became: What should they do with the fifth day? Alan's first thought was to cut back on shifts and downsize the workforce (labor costs). Wrong thinking—old thoughtware.

Excess capacity is an opportunity, not waste.

Originally, the problem had been that the production process could not meet demand in five days and now that that was solved, the old thoughtware kicked back in and figured the smart thing to do would be to reduce capacity, particularly since they could not increase demand immediately. The excess capacity was seen as waste. I told him, if you downsize the workforce, you will lose everything you have gained. First, the people's knowledge of the process and problem solving goes out the door with them and your process will slide backwards. Secondly, the very minds that improved your process and made you more money, will ask themselves: "What kind of reward is that?" For them, it will be the last time they contribute to improving a business that then lays them off. It makes no sense. So, what we did (i.e., another management learning experience) was run four days of production and on the fifth day focus on increasing demand to fill the new capacity.

Alan's first reaction was typical—old thoughtware. It seems like the natural thing to do. If you can't immediately get more volume through to absorb the extra 20% capacity, then you should cut the capacity. Many CEOs or vice presidents of manufacturing would think, I can now report that I saved 20%, so why not? You can do that, but you will never achieve it again. What you want to do is do it again and again. Either reduce costs by another 20% or go to another plant and repeat the process. That's what ABC did. They went and reduced costs by 20% in plants across the country. It was a $12-million cost reduction in one year without any headcount reduction. The following year, their ability to deliver faster (shorter lead times) and better (quality) allowed them to completely fill the freed-up capacity generated through process thinking. They focused on getting better at the demand generation process for the plants with increased capacity. And, they continued to have employees problem solve the process and Kaizen their respective areas. That's continuous improvement—on a daily basis.

The other crucial piece of this is the respect for people. Whenever I state, "People are the heart and soul of the organization," I get CEOs nodding in agreement. Then I ask, "If you respect your people, then how can you give them a lousy process? And, worse, not ask them how to make it better?" Bad processes are tangible evidence of a lack of "respect for people." And the highest form of respect is asking people for their help. And, because only the people who live in the process understand it and can fix it, it makes sense to get them to do it. I address this critical issue in Chapter 5 (Process Design and Respect for People). As mentioned in the Prologue, respect for people is the conviction that employees have the right to be successful every time they do their job. The art of doing their job is to find problems and make improvements, which is tough to do in a layoff-thinking culture.

At ABC Adhesive, they get it. After experimenting, they understood that the point of redesigning the process was not to eliminate people, rather it was to increase throughput with the same people. The only way they could do that was by respecting the people and asking them how to do it. The main reason the people helped was because the process they had was a pain in the ass, and they knew it. Alan made the commitment to understand the primacy of process and take the perceived risk (virtually none) of having employees focus on improving the process. Process thinking now permeates the ABC workplace and frontline people are continually identifying variances, removing them, learning from them, and experimenting again, continuously building a mousetrap better. What ABC achieved in their initial model line (i.e., experimenting with $20 million product line) summarizes the power of process innovation (Figure 2.2). It demonstrates how the focus on customer value leads to improved financial value and how "respect for people," instead of laying them off, lets them continuously improve the process, which leads to process innovation, product improvement, and productivity gains.

Before Process Thinking	Measure of Success	After Process Thinking
Demand > Supply	Customer Experience	Supply > Demand
30	Throughput (*Pallets/Shift*)	52
16.10%	Perfect Order (*On-time In-full*)	93%
$2–4 million	Backlog (*Unshipped*)	$0
4 weeks	Lead Time (*Peak*)	5 days
300k over budget	Quality (*Product scrap*)	On budget
1.1	Inventory Turns (*Raw Material*)	10.7
1.3	Inventory Turns (*Finished goods*)	9.1
Apart from the process	Safety	Part of the process
	Productivity (*Throughput per employee*)	Increase of 73%

Results after 18 months of process thinking application.

FIGURE 2.2
ABC Adhesives: Performance improvement.

A CAUTIONARY TALE

In a recently published paper by William Lazonic ("Apple's Changing Business Model: What Should the World's Richest Company Do with All Those Profits?"), the author says, "Apple is undergoing a personality downgrade … captured by the shareholder value ideology and Cook and his team are now supporting value extraction rather than value creation." This use of capital can "signal that management lacks incentive or imagination to put the money to better use, such as R&D or employee development, … and they reward those who sell their shares not those who hang on to them."[32] What happens at Apple is still to be determined, but to borrow from one of Warren Buffett's principles, I say that we can't run businesses by trying to run up the stock all the time, we have to address the long-term value we are trying to create. And, it is one of the reasons Michael Dell took his public company, Dell Computers, private (Charlie Rose interview, PBS, 2013). He wanted to allow the company to focus more on the long term, be more innovative, and not always have to respond to the stock price. Process thinking and a business model built on the primacy of process are essential in creating and sustaining long-term shareholder value by focusing on everyday customer value. However, firms may shun the longer term view promoted by the process mind. They may be shy to invest these stock piles of cash, which are earning next to nothing in interest, as the incentives for management are misaligned with the process mind. One study indicates that in businesses where executives have share options as part of their pay package, when vesting time arrives (i.e., eligible to cash them in), R&D spending drops, along with outlays on capital expenditure and advertising. The study also finds that firms are more likely to top their earnings targets in quarters when options are about to vest. Are executives then fiddling with profits at the expense of the short-term customer value and long-term enterprise prosperity?[33]

REFERENCES

1. Much of the information on Apple is drawn from several articles (e.g., Re stock – Macworld, Feb.21, 2013: http://www.macworld.co.uk/news/apple/why-does-everyone-hate-apple-right-now-3427976/.
2. Carr, A. Feb.14, 2013, Fast Company, Death To Core Competency: Lessons From Nike, Apple, Netflix. http://www.fastcompany.com/3005850/core-competency-dead-lessons-nike-apple-netflix.

3. Govindarajan, V., and J. Desai. 2013. *Innovation isn't just about products. Harvard Business Review* blog. Online at: http://blogs.hbr.org/2013/09/innovation-isnt-just-about-new-products/.

4. Velazco, C. 2013. *BlackBerry reports $1.6B in revenue and a $965M loss in Q2 2014.* Online at: http://techcrunch.com/2013/09/27/blackberry-reports-1-6b-in-revenue-and-a-965m-loss-in-q2-2014-earnings/.

5. DeGraff, J. 2013. The Management Innovation eXchange (MIX). *Why most innovative companies aren't.* Online at: http://www.managementexchange.com/blog/why-most-innovative-companies-arent.

6. Andon, J. P. et al., 2010, Boston Consulting Group, Innovation 2010: A Return to Prominence and the Emergence of a New World Order, www.BCG.com/Documents/File 42620.pdf

7. Isaacson, W. 2011. *Steve Jobs.* New York: Simon & Schuster, 361.

8. Economist.com/blogs/Schumpeter/Nov.23/13/Management Thinkers Disagree on How to Manage Complexity. http://www.economist.com/news/business/21590341-management-thinkers-disagree-how-manage-complexity-its-complicated.

9. Ibid.

10. Martin, R. 2009. *The design of business.* Boston: Harvard Business Press, 37.

11. Ibid., p. 38.

12. Ibid., p. 40.

13. Livingston, J. 2007. Interview with Steve Wazniak in Founders at Work: Stories of Start-ups' Early Days (published by Apress).

14. Harreld, H. 1997. Apple gains tech agency customers in next deal, Federal Computer Week, January 5, 1997.

15. Segal, D. 2013. Apple's retail army, long on loyalty but short on pay. *The New York Times.* June 23, Business Day.

16. Isaacson, *Steve Jobs,* p. 359.

17. Miller, H. 2013. BlackBerry Ltd. Poised for writedown as inventory of unsold smartphones swells to almost $1-billion, Bloomberg News, September 19, 2013 http://business.financialpost.com/2013/09/19/blackberry-ltd-poised-for-writedown-as-inventory-of-unsold-smartphones-swells-to-almost-1-billion/? lsa=19db-b8a0

18. Petty, C. 2012. Gartner announces rankings of its 2012 supply chain top 25. Paper presented at the Gartner Supply Chain Executive Conference, Palm Desert, CA, May 21–23. Online at: http://www.gartner.com/newsroom/id/2023116 (Table 1).

19. Ibid., p. 2.

20. America's top stores. 2010. *Consumer Reports Magazine*, July. Online at: http://www.consumerreports.org/cro/magazine-archive/2010/july/shopping/retail-stores/overview/index.htm.

21. McCorvey, J. J. 2013. The race has just begun. *Fast Company* (September), 68–76.

22. Ibid.

23. Ibid.

24. Lapin, D. 2012. Lead by Greatness!: How Character Can Power Your Success, Avoda Book, pp. 135–138.

25. Frank, W. S. 2006. Leaders Should Be Aware of Uncontrolled Growth, Denver Business Journal, Oct. 30, 2006.

26. Freiberg, K., and J. Freiberg. 1996. *Nuts! Southwest Airlines' recipe for personal and business success.* New York: Broadway Books.

27. Marelli, S., G. Mattocks, and R. Merry. 2000. *Role of Computer Simulation in Reducing Airplane Turn Time.* www. Boeing.com/commercial/aeromagazine, 2000.

28. Sofell, J. 2013. Airlines and airports look to take the pain out of boarding plane. CNN *Business Traveler* (December 18). Online at: http://www.cnn.com/2013/12/17/travel/four-innovative-ways-cut-boarding-planes/index.html?iref=allsearch.

29. Martin, R. 2007. *The opposable mind*. Boston: Harvard Business School Press, 6.

30. Schrage, M. 2003. Daniel Kahneman: The thought leader interview. *strategy+business* (Winter), 121–126.

31. Vozza, S. 2014. Nine levels of work hell. *Fast Company* (footnote A), 55. Online at: http://www.fastcompany.com/3026579/work-smart/the-nine-levels-of-work-hell.

32. Lazonick, W., M. Mazzucato, and O. Tulum. 2013. Apple's Changing Business Model: What Should the World's Richest Company Do with All Those Profits? (July 1, 2013). Accounting Forum, Forthcoming. Available at SSRN: http://ssrn.com/abstract=2310608 or http://dx.doi.org/10.2139/ssrn.2310608.

33. Edmans, A., et al. 2014. *Equity vesting and managerial myopia* (footnote B, p. 61). Online at: http://ssrn.com/abstract=2270027.

3

History Repeats Itself—Unfortunately

History repeats itself, first as a tragedy then as farce.

Karl Marx

FIVE HUNDRED YEARS OF THEORIES

There is nothing more difficult and dangerous, or more doubtful of success, than an attempt to introduce a new order of things. For the innovator has for enemies all those who derived advantages from the old order, while those who expect to be benefitted by the new order will only offer lukewarm defense.

Niccolò di Bernardo dei Machiavelli (1469–1527)
Author of *The Prince*

It is said that a clever person asks difficult questions and a *very* clever person asks profoundly simple questions. You can be the judge as to whether this question is difficult or simple:

If, as we have seen in the previous chapter, a business model's success is rooted in its ability to design and drive a process-focused organization and allow for the development of process thinking management—required to bring the model to life—then why are more enterprises not racing to introduce such fundamental change; change that is necessary for dramatic performance improvement?

It is a simple question and the answer has been available for over 500 years and, yet, it is difficult because few have deeply understood the answer, and therefore, have not implemented the necessary change.

In 1513, Machiavelli observed in his treatise, *The Prince,* why organizations (colonies) introducing new management change programs (change in administrative procedures introduced by the new conquering Prince) rarely resulted in real improvements. His conclusion: The existing order of things is simply more powerful than the proposed new order.

Today, the relevant question is: How much real impact has continuous process improvement realized in comparison to the gains it was designed to achieve? The answer is: very little, particularly, if counted in terms of return on investment. Studies repeatedly reference Lean and Six Sigma failure rates in the 60 to 74% range[1] and those failure rates are consistent with and similar to other process improvement methods. A recent survey of executives confirmed 75% of companies have a continuous improvement program,[2] only 58% report even a minimal financial impact, and 70% believe their program needs a complete overhaul.[3] Generally, the failure rate, when measured against expected results, can be upward of 70%. Even laser-focused, continuous process improvement techniques like Quality Circles (our first real exposure to process thinking in the 1980s) were unsustainable in the face of *"all those who derived advantages from the old order."*[4] In the United States, 75% of all Quality Circle initiatives that started in 1982 had been abandoned by 1986.[5] In the 1990s, the reengineering movement took the business world by storm, gathering speed and peaking in 1994. According to an article by Holtham and a book edited by Coulson, it then moved on to public services and disappeared as a hot topic around 1997.[6] It is apparent that grafting these process-focused programs onto functionally-designed structures just does not work. These efforts are like weight loss programs that typically start off well, generating excitement and progress, but then fail to have a lasting impact as participants lose motivation and fall back into old habits. I am not suggesting performance improvement programs are entirely ineffective; in fact, for the most part, each one is theoretically sound, well researched, and clearly articulated. There are well-regarded authors, speakers, trainers, and consultants who bring extraordinary credibility to each program and their success stories cite dramatic increases in profits through recipes for workplace satisfaction and productivity. And yet, when these change programs are embedded in the organization's traditional business model, the organization's immune system, made up of well-entrenched policies and processes, encourages the body to reject them. The problem is not the managerial science behind the programs, it is that these transformational efforts are doomed to failure when set in legacy organizational structures operated with perfunctory management thinking. What is required to make them work is a different type of management thinking—new thoughtware. The new thoughtware is all about process thinking, process flow, and a problem-solving culture that identifies and eliminates disruptions to the flow. Absent a change in business process design, improvement is not possible. History has shown that any other method of trying to leverage improvement is arbitrary and doomed to failure.

CRUSHING OLD ALLEGIANCES

Improvement comes from changing management's perspective, not simply changing specific practices. It comes from altering their instincts and reasoning about how to run the business, and that means developing a process mind that can overcome management's resistance to understanding. It means listening to Machiavelli's message of "crushing" all allegiance to functionality in an organization and demanding fidelity to the business processes that deliver customer value. It appears that much of the twentieth-century management science we apply to improve organizational performance is only a continuation of the old art of government, a 500-year continuation. Let's, for the moment, set aside our economic or accounting mind and look at the business enterprise through the lens of a historian or political scientist.

As secretary to the second chancery of the Republic of Florence, Machiavelli was the first in a long line of management consultants who attempted to improve his client's organizational performance. As a consultant, he was responsible for introducing new rules designed to avoid the *"slow pace of change,"* by using the latest research in theories of management; at that time, political science. He explained why organizations had such difficulty with introducing change, which is the same challenge managers experience today when attempting to lead a continuous improvement program. *The Prince* is about Machiavelli's thinking on how to gain and sustain organizational success by overcoming the reality that managers favor the existing order of things and have no faith in anything new that is not the result of well-established practice. People do not easily relinquish well-established practices and, 500 years later, Machiavelli's observations hold true. Today, management continues to hold tight to the status quo despite irrefutable evidence of the need for organizations to adapt or perish. Why else would continuous process improvement initiatives be so ubiquitous? Such programs have become necessary tools of corporate management in their attempt at renewal and improvement. And yet, these tools and techniques do little to facilitate innovation and performance improvement when there is an inherent bias to the status quo; functional optimization and policy and systems support that is obsessed with risk-free reliability, which, in turn, feeds on short-term financial performance mandates. This status quo is dressed up as a sheep, but the underlying wolf maintains a perverse pedagogy rooted in the fear of failure that says, "Prove it works before doing it."

Machiavelli's proposed approach to the program failure dilemma was to weight the dice heavily in favor of success by treating those who supported the change with enormous respect and to "crush" those who did not. No gray area here. He observed that anything short of such a complete removal of nonsupporters would allow them to sabotage the improvement effort and the organization would then spend untold energy in accommodating these "naysayers," eventually succumbing to the sheer exhaustion of obliging their resistance. Sound familiar? Machiavelli suggested that the Prince replace the "enemies of the change initiative" (i.e., functional managers) with loyal leaders (process believers) in charge of one or two business processes (i.e., value stream managers covering all functions required to deliver value to the customer) with the ability to "crush" (overrule) all functional or departmental rulers. For example, a functional sales manager, with allegiance to departmental budgets and commission targets, might be replaced by a process-focused demand generation leader with allegiance to the customer. This is the expedient and cost-effective way and the only people who will be upset are the former functional managers whose jobs they have taken over. And, because they are no longer in the organization, they cannot cause trouble. And, the rest of the value stream members will not protest because they still have their old jobs, albeit, with a new allegiance to the horizontal process, particularly while they have the example of the sacked managers to keep them in line. Thus, when a continuous process improvement program is introduced, incumbents will either be warmly embraced and encouraged or sacked. After all, anyone kept on or accommodated would remain true to their legacy function (department) and continue to subvert any attempt to introduce a new order of things, usually while being politically correct and nodding support within earshot of the boss man. This is usually why most people are repelled by the cynical approach associated with the Machiavellian term that refers to cunning and deceitful tactics commonly known as *the end justifies the means.*

IT'S NOT THE PEOPLE, IT'S THE FUNCTIONS

There's no doubt that such a Machiavellian shock approach today would violate what we have learned about modern change management because unilateral dismissal is not just illegal, it is immoral. Nevertheless, the lesson is important. Machiavelli's approach is right; we must eradicate the old to allow for the new. Without a complete dismantling of the silo mentality, ingrained in the legacy organizational structure, improvement efforts will continue to experience outrageously high failure rates and the process mind will not evolve and emerge. It is not the people that need elimination, it is the dysfunctional, functional walls that are damning up the flow of the process that need to be blown up. So, before enacting Machiavellian layoffs, the understanding must be that it is the functions and nonvalue-adding activities they do, not the people, that need to be "crushed." That's the correct contemporary application of the Machiavellian principle. It's the process, not the people.

The principle, however, has to be applied within the two foundational elements of a process-focused organization: (1) the principle of waste elimination and continuous improvement, and (2) a profound respect for people, which is the full utilization of all human talent. Continuous improvement of the business process means understanding the entire system that provides value to the customers and the inherent range and cause of variation (disturbances to flow) in that system. Because there are limits to what we can know, there is a need for the engagement of people in that system, moment to moment, to address the variation. Process innovation requires employee engagement. It is mandatory. This is the "respect for people" principle and that means not giving employees broken processes, processes that have no chance of success. It means providing people the ability to detect when a variance or abnormal condition occurs and the ability and willingness to right the situation. Recall the process-focused organization runs on an operating thoughtware platform (circulatory system), which means allowing each employee to see the flow of value to the customer, and having the information, authority, and skills to fix any breakdowns in that flow before it reaches the customer. Fortunately, the contemporary version of Machiavellianism does not require that we eradicate our employees to achieve meaningful performance improvement, it means we destroy our functional silos and the associated thinking that blocks the ability of people to learn and to see their entire end-to-end process with clear line of sight to the customer. People are not our problem, lousy processes are. Note ABC Adhesives did not lay off its way to performance improvement, it streamlined its way there.

> Brilliant process management is our strategy. We get brilliant results from average people managing brilliant processes. We observe that our competitors often get average (or worse) results from brilliant people managing broken processes.
>
> **Toyota executive**

The interpretation and application of Machiavelli, 500 years later, means a focus on addressing two main limitations to improving the process. The first is overcoming our inability or unwillingness to let go of functional structures, and the second is our need to dispel management's resistance to understanding how to succeed in a process-focused organization and develop a process mind. Both require a pivot in perspective, the way managers see and think about the organization, and that change in perception is counterintuitive to their managerial instincts and reasoning. Traditionally, management practices have concentrated on being good at gathering information and making decisions based on facts and figures, and acting on proven and reliable procedures in order to contain—read, hide—problems. Conversely, process thinking concentrates on experimentation and discovery, where problems are exposed so they can be prevented. Most managers aren't trained in discovery because it cannot be reduced to a set of rules or specifications. Discovery is more about intuition and seeing beyond the hard information; a lot of gut instinct. It's what Daniel Pink refers to in his book, *A Whole New Mind,* when he writes, "… the MFA (master of fine arts) is the new MBA (master of business administration)." He says, "Today, we're all in the art business," where the future belongs to a different kind of person with a different kind of mind: artists, inventors, storytellers, creative and holistic right-brain thinkers. Pink points out that the recruiting demand for MBAs has dropped significantly since 1993 and more art grads are occupying key corporate positions.[7] These people are better equipped to better understand process thinking. It is all but impossible to experiment and discover our way forward when management is asking questions like: Can we prove it will work? How can we be sure of the outcome? What proof do we have that it will work? However, experiments can only be proven by future events. If all decisions by management are made on using past experience to predict the future, then experiments are out, which means we will not expose disruptions to flow, and, thus, cannot resolve them. We will continue to conceal the waste and maintain the status quo.

The other impediment is our inability or unwillingness to let go of our functional structures. Before I delve further into this organizational design impediment, let's look at how we got here. How, in our current business structures, we allowed the whole end-to-end process to become subjugated to the discrete parts, where the efficiency of functional—suboptimization—is valued more than optimizing the whole of customer value, and where we separate thinking from doing and deciding from acting. It is where we have buried the process mind.

PROCESS THINKING IS NOT NEW

Automobile manufacturing has been called "the industry of industries" by Peter Drucker.[8] In the past 100 years, it has been the driving influence on how we make things. Henry Ford had been experimenting for years to drive down product cost by overcoming well-established manufacturing practices that were a carryover from the craft-production world. Many of his cost-reduction innovations were based on the simple principle that it's better to bring the worker to the work than bring the work to the worker. Create a process and make the process flow and remove impediments to that flow.

In late 1913, in Highland Park, Michigan, the first moving assembly line winched a chassis across the floor of the factory as workers affixed parts to it. It cut in half the 12 hours it had previously taken to make a Model T. A year later, it was down to 93 minutes (from 720 minutes). It made the automobile affordable for most Americans with the price of a Model T falling from $700 in 1910 to $350 in 1917.[9] That was a rare happening (i.e., a process improvement focused on enhancing customer value with a financial outcome favorable to both the consumer and the shareholder). The process achieved the purpose of fulfilling customer demand, while meeting the process specification of profitability and shareholder value. Henry Ford often said that it wasn't the employer who paid the wages, they only handled the money; it was the customer who paid wages.

This visible manifestation of Henry Ford's thinking, the moving assembly line, was only possible because, since 1908, his team had been thinking process flow and exposing disruptions to flow and creating a horizontal cross-section view that cut across traditional functions. Ford had a process mind, continually experimenting, discovering, and learning how to reduce time. He did not demand proof to protect the status quo, and he failed often ... but effectively. He experimented his way to the 93 minutes and achieved a great deal:

- Interchangeability of parts (the first time in volume production)
- Go/no-go gauges to catch defective parts
- Single-piece flow in fabrication by locating technologies in process sequence
- Standard work and precisely repeatable cycle times
- A primitive pull system for parts supply[10]

Ford believed the only real mistake was one in which you learned nothing. All of these elements had previously been tried in some form, but it was their combination, the whole end-to-end process designed with continuous flow as its central objective that produced this order of magnitude leap in productivity and cycle time.

> Life is a series of experiences, each one of which makes us bigger, even though sometimes it is hard to realize this. For the world was built to develop character, and we must learn that the setbacks and grieves which we endure help us in our marching onward.
>
> **Henry Ford**

But Ford failed in one significant way. Although he put in many elements of process thinking, he never created an overarching system, a foundational, thoughtware system to support his business model, to hold it all together and sustain his methods. He failed to prescribe the right diet and exercise for the ongoing health of the circulatory system (i.e., he didn't empower workers to make improvements and there was no concept of continuous improvement). So, when variety raised its inevitable head, he was not able to learn and adapt. Not only was the Model T limited to one color, it was limited to one specification and all Model T chassis were identical through the end of production in 1926.[11] After Ford's departure, others installed a formal management-by-results system that replaced the management-by-process that he had pioneered, and that replacement model has been the established practice ever since. The replacement model is premised on the optimization of the parts, not the effective flow of the whole. The automakers' response to variety (i.e., many models with many options) was to regress back to discrete process areas with longer and longer time lags between these steps. As machines got larger, they built larger batches, disrupting flow and increasing both inventories and throughput time. Only now, in the twenty-first century, is Ford Motor Company returning to its roots, trying to embrace process-focused management, and they are not alone. In the early 1990s, the assembly of Boeing's 737 family of airplanes followed well-established practices. They were assembled at stationary positions, in a vertical structure with the total assembly time taking in excess of 30 days. Now, based on process thinking, they have built a moving assembly line process that takes the planes from start to finish in eight days.

THE TOYOTA "THINKING" SYSTEM

No illustration of the power of process thinking and its elements of continuous improvement and respect for people is more insightful than Toyota, indisputably the world's greatest car company. Toyota, despite operating in the cyclical automotive industry, has increased profit margins each and every quarter for more than 50 years.[12] The superiority of the Toyota Production System (TPS) is proven. Period. And, as such, it deserves to be a model that the process mind can learn from and adapt to our enterprises. Toyota has had year-over-year sales growth for decades and its profits exceed that of all other automobile companies and its capitalization exceeds that of GM, Ford, and Chrysler combined. "No organization outside Toyota's family of companies has ever come close to matching Toyota's stellar performance."[13] Originally, as Kiichiro Toyoda, Taiichi Ohno, and others at Toyota looked at the challenge of variety (i.e., mass customization), it occurred to them that a series of simple innovations might make it easier to provide both the continuity in process flow that Henry Ford had pioneered and a wide range in product offering. They thought that they could marry variety and customer value (cost and quality). They revisited Ford's early thinking and conceived the TPS, where the focus shifted from individual machines and their utilization to the flow of the product through the entire process. Interestingly, the simple innovations of process thinking embedded in the TPS (sometimes referred to as the Toyota Thinking System) date back to the early 1890s when inventor Sakichi Toyoda designed and patented a manually operating loom for weaving cloth. It greatly improved worker productivity and quality. In the 1920s, Sakichi's son, Kiichiro, designed and patented new loom features, including improved mechanisms that would automatically stop the machine when the thread broke (a concept known as *Jidoka* or error proofing). *Jidoka*, which is the genesis of the respect for people principle, allows for visible detection and resolution of disruptions to flow by the employee. It is a fundamental pillar of process thinking because it is designed to expose disruptions to flow. It maintains that the output of a specific process (within a desired range) can be improved by exposing and eliminating variances *as they occur*. This is not only critically different thinking, it is indispensable in overcoming management's inability or unwillingness to let go of its functional structures and established practices. This is real continuous improvement (exposing disruptions to flow and allowing people who are willing and able to countermeasure those disturbances) and the essence of process thinking in the automotive industry, and in all business processes. It's simple and straightforward, but it's not easy.

> Simple can be harder than complex: You have to work hard to get your thinking clean to make it simple. But it's worth it in the end because once you get there, you can move mountains.
>
> **Steve Jobs (1955–2011)**

LEAN

Perhaps the closest we have come to codifying this idea of process thoughtware is in the body of knowledge called *Lean*. Lean is best described as a business system for organizing and managing the enterprise by correctly specifying value from the standpoint of the end customer, removing wasteful actions, and making those remaining actions that do add value occur in a continuous flow as pulled by the customer. Applying Lean requires moving from a vertical structure to a horizontal process-focused structure and is best done by experimenting with an initial process; a model line (i.e., a stream of value an inch wide and a mile deep). We will cover this in more detail in later chapters; however, let's go back to the lessons of Ford and Toyota to better understand the idea of process-focused organizations. Lean is not just how it works, it's about how to design the process and to fulfill customer demand. Lean is about building horizontal process flows of value, sometimes called *value streams, continuous flow processing*, or *cellular production*. Whatever the nomenclature, Lean is, at its essence, a problem-solving mindset that is embedded in process thinking. Lean requires a process mind to create a continuous flow of value, with no interruption, from customer request to customer fulfillment. Much of the soul of process Thoughtware is derived from Henry Ford's thinking based on the dictum that the longer something is in the factory, the more it costs.

Figure 3.1 lists the seven sequential steps required to move from the traditional "batch and queue" vertical design where optimizing the discrete functions does not allow for continuous flow, to an uninterrupted constant flow. Think of these discrete functions as dams in the river, blockages that can only be removed through these seven steps.

Figures 3.2 through 3.5 illustrate the visual transformation as this sequence of steps is deployed. These steps are the experiment that provides ongoing learning and adapting through continual exposure and resolution of problems.

Seven Steps to Create a Continuous Process Flow
• Locate people and equipment in the proper sequence
• Design for minimum distance between people & equipment
• Process and move one piece at a time
• Separate people from equipment/workstations
• Train people to perform multiple tasks
• Produce at the rate of consumption
• Distribute work evenly

FIGURE 3.1
Seven steps to create a continuous process flow.

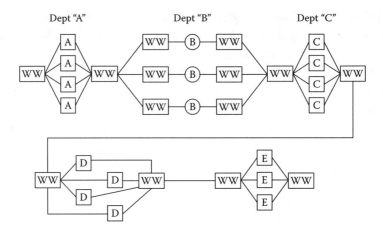

FIGURE 3.2
Stage 1: Functional organization with specialized functions.

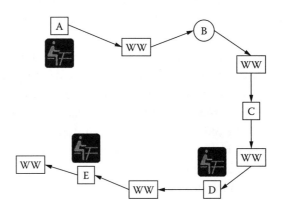

FIGURE 3.3
Stage 2: Creating a process-focused organization.

Figure 3.2 (Stage 1) depicts a traditional "batch and queue" organization design where each department supplies the next department (e.g., Dept. A supplies Dept. B, Dept. B supplies Dept. C, etc.) completing their unique assignment individually and in isolation of the other departments. (ww =waste of waiting)

Figure 3.3 (Stage 2) depicts the initial stage of a process-focused organization. One human resource (ie. an operator) is taken from each of the five discrete departments (A–E) and placed in a single process. Each operator's allegiance shifts from the functional department

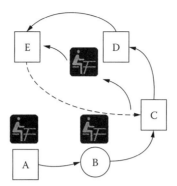

FIGURE 3.4
Stage 3: Eliminating "waste" with one-piece flow (no WW).

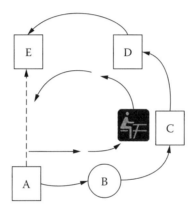

FIGURE 3.5
Stage 4: Continuous process flow. People aligned with process not function.

(i.e., Dept. A) to a focus on the end customer (either A, B, C, D, or E). In time, we can process with three employees rather than five. "Waste of waiting" (ww) between functional departments is reduced as we work less to a "batch and queue" model where the parts (departments) are optimized, and work more to a continuous flow model where the purpose is to reduce the waiting by only producing what the next department can absorb, allocating our resources to the place in the flow where the "constraint" to flow occurs.

In Figure 3.4 (Stage 3), as waste is eliminated, the velocity of the flow increases, throughput goes up and processing time goes down. We are now building one-at-a time versus "batch and queue". This is the essential business model of the process mind.

By Stage 4, (Figure 3.5), we achieve continuous process flow, aligning people with the process that adds value to the customer, not the discrete department that simply addresses the efficiency and utilization of that independent department.

These four "stages" of evolution from the traditional, vertical "batch and queue" to a horizontal flow of customer value can only be deployed through a deliberate, patient, and focused application of the seven steps outlined in Figure 3.1.

The Japanese learned from what they saw in Henry Ford's Detroit and honed the assembly line concept with a high-quality, Lean production system. The Toyota Production System (TPS), commonly branded as Lean, is widely recognized for having created a new production system founded on process thinking. But (another important *but*) the everyday, off-the-shelf practice of Lean that I see today is a faint echo of the essence of the TPS. The vast majority of organizations that say, "We are doing Lean," still have deeply entrenched siloized organizations. At most companies, Lean is usually introduced into the manufacturing organization and gains some quick wins using common tools on the shop floor. However, the effort eventually gets bogged down because it requires support from the other functions as the implementation process moves to the next level. Without a process mind, it is not possible. Top leadership either does not understand it or is unwilling to commit to a process-focused organization as a prerequisite to successful implementation of Lean. Today, only Toyota, Honda, and Danaher are truly Lean enterprises, while others dabble with Lean tools when they are convenient and then the efforts fade over time. It's hardly a mystery as to why only 2% of companies that have a Lean program achieve anticipated results. These Lean practitioners proudly display visible tools, techniques, and seem to be able to articulate the principles; however, the behaviors, customs, sequences, and thinking of the process mind are rarely evident. Properly applied, Lean is about an organization's ability to learn, and although the ability to learn does not require Lean, an organization does require a focus on process rather than on functions in order to learn the new thoughtware.

The term *Lean* was coined by John Krafick, a researcher with the International Motor Vehicle Program (a five-year, 1985–1990, study of the differences between mass production and Lean production in the motor vehicle industry). Lean describes a production system that uses less of everything compared with mass production—half the human effort, half the space, half the investment in tools, half the engineering hours in new product development, less than half the inventory, and significantly fewer defects. Ever since the concepts of Lean were clearly articulated by James Womack, Daniel Jones, and Daniel Roos in their pivotal book, *The Machine That Changed the World* (Free Press, 1990), organizations of all types have been trying to embrace Lean. And, yet, a quarter of a century later, companies continue to find it a rough go. Of the tens of thousands who have adopted some form of Lean program, the failure rate is staggering. Only 2% have achieved anticipated results.[14]

In 1980, American car executives were so shaken to find that Japan had replaced the United States as the world's leading carmaker that they began to visit Japan in droves to find out what was going on. How could the Japanese possibly win in both price and quality? It made no sense because the prevailing thinking was that those two characteristics were mutually exclusive. Also, they were befuddled as to how the Japanese got new models out so quickly, in less than half the time the Americans did. It was thought that it must be their industrial policy or state subsidies or the uniqueness of the Japanese culture. Guess what? It turned out not to be any of these. The secret was a process-focused, horizontal system for making things, where the daily practice of identifying and deploying better ways is a product of the daily habits and routines of the people in the organization—the thoughtware. It is about human thinking and behavior, which should have been the lesson of Lean. Unfortunately, for most North American adherents, Lean today means tools and techniques, not process thinking and human behavior. And even more remarkable is the myth that Japanese manufacturing techniques were uniquely developed for, and suited to, the Japanese culture and unsuited for the American culture. In fact, much of Lean process thinking came from the West and, as we have seen, the Toyota Production System was greatly influenced by American industrialists like Henry Ford. Moreover, it was an integral part of the teachings of an American statistician, Dr. W. Edwards Deming.

THE QUALITY REVOLUTION

In Japan, from 1950, Deming taught Japanese management how to improve design, product quality, testing, service, and sales through various methods, including the application of statistical methods. He taught: (1) identify the process, (2) identify variances from the process, and (3) countermeasure the variances with a problem-solving discipline. It became known as the Deming Circle of Plan, Do, Check, Act/Adjust (Figure 3.6). His System of Profound Knowledge suggested that management must understand the overall processes involving suppliers, producers, and customers, and the range and causes of variation in those processes. It meant that business managers and leaders must undergo a profound transformation that breaks down barriers in our organizations and sees every activity and every job as part of a process. Deming believed in transformational learning, which he described as creating a shift in context, a shift from functional

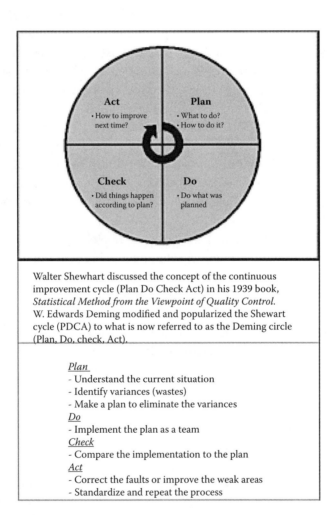

Walter Shewhart discussed the concept of the continuous improvement cycle (Plan Do Check Act) in his 1939 book, *Statistical Method from the Viewpoint of Quality Control.* W. Edwards Deming modified and popularized the Shewart cycle (PDCA) to what is now referred to as the Deming circle (Plan, Do, check, Act).

Plan
- Understand the current situation
- Identify variances (wastes)
- Make a plan to eliminate the variances
Do
- Implement the plan as a team
Check
- Compare the implementation to the plan
Act
- Correct the faults or improve the weak areas
- Standardize and repeat the process

FIGURE 3.6
The Deming Circle.

suboptimization to process control. Deming's teaching turned out to be a monumental contribution to "the machine that changed the world." This is the invisible part of Lean thinking that accounts for the underwhelming results.

On June 24, 1980, NBC News broadcast, as part of the television show *NBC White Paper*, a television episode called, *If Japan can … Why can't we?* That event has been credited with beginning the "quality revolution" and introducing the methods of Japanese manufacturing to America. Remarkably, the concept of quality management was, up to that point, not part of the daily business lexicon. The show detailed how the Japanese captured the world automotive and electronics markets by following the advice of W. Edwards Deming. It said that the Japanese techniques had been "largely ignored by American management." Of course, they snubbed the lessons of Deming. For the most part, Western managers were too absorbed in hubris and hierarchy and a short-term view that often rewarded individuals more than the company or the consumer.

If we take a look at General Motors and the basic assumptions on which it operated at that time, we can see the stark reality. Ian Mitroff and Harold Linstone in their book, *The Unbounded Mind: Breaking the Chains of Traditional Business Thinking*,[15] talk about Thomas Murphy who was the CEO of GM in the 1970s and on the board until 1988. Murphy articulated GM's business model, the way it operated within its credo:

1. GM is in the business of making money, not cars.
2. Success comes not from technological leadership, but from having the resources to quickly adopt innovation successfully introduced by others.
3. Cars are primarily status symbols; styling, therefore, is more important than quality to buyers who are, after all, going to trade up every other year.
4. The U.S. car market is isolated from the rest of the world. Foreign competitors will never gain more than 15% of the domestic markets.
5. Energy will always be cheap and abundant.
6. Workers do not have an important impact on productivity or product quality.
7. The consumer movement does not represent the consensus of a significant portion of the U.S. population.
8. The government is the enemy; it must be fought tooth and nail every inch of the way.

9. Strict, centralized financial controls are the secret of good administration.
10. Managers should be developed from the inside.

Obviously, there has been a significant reversal in thinking at GM, especially after it went through its transition as "Government Motors" and came out the other side with new operating principles. Now, their operating principle is captured in a quote made by the new management that says, "We win when the customer says we win." Officially, there are now five principles, which the newly reorganized, postrecessionary GM uses to guide its business:

1. Safety and quality first
2. Create life-long customers
3. Innovate
4. Deliver long-term investment value
5. Make a positive difference

This is a huge shift from where they were to where they want to be. Also, the shift would never have happened without the influence of Deming and the process-focused thoughtware he preached. It will not be accomplished without a surgical intervention to address the chronic condition of conventionally managed organizational silos. Perhaps Mary Barra, appointed CEO of GM in 2013, will actually understand that to enact the five new principles, a Machiavellian approach to GM's notorious fiefdoms will be needed to crush their hold on the organization and if they do, they will never again need the financial security blanket of the government to hide behind.

Deming made a significant contribution to Japan's reputation for innovative and high-quality products. He is regarded as having had more impact upon Japanese business than any other person of non-Japanese heritage. He is somewhat of a hero in Japan and the country's highest industrial award for quality and productivity is named after him. Despite this, at the time of his death in 1993, he was only just beginning to win recognition in the United States. However, his contribution and impact have been affirmed over the past two decades.

In 1985, the U.S. government funded a $5 million, five-year study at MIT called the "International Motor Vehicle Program." Its objective was to understand why Japanese automakers were so much more productive and produced better quality products at competitive prices compared to the big three in Detroit. In 1990, based on the study and the dissemination of the learning in *The Machine that Changed the World,* we discovered just how influential Deming's teachings were in breaking down organizational barriers and regarding every activity and every job as part of a process. His book describes the Toyota Production System; unfortunately, it only described "what" process-focused production looked like, but gave no details of "how" to do it.

As Deming demonstrated, the gains are achieved without additional investment in either machines or people. Deming was prophetic when he warned the West that they could not copy the Japanese because they "… don't know what to copy." He went on to explain that the key to success was a "learning system" made up of reliable standard methods, reliable standard problem solving, and experimentation. It was this understanding that was "to Japanese production workers all the way through the company, a second language." He was right. The West copied the tools and techniques, but not the culture. The main reason it couldn't be transferred was related to another Deming maxim, "… management causes 85% of all the problems." He also said, "There's nobody that comes out of a School of Business that knows what management is, or what its deficiencies are. There's no one coming out of a School of Business that ever heard of the answers that I'm giving your questions—or probably even thought of the questions."[16] Process thinking is not taught in the MBA curriculum and developing a process mind is not a prerequisite to graduating.

THE EVIDENCE IS UNDERWHELMING

The point here is that there is no direct connection between the development of Western management thought and the evolution of the process mind, whether labeled as Lean or something else. It has only happened in a few corners of the Western industrial complex, continuing to reinforce, centuries later, Machiavelli's principle: Reality trumps idealism. Regardless of thousands and thousands of tours through the Toyota Production System, by some of the brightest and most influential figures in industry; despite tens of thousands of articles, books, courses, belt certifications programs, seminars, consortiums, benchmarking tours; and dedicated institutes, all preaching the power of TPS/Lean, it is all in vain without the ability to see beyond the tools and techniques. Most have never recognized that the organization is first and foremost a collection of core processes involving many steps that must be performed properly, in the right sequence, at the right time, as defined by the customer. I repeat, until they see this reality, the unfertile grounds of the conventional siloized organization cannot possibly sow and grow the seeds promised by Lean or any legitimate continuous process improvement undertaking.

Although today's management talks a lot about the customer being the center of gravity, the shareholder still rules in too many organizations. Slow, steady continuous improvement does not lead to immediate recognition, quick promotions, or soaring share prices. Managers are still looking for the "big bang" project that sounds good and comes with great fanfare even though these initiatives are usually not sustainable. And yet, everywhere I go, everyone agrees that continuous process improvement is the most formidable weapon an organization can acquire and many believe they are doing it. They have Lean, Six Sigma, and other reengineering initiatives, but they continue to live in a vertical world and do not understand process thinking. They must first develop a process mind and dismantle the functional structures.

Cliff Ransom, vice president at State Street Research in Boston, is one of a few stock analysts who analyzes manufacturing companies through a Lean lens. He stated in Association for Manufacturing Excellence's (AME's) *Target Magazine*: "Very few companies have advanced with Lean manufacturing until you can see the results financially—perhaps one or two percent at best. Another two–three percent are getting there—okay, but not outstanding ... another 10–15 percent mostly just talk Lean. The majority, 80 percent or so, don't even have the buzz words straight."[17]

Jeffery Liker, a prolific researcher on Lean, and Mike Rother, who has done extensive research on Toyota management practices, claim that only 2% of companies that have Lean programs have achieved their anticipated results.[18] And, Robert Miller, the executive director of the Shingo Prize (the most rigorous standard of demonstrated operational excellence), revealed that a large percentage of Shingo Prize winners had not been able to maintain their gains, and, in many cases, lost ground. It was discovered that the winners had been experts at implementing tools of Lean, but had not embedded them into their culture. I always say, "Beware tool heads and Kaizen cowboys for they know not what they are looking for." Process thinkers do not teach the tools and skills, they teach the employee to see the process. The employee will then use the tool needed to remove disruptions to that process. The old thoughtware embraces tools; the new thoughtware creates a business process. Mastering the tools is the easy part, the 10-cent answer; the hard part is installing new thoughtware. The challenge is not to teach employees the skills of process thinking, rather teach the employees how to develop a process mind and then they will discover the skills required. Develop the people and let them develop the process.

PROGRAM ADDICTION

In more recent history, we have experienced a plethora of quick-fix, short-term, flavor-of-the-month programs: Theory X, Theory Y, Theory Z, Excellence, Grid Management, MBO (management by objectives), Situational Leadership, T-groups, Team Building, etc., etc. Richard Pascal in his book, *Surfing the Edge of Chaos,* counted 30 distinct "fads," programs that were offered between 1950 and 1990 that might be labeled business improvement programs, all of which were designed to change at least one business practice.[19] Then in the 1990s, there was an explosion of Reengineering, TQM, and Six Sigma, to name a few. Many of these programs were developed with management science that had process improvement principles at their core, but (and this was the flaw) they were dependent on a pedagogy that applied them to existing vertical structures and control systems. They didn't take. Why? Because of what I call the organization's immune system: vertical structures and established practices and policies designed to hide, not expose problems. Immune means to exempt. And, as we learned from Machiavelli, any part of the organization exposed to change will "exempt themselves" because they "favor the existing order of things" and "have no faith in anything new that is not the result of well-established practice." This immune system protects the status quo and perpetuates ingrained thinking that cannot—will not—adopt the process mind needed to change existing systems. If, after all, the business culture is to ensure that tomorrow consistently and predictably replicates yesterday, it follows that the business will be designed as a structure with long-term, ongoing operating procedures, specialty department roles, and assignments that are not designed to change. In the early 1990s, what Michael Hammer's reengineering set out to do was make invasive change, major surgery that tried to overpower the immune system with his "flatten the organization" concept. It didn't work because the immune system is systemic and buried in processes running throughout the organization. The people's thinking and the processes are inextricably linked and one cannot change without the other.

Pennies don't fall from heaven; they have to be earned.

Margaret Thatcher
U.K. Prime Minister (1979–1990)

There is no big bang solution here; you just can't pop a pill and dissolve ingrained thinking and established practices. I often tell people that if there was a penny on the floor as you are walking through a factory, you might not see it and walk past it. Or, even if you did see it, not stop to pick it up. However, if there were a $20 bill, you would probably see it, stop, and pick it up. It's the same with performance improvement. You are not going to find many $20 bills on the shop floor or in the office, but there's much more than $20's worth of pennies, *if you look*. Problems, disruptions to flow, variances in the process, and waste are hiding in plain sight in every employee's "I-told-you-so" eye roll. Process improvement is in seeing the problems and building the habit of addressing them, not ignoring them. From my experience, most corporate leaders either do not have the patience or control to implement continuous improvement programs successfully. Successful implementation requires something that is rare in both people and organizations: constancy of purpose. However, regardless of the flavor of continuous process improvement selected, if you stick with it, it is amazing how the little, day-to-day improvements add up over time; after a few months, you look back and realize how much has been accomplished. Once you have the habit, you can do whatever you have a mind to do. Process is not just how you structure the organization or how you execute production, it is how you think; it is the process mindset of how you improve things. However, discovery is not natural to businesspeople, logic is, and those pennies are more readily available by discovery than by logic, which is what Roger Martin demonstrates in an organization's "reliability bias": an innate means of protecting the status quo. He writes:

A business that is over-weighted toward reliability will erect organization structures and processes that drive out the pursuit of valid answers to new questions. Inevitably, such organizations come to see maintenance of the status quo as an end in itself, short-circuiting their ability to design and redesign processes continuously.[20]

WE GOT SOME THINGS RIGHT

Despite the shortcomings, everything has not been wrong and we have moved along the learning curve of what works and what doesn't. In the 1990s, we began to understand process. Reengineering, TQM, Six Sigma, and Lean initiated a shift toward continuous process improvement principles. Hammer's message on reengineering was directionally right, but missed a critical point by thinking information technology was the secret sauce to make it all work. The idea of reengineering was to tear down the silos and look at the business as process flow, which was right, but believing it could be replaced, or at least accelerated, through the application of enabling information systems, lead to some gross malpractice of Hammer's thesis. Organizations got so caught up in the emerging technology of the 1990s that they skipped the breaking down of the vertical structure part and jumped directly into applying generous amounts of information technology (IT) (e.g., complex, elaborate firmware software). It didn't always work because much of what was done was what I call "automating rework." Management applied technology to broken processes. The technology was designed to enhance the work itself, but it did not focus on the stuff that gets in the way of work. Elaborate, company-wide software like Enterprise Resource Planning (ERP), although it might track the resources used efficiently on 5% to 10% of the work activities, it doesn't address the 90% to 95% of stuff that gets in the way of work. It doesn't tell you if you are adding value to the customer or if you are working on strategy.

Similarly, with Customer Relationship Management (CRM) software, one might use the past to provide general rules or assumptions about the future, but it offers little on how to build an effective, demand generation process. Users of these automated information management systems have implicitly accepted the notion that information is good, more is better, and all possible information is best. It's about controlling operations. Conversely, the process thinker sees this control of operations as wasteful, and therefore, tries minimizing not maximizing the need for these "information factories." Again, this goes back to the Chennai Paradox. Of course, we must embrace technology that allows enterprises to manage supply chains in real time and analyze massive amounts of data at the touch of a button, but, in the dynamic and complex world of high variety and "I-expect-it-now" product and service proliferation, technology alone is not enough (e.g., the November 2013 Global Electronics Forum in Shanghai featured 22,000 new products). We need to be cognizant of the fact that most analysis, no matter how high-tech, is based on passive data that are wrong the moment they arrive (i.e., transport problems, customs clearances, feedback on current conditions, inventory accuracy, factory uptimes, material requirements accuracy). For example, the constant recalculation of a supply chain schedule is still reliant on a not very accurate forecast schedule and information that is already a day, a week, or more, late. And the impact is amplified the farther we get downstream in the supply chain, which means the consumption at the end of the supply chain (i.e., customer value) might be somewhat useful for big picture capacity planning, but is useless for near-term, detailed supply chain scheduling.

Although the overall forecast is accurate, at any point in time, it is not. No amount of automated information system management will change this. Only by using as little guessing information as possible, and more real, pure signals based on actual, visible end-of-supply-chain demand—and no noise in the information flow beyond that—can we create world-class process management. That means blowing up the wasteful information factory and bringing it down from specialized IT offices to the trenches and coalfaces of the process itself, where each step can signal the previous step about its immediate needs. The entire process must be designed so that it only responds to the most downstream point in that process, customer demand. All needs to fulfill that customer value are pulled back up through this point.

Process control is difficult if we can't see the proverbial process forest for the functional trees.

TOTAL QUALITY MANAGEMENT AND PROCESS THINKING

Total Quality Management (TQM), which was really the extension of Statistical Process Control (SPC) to the whole company (later reinvented as Six Sigma) also was directionally correct, and no more than what Dr. Deming was trying to tell organizations, whose ears were plugged with hubristic wax in the early 1950s. The message of TQM and its various manifestations was powerful. The TQM premise is that poor quality (e.g., defects) is the result of unreliable processes creating the defect (e.g., reliability might best be defined as a process that adheres to a standard 99 out of 100 times). Thus, if we can determine the range and cause of variation (through statistical sampling), we can eliminate the defect (increase quality). However, applying TQM (process control) requires a deep understanding of the overall processes involved, including suppliers, producers, and consumers. Without the ability to see the entire workflow, the application of TQM is dramatically diminished. TQM requires a process focus. Again, as in reengineering, we developed the right thinking, but failed to change the organizational structure so we could see the process. We were unsuccessful in developing the process mind. We continued to look upward at our own specialist function not outward to the customer. Process control is difficult, if we can't see the proverbial process forest for the functional trees. Six Sigma is no different. Fixing any and every shade of variation that would potentially impact the consistency of the result, without knowing how all the dependencies in the workflow relate, just reduces the effort to a never-ending game of Whack-a-Mole (Hasbro's popping-the-mole-back-into-his-hole game).

TQM also suffered from a flawed pedagogy. Historically, these change initiatives were applied as an episodic exercise, as an add-on to the existing way of doing business. And yet, the delivery method is as important as the content and management never changed the fundamental teaching delivery method. The tools and techniques of TQM and reengineering were bolted on to the existing structures, creating vice presidents of quality, another department to focus on things that caused defects. Continuous improvement (CI) was seen apart from, not part of, the way business was conducted. External information factories introduced spreadsheets to record after-the-fact nonconformances, and employees were pulled out of their day job once a week to sit for an hour or so on a Quality Circle team, or a CI task force and then sent back to work in their walled fiefdoms. It was sort of like going to piano lessons once a week, but having no piano at your home, or going to a weekly weight loss clinic and spending the rest of the week on the couch eating fast food. Six Sigma is a good example. It's an expert-based model that does not address process thinking. With Six Sigma, organizations spend many months and a gazillion bucks training someone as a "Black Belt" (i.c., expert). First, why so long? Why so many tools? If I was a cynic, I might suggest that it's necessary to teach 30 or 40 tools to justify the cost and time to train a Black Belt. However, is this necessary to improve the process in terms of quality and costs? Do more tools make a better tradesperson? Professor Kaoru Ishikawa (a Japanese organizational theorist) stated in 1985, "The seven quality tools, if used skillfully, will enable 95% of workplace problems to be solved."[21] Nothing has changed. Meanwhile, during this "Six Sigma belt training" nothing is happening, mainly because there is no connection between the people and the process. Why do we need "expert" black belts? Is this type of specialty and elitism not contrary to the basic process-focused principles of breaking down barriers between departments and employee engagement through a respect for people? The process-focused organization is designed to enhance cross-boundary communications and allow people from different areas to work better together to solve problems. The overall goal of bringing the process under control was right, but the means was wrong. If we are to improve processes, we must listen to the process. The voice of the process is the control limit. At the risk of being charged with heresy, I personally have seen no real impact from Six Sigma, even though I dogmatically deploy the teaching of Dr. Deming on process variation in which control limits have been, and always will be, 3 Sigma. It is interesting that Toyota continues to make the no. 1, quality-rated car in the United States (as per J. D. Power) and, yet, unlike Ford and General Motors, strong followers of Six Sigma, Toyota does not use Six Sigma.

KEEP IT SIMPLE

Again, these continuous process improvement tactics based on sound management science did get smarter and more in tune with what was going on in a faster, globalized Internet world, but major surgery as proposed by Hammer's reengineering, or heavy artillery as required by Six Sigma was not really workable. What was needed was microsurgery and right-sized munitions at multiple points in the process that would have allowed people who lived in the processes to change them. Reengineering went for the big bucks (i.e., $20 bills) and missed a gazillion pennies, right in front of them.

From personal experience, covering well over 100 companies in 15 countries, incorporating over 1,600 business processes, I have empirical evidence that 75% of all problems are visible and can be remedied with the common-sense and face-to-face communications of the people who live and work in that process, *if* the organization designs and executes across functions as an integrated process and is maniacally obsessed on delivering value to the customer. Another 20% will require more rigorous root cause analysis; however, only 3% will require anything near the heavy artillery of Six Sigma or its derivatives, design of experiments, statistical analysis, and others. Another 2%, where there is complex material or information exchange, may need a complete process redesign.

The past 50 years have added to our understanding and advancement of organization development and management science, but if we contrast the preponderance of programs with the dearth of results and their short life span, on average four years,[22] then I suggest we have not achieved near what we are capable of. These prescriptions and the antidotes for the prescriptions have made many corporate leaders look more like addicts in need of a quick fix than long-term visionaries, as they have jumped from one change program to another, sometimes not even pausing to take an organizational breath. Subsequently, many have become skeptics. Of course, there has been some success, but what I have seen, around the world, is a not a lack of sophisticated, problem-solving implementations, but an inability to see the root cause of those problems because they are hidden under a mountain of discrete departments, specialized functions, and misaligned policies and practices designed to conceal the root cause. Old thoughtware covers up problems, but new thoughtware exposes problems.

> There is nothing man will not do to avoid the difficult task of thinking.
>
> **Thomas Edison (1847–1931)**

SIMPLE IS HARD

Why are change programs and continuous improvement so ubiquitous when, by documented account, they fail at least 70% of the time?[23] Especially when, from the employees' point of view, the parade of faux change has been embraced "like the stench of a dead woodchuck under the porch," to borrow from the vernacular of Dilbert. Today, most companies remain heavily engaged in such programs, often under the umbrella of continuous improvement, and, by and large, they are accepted as necessary to modern business survival. Everywhere I go, executives, managers, and frontline people are bemoaning the lack of success of these practices and when I ask why the failure, there is a consensus in the rationalizing, which, in order of frequency, is as seen in Figure 3.7.

Obstacles	% of Companies
1. Backsliding to old ways (*hello, Machiavelli*)	85%
2. Lack of Implementation (*lack of know-how*)	61%
3. Employee Resistance (*failure to remove "ankle draggers" who resist change*)	42%
4. Viewed as Flavor of the Month (this too shall pass)	36%

FIGURE 3.7

Obstacles to continuous process improvement. As reported in the HPM Consortium Publication (October 2007) based on a Survey of 1000 Canadian Companies who claimed to have a Lean/C.I. Program in place, that is failing to meet expectations.

Notice no. 1, backsliding to old ways (experienced by 850 of the 1,000 companies reporting). This is not a financial issue nor a strategy or competency or technology issue, it is *backsliding to old ways*. It is indigenous to the current organization structure and management thoughtware.

If we are to change the effort to improve performance, then we must look closely at these apparent reasons for failure. I say *apparent* because for me these so-called reasons are just excuses, comfort for sluggish management thinking that gets caught up in the symptoms and avoids reality. Lack of know-how really means the inability to expose problems, the refusal to see the process flow. Employee resistance to change is the mother of all excuses, when, in fact, employees will enthusiastically embrace change that allows them to remove the silly things that get in the way of their work. As for flavor of the month, that's a leadership issue. In the end, all of these rationalizations are part of a bigger problem—management's resistance to understanding. What most leaders fail to realize is that any true continuous improvement, problem-solving methodology is a management philosophy, not simply a collection of tools and techniques.

IT'S MORE THAN EMPOWERMENT

Continuous process improvement is a scientific method applied to business problems and scientific thinking is counterintuitive to most management steeped in a mind-map of proof and analytical thinking.

One never learns something new, rather one refines one's understanding of the situation around them by testing a hypothesis and learning to know when to apply and how much. This is the essence of the process mind. The new thoughtware is not about absolutes, but as Taiichi Ohno, the father of TPS, taught us, it is about getting rid of our misconceptions. Most of what we believe is neither right nor wrong, it is appropriate or inappropriate to the situation. Process-focused organizations use experimentation to determine which is which. Even motherhood and accepted dogma like servant leadership or collaborative, consensus-seeking management is not right or wrong, rather it may be, or may not be, appropriate to any particular situation. If I am pinned down in a trench with enemy fire raining down on me, I am not looking for my manager to call a team meeting. That would be inappropriate. I am looking for a benevolent autocrat who will decree the next steps to get out of there. In studying the impacts of endless collaboration, Morton Hansen of the University of California, Berkeley, analyzed 182 teams who were trying to win a contract on behalf of a professional services firm. He found the more time they spent consulting others, the less likely they were to win a deal. Collaboration and consensus has costs as well as benefits and those need to be weighed against each other instead of blindly assuming more teamwork is better. The process mind has no dogmatic allegiance to management styles, whether modeled on the hierarchy of the armed forces or the learning-through-play school of Montessori. The only rule is: What is the best way to provide sustained ability to meet customer demand? The new thoughtware thesis says: It is by making visible to employees the uninterrupted flow of value to the customer and providing those employees with the respect they deserve to fix breakdowns in that flow, before it reaches the customer. Machiavelli would agree.

The process mind is not dictatorial (do it my way) nor is it a pure expression of empowerment (do it your way). Rather, it is a mutual expression of leadership that says, follow me and we can figure this out together. One person cannot effectively tell hundreds of others what to do and when to do it nor can hundreds of people just do as they wish. We need to find the right balance of control and flexibility and direction and adaptability. We need to make it easy for employees to see and solve problems and learn from their mistakes and we need to solicit constant feedback from them on what prevents the flow of value to the customer. It means giving them the freedom to come up with new ideas while making sure they operate within the parameters of the overall purpose. It's a tough line to define and walk, requiring constant balancing, but it is an incredibly worthwhile and valuable journey.

REFERENCES

1. Lassiter, B. S. 2012. *Improving how organizations improve.* Performance Excellence Network, November 29. Online at: http://performanceexcellencenetwork.org/the-presidents-blog/improving-how-organizations-improve/
2. Sharma, M., *Is Your Continuous Improvement Program Delivering As Promised?*, September 2010, Accenture, www.accenture.com/global/consulting/processinnovationperformance
3. *Manufacturers Are Failing to Garner Long-Term Productivity Benefits Despite Retrenchment Efforts Amid Weak Economy.* Lean manufacturing/Six Sigma programs seen as a poor investment for most companies September 28, 2011. http://www.alixpartners.com/en/MediaCenter/PressReleases/tabid/821/articleType/ArticleView/articleId/154/Manufacturers-Are-Failing-to-Garner-Long-Term-Productivity-Benefits-Despite-Retrenchment-Efforts-Amid-Weak-Economy.aspx#sthash.fQ4GzsiO.dpuf
4. Machiavelli, N. 1513. *The Prince.* Adolph Caso (Ed.), Rufus Goodwin (translator) 2003. Wellesley MA: Dante University Press, 46.
5. Pascale, R. T. 1990. *Managing on the edge: How successful companies use conflict to stay ahead.* New York: Simon and Shuster.
6. Holtham, C. 1994. Business process reengineering: Contrasting what is and what is not. In *Business process reengineering: Myth and reality,* ed. C. Coulson-Thomas. London: Kogan.
7. Pink, D. H. 2005. *A whole new mind.* New York: Riverhead Books, 54–55.
8. Drucker, P. 1946. *The concept of the corporation.* New York: John Day, 149.
9. Womack, J. P., D. T. Jones, and D. Roos. 1990. *The machine that changed the world.* New York: Harper Collins, 29.
10. Ibid., p. 27.
11. Ibid., p. 26.
12. Magee, D. 2007. *How Toyota became #1: Leadership lessons from the world's greatest car company.* New York: Penguin Group, 8.
13. Rother, M. 2013. Keynote speech at the International Lean Conference in Toronto, Canada, October.
14. Pay, R. 2008. Everybody's jumping on the Lean bandwagon, but many are being taken for a ride. *Industry Week* (March 1).
15. Mitroff, I., and H. Linstone. 1993. *The unbounded mind: Breaking the chains of traditional business thinking.* Oxford, U.K.: Oxford University Press.
16. Deming, W. E. 1980. *If Japan can ... Why can't we?* Quote on NBC News as part of NBC *White Paper,* June 24.
17. Ransom. C. F., II (VP State Street Research). 2008. Lean manufacturing: Fat cash flow. Interview in AME *Target Magazine.*
18. Liker, J., and M. Rother. 2011. *Why Lean programs fail.* Cambridge, MA: Lean Enterprise Institute.

19. Pascal, R., M. Millemann, and L. Gioja. 2000. *Surfing the edge of chaos.* New York: Crown Business, 12.
20. Martin, R. 2009. *The design of business.* Boston: Harvard Business Press, 43.
21. Ishikawa, K. 1985. What Is Total Quality Control? The Japanese Way (1st ed.), Englewood Cliffs, New Jersey: Prentice-Hall, p.198, "From my past experience as much as ninety-five percent of all problems within a company can be solved by means of these tools."*
22. Jones, M., and R. Thwaites. 2000. Dedicated followers of fashion. In *The reengineering revolution,* eds. D. Knights and H. Willmott. London: Sage Publication.
23. Maurer, R. 2010. Why 70% of Changes Fail, Sept. 19, 2010 www.reply-mc.com/2010/09/19/why-70-of-changes-fail-by-rick-maurer/

---

* Note: The seven tools Professor Kaoru Ishikawa references are: Cause-and-Effect Diagram (also known as the 'Fishbone' or Ishikawa Diagram), Check Sheet, Control Chart, Histogram, Pareto Chart, Scatter Diagram, Stratification (alternatively, Flow Chart or Run Chart)

4

The No. 1 Root Cause

We need to stop trying to make processes useful and start creating useful processes.

FIFTH-GRADE MATH EXPOSES THE PROBLEMS

I present many talks and workshops on the dysfunction of functional thinking and sometimes I illustrate the problem. I ask a participant to come up and help me demonstrate how a vertical organization and its inherent "white space" is perhaps the biggest impediment to continuous process improvement.

White space is defined as the interaction between departments, which shows as white space on traditional organization charts.[1]

Let's call the participant Andy. Andy is going to start a shirt factory. I sketch out on a flipchart how Andy is going to set up his company based on well-established practices (Figure 4.1). Andy is the boss and he decides that there will be a department for designing shirts, and he is hiring four designers. He also wants a head of design reporting to him. I draw this with Xs as illustrated in Figure 4.1. Then, he's going to hire some cloth cutters, so I put four more employees under the cloth-cutting department, and then a department of sleeve attachers, and a department of assemblers who sew the shirts. Andy has now structured a 4 × 4 matrix, and he is ready to go. Then, the first customer buys a shirt and guess what? The first shirt out of Andy's factory is poorly made. Its collar is poorly attached, some buttons are missing, and the cloth easily rips after the first wash. Andy promises to fix things. Now, if you go back to your fifth-grade math, that 4 × 4 matrix structure built by Andy has 64 boundaries,

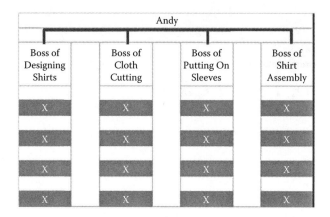

FIGURE 4.1

Traditional vertical organization structure.

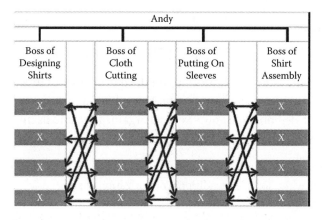

FIGURE 4.2

Opportunities are in the "white space."

or 64 interfaces among 16 employees in 4 departments where liabilities can occur, 64 areas of *white space*. Andy needs to look at those 64 opportunities to determine the root cause (Figure 4.2).

Unfortunately, there is no visibility of those white spaces. They are hidden. So, he responds in traditional fashion, assuming the cause of the defect is bad material from a supplier and countermeasures the supposed problem by establishing a new "set of Xs," a purchasing department, a new silo. Andy has just created a 5 × 4 matrix. Andy has just added white space and buried the problem deeper. Continuing to be frustrated by ongoing quality problems and customer complaints, Andy adds a Quality Control department, another function, creating a 6 × 4 matrix and more white space, burying the root cause even deeper (Figure 4.3). All Andy has done is exacerbated the problem. He has added more functions (and cost) that added more white space between functions, which doesn't solve the problem. Andy can keep adding onto this old mechanical, functional structure, but it won't get at the fundamental problem hidden somewhere in the process. There is no "manager of white space" to look after all the points of interface between functions, thus the problems continue. Even if there were managers of white space, it would create more white space. It's obvious and, yet, we ignore the fact that we can't get there from here.

A fundamental redesign of Andy's drawing is required. Of course, most organizations have a much larger matrix and infinitely more white space than Andy's illustration. At this point, I suggest to Andy that he turn the matrix sideways and look at it horizontally so that designers, cutters, sleeve putter-on-ers, and assemblers are all working in the same direction—toward customer value (Figure 4.4). Now, Andy sees his entire organization differently—horizontally.

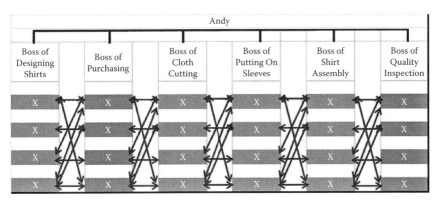

FIGURE 4.3
Every new "silo" creates twice as much additional "white space."

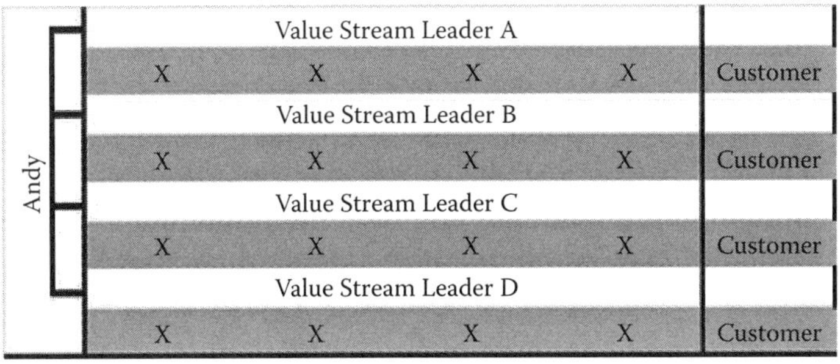

FIGURE 4.4
Focusing horizontally in value streams eliminates the "white space."

LESSONS FROM THE SHIRT FACTORY

Andy's designers and cutters are no different than your engineers, accountants, purchasing managers, CAD designers, software coders, software testers, and marketing people, in that they are all working vertically and no one is managing the white space. They are not thinking flow and working together to fill customer demand, which is, and must be, the purpose of the process.

Andy could have had the best designers, cutters, and assemblers in the world, but that would not have solved his problem. The sleeve was the sleeve department's responsibility, but the problem was in the cutting, which was connected to a design problem. And, the buttons were an assembly problem and "never the twain shall meet." The problems were lost in the no-man's land of no responsibility. Therefore, they never got exposed. However, when Andy turned the chart horizontally, he had design, cutting, sleeve, and assembly people working together, in a stream of value delivery with a common purpose: customer fulfillment. It's the same way Southwest Airlines brings together whoever it needs to get the plane back in the air. It's what I call a "river of value," where everyone is working in concert along the process.

Once Andy begins seeing and thinking horizontally, he can easily add to his organization without adding complexity. He can have value streams like A, B, C, D, which are distinguished simply by time and sequence. This represents a shift in how things are organized, cycled, sequenced, and done in order to continuously create more customer value and drive revenue. In its simplest form, process thinking is about supporting any factor that accelerates horizontal movement of information, product, and services toward customer value. Andy could now make golf shirts or dress shirts or even jackets or dresses as long as he adheres to the rules of time (i.e., the time any particular activity takes in the process) and sequence (i.e., the order in which the activities need to take place). He might have a continuous processing cell—often called a *value stream* or *river of value* or a *cellular design*—for each type of shirt, but he would *not* have to have one for normal variations in dress shirts. For example, he could have one for dress shirts with pockets, long sleeve, and short sleeve because the flow for the dress shirts, with or without pockets, with long sleeves or short sleeves is common. Just because he's adding a pocket doesn't mean he's changing the time or sequence of the process (river of value). However, if he decides to design and sell and stitch together hats, he might require a different value stream. Any organization, service, or manufacturer may have hundreds, even thousands of variations in its offerings, but it only has a few processes. The process only changes, and a new process or value stream is required, when the time or sequence of the work dramatically changes. Think of our friends at McDonald's. When you order a Big Mac, you get it in two and a half minutes (time to cook and construct) because that's the standard. However, if your daughter wants a hamburger with nothing on it, you might think that would be faster because it has fewer parts and steps, but it's not true. It's within the standard and can be made in that normal process (by simply skipping the mustard, tomatoes, onion, etc.) when it's going through. It's not a disruption to flow. But, if your son wants a hotdog, that's different. Most organizations will try to run a hotdog through the hamburger process rather than build another process for hotdogs. That is a serious disruption to flow. The choices the organization needs to make in response to a hotdog order are (1) don't sell hotdogs; or (2) knowing there's a big hotdog market, build a separate process for hotdogs and scale it up; or (3) cram the hotdog down the hamburger line and screw everything up. Ninety-nine times out of a hundred, traditional organizations with well-established practices pick method three because they think it is extra revenue and cost effective to run it through the same normal (reliable) process. After all, it's the same as ... *but* .... These organizations almost never calculate the hidden cost of the disruption to flow and the cost of screwing up the process every time a hotdog is ordered. How many times have you forced a hotdog down a hamburger process?

Remove the things that get in the way of work and organize the work that remains in streams of value with common time and sequence characteristics.

SIMPLIFY, SIMPLIFY, SIMPLIFY

Andy's original vertical design and need to continually bolt on more parts creates more complexity. Andy only has a small 4 × 6 matrix, so think of the number of discrete departments in your organization and the number of roles within those functions and your organizational matrix of white space gets daunting. Like Andy, you may not have thought about it this way because you are probably not exposed to a process view of the organization. For instance, how often do you say, "I work in the demand generation process," or "I work in the data conversion process where we create decisive information." Or "I work in the raw material transformation process." This is process-thinking language. The matrix of complexity becomes more acute as the customer demands more and more variety and more customization of products and services. The refrain of the process-focused organization is simplify, simplify, simplify, by removing the things that get in the way of work and organize the work that remains in streams of value with common time and sequence characteristics. Many successful companies have used simplicity to drive their business performance: Ikea with its flat packs; McDonald's with its burgers; Berkshire Hathaway with its buy, improve, and hold strategy; Southwest Airlines and its clones with its low-cost airline service; and Apple with the same process for a succession of iProducts. This simplicity is driven by the need to create reliable processes, meaning "one size fits all." The lesson, however, is in the process simplicity, not the products and services resulting from that process. Even simplified processes can produce a host of different products or service outputs. The key to simple processes is understanding that complexity is created by small variations in the process that cause disturbances to flow. The problem is that these variations are often invisible. There could be a million cars on the road, but it only takes a couple to create gridlock. Also, if the breakdown that caused the gridlock was not forecast or scheduled, there would have been no reason to create an off ramp because it was assumed that the process worked yesterday when there was no traffic jam, so it should work today; after all, it's a reliable process.

ROOT CAUSE

It's worth repeating: The root cause of the epidemic failure of continuous process improvement programs is management's *resistance to understanding process* both in terms of its organizational structure and its inability to adopt a process mind. When I state this to an audience or a CEO, the uneasiness is palpable. There's a shuffling in the chairs. Most managers think they have this "process thing" figured out and I always see that look on their face of, "Oh no, not process again." That's when I say, "If you aren't out-performing your competition like Apple is, then you don't have a good understanding of process. And, if you can't describe what you are doing as a process, you don't know what you are doing." I add, "And, don't tell me it can't be done."

The evidence is in and the results are indisputable. When an organization makes a commitment to understanding the *primacy of process*, the performance improvement can be substantial. The toughest part is trying to understand something that is not obvious. If you don't know what you are looking for, it is hard to see, hard to follow, and hard to fix, unless you change the thinking. Change the thinking and you change understanding. Change the understanding and you begin to change practices. Change practices and you begin to change performance. Here's an anatomical metaphor that emphasizes the critical nature of the thoughtware. Change the operating thoughtware by infusing a healthy circulatory system into your organizational body that continually changes and enriches the organization with ongoing exercise. The system directly observes the disruptions to flow and adheres to a good nutritional, problem-solving diet to countermeasure and prevent those at-risk arteries; thus, you are creating streams of value, not functional silos, which always lead to stenosis, even atresia. Your organization's future health depends on it. And, in Chapter 12, we talk more about the requisite "carrot diet."

THE IMPERATIVE IS IMPERATIVE

On a macro basis, technology has been driving exponentially the proliferation of change around the globe, at rates Machiavelli would never have imagined. It is everywhere, from the offshoring of jobs and the rise of China and India to the disruptions of terrorism and the calamity of the 2007–2009 recession. On a micro basis, most change is anchored in the merry-go-round of programs (more like a rollercoaster) that we have endured over the decades. They have generated little sustainable change and we can no longer blame employees for resistance to such change efforts. In fact, most employees have moved past the corporate addiction stage to the torpor of acceptance. They have experienced the ineffectiveness of the latest whim and they know there is no sustainable improvement to come. Their resistance is *not* to the change, it is to the failure; the inability to overcome the status quo of *prove it before you do it*. And, rightly so. Especially since those who live in the "gemba" (the actual place where the work gets done, in the trenches, at the coalface, plowing fields, mending fences, and generating value) know the solutions. They just need a problem-solving methodology that gives them permission to look into the "white space" without the status quo rearing its departmental head to defend their particular specialty empire.

I mentioned earlier the problem of the immune system protecting the status quo and how it fights to keep its fiefdoms. Well, I have another term for the pathology that permeates an organization at the management level. It is the collective, old thoughtware that hangs over the business like smog hangs over Beijing. I call it the *bozone layer*. It's a symptom of the immune system, a fog of inertia that infects people who are stuck in status quo thinking. It is designed to resist the process mind. Managers in the bozone layer find it difficult to accept new thinking, as discovered in Daniel Kahneman's (psychologist and winner of the 2002 Nobel Memorial Prize in Economic Sciences) research, especially if the thinking breaks through the bozone layer and sheds light on problems that have been there all along. The bozone layer is not only embarrassing, it's crippling. The bozone layer chokes new thinking off at the top of the organization and stops new ideas from bubbling up from the bottom. The only way to rid an organization of its bozone is by the company manifesting a deep respect for people and taking a healthy injection of new thoughtware. What do we need to do to create process-focused management thinking and to allow the process mind to evolve? Install a new business model because it is not just a structural change from vertical to horizontal, it is a wholesale rebuild of the operating thoughtware, the engine of any business model. The new thoughtware is an archetype shift in emphasis, from a focus on resources to workflow, from a fixation with targets to process capability, from obsession on shareholder value to customer value, from hiding problems to exposing disruptions to flow, and from the analytical to the experimental.

I was to learn later in life that we tend to meet any new situation by reorganizing, and a wonderful method it can be for creating the illusion of progress while producing confusion, inefficiency, and demoralization.

Petronius Arbiter (66 CE)

UPGRADE THE ORGANIZATION'S THOUGHTWARE

Not since the industrial revolution have we seen a longer list of companies whose business models are now obsolete and the speed of change in the digital age is accelerating this obsolescence. Only 13.4% of the Fortune 500 companies (ranked by gross revenue) in 1955 were still on the list 56 years later in 2011—even though it was an era when American automotive companies owned 95% of the world market and Japanese was a synonym for poor quality. Also, almost 87% of those companies have either gone bankrupt, merged, gone private, or fallen from the top 500. That is a lot of churning and no doubt the next 56 years will bring another churn with the same number of new companies in new industries.[2] In 1958, companies in the S&P 500 had typically stayed in the index for 61 years, but, today, the average is just 18 years. Nokia produced a quarter of the world's handsets in 2000 and, in September 2013, it sold its handset business to Microsoft (another shadow of its former self).[3] Just as Cisco, eBay, McDonald's, Microsoft, and Yahoo replaced American Motors, Studebaker, Detroit Steel, Maytag, and National Sugar Refining, their replacements, the next Facebook and Twitter, will emerge, and quickly. Today, many enterprises are rethinking their business models (i.e., media, publishing, music, advertising, retail). The education system and healthcare industry need new models and so do banks, the legal profession, the post office, computer makers, and the telecoms. All are having a hard time finding the right model, perhaps because they do not have the right operating thoughtware system. Process thinking is simply *not* a competency that exists in most companies, mainly because it never had to. Fifteen years ago, I talked about the need for new thinking in my book, *Thoughtware: Change the Thinking and the Organization Will Change Itself* (Productivity Press, 1997), and yet, here I am today still saying we need a serious upgrade in process-thinking thoughtware in most organizations.

> Men occasionally stumble over the truth, but most pick themselves up and hurry off as if nothing happened.
>
> **Winston Churchill**

I have found, as W. Edwards Deming did 40 years ago, that whether the leader is a steeped-in-experience guy or a spit-and-polished MBA, most are still operating with a business model rooted in the traditional baggage manifested by vertical thinking. Of course, we have added state-of-the-art technology and advanced managerial practices, but somehow that "damn process thing" continues to be misunderstood and ignored. In his book, *Competing for the Future*, Gary Hamel, an American management consultant, said, "Put a 1960s-era CEO in a time machine and transport him to 2010, and that CEO would find a great many of today's management rituals little changed from those that governed corporate life a generation or two ago." He's right. Old thoughtware holds us in its grip and prevents us from keeping pace. The irony is, most everyone agrees that it's a new world—fast, furious, and unpredictable—and, yet, we continue to operate with encrusted and wasteful processes, with self-inflicted blood clots resulting from legacy policy thinking and proliferating organizational white space. This organizational pathos is evident in the refusal of management to surrender its obsolete departmental kingdoms. Again, there is blind obedience to a top-down, inside-out perspective, which is often driven by shareholder value rather than a sustained process-focused approach that unwaveringly defers to an outside-in customer perspective. Many companies mouth the "customer first" rhetoric, but if they are not focused on the value delivery process that fulfills the customer's demands, then it is just talk.

For more than 20 years, I have been walking the workplaces in many-industries, businesses, and geographies; in back offices, factories, laboratories, and service centers; in mines, banks, distribution centers, supply chains, and manufacturers—whether discrete, batch, or process producers—and I consistently see the same thing—competent, skillful, functional managers, each trying to improve productivity and performance by optimizing their silo, while marveling at the disruptions to the flow imported into their functional compartment from somebody else's department. What is remarkable is that these managers intuitively know, just below the surface, just outside their reach, that the real value flows horizontally and that customers are hindered by the vertical constraints that interrupt flow. They know it, but can't, or won't, address it. It just seems too hard, too outside the norm and the expected. Until we devise a model that marshals the collective thinking around the horizontal flow of value to the customer, then we will continue to act as we have, optimizing our own particular vertical responsibilities and interests that work against the flow of the whole.

WHITE SPACE

Most disruptions to flow cannot be seen from a vertical perspective. Andy learned that in my classroom and he also learned that in contemporary business structures; it has proved to be more difficult than most can handle. The term *white space,* coined by the late Geary Rummler, is the system, the connections that flow *between* parts, not the parts that are important. We pay attention to the wrong parts—the boxes, not the white space.[4] We have to learn to look at the white space. This is where significant improvement can be achieved and sustained over time. Rummler's term *white space* and its companion, *waste,* go hand-in-hand and are critical in process thinking. To see the landscape of white space, we need to look at and listen to the noise created by white space.

RESHORING

Another good example of old thoughtware is labor arbitrage, the maniacal chase across the globe for the lowest wages. Amazingly, we have been content to make this deal with the devil and trade off low labor rates in exchange for elongated supply lines. The process mind would not accept this. This reflects a critical aspect of modern management failure because it further exacerbates the separation of thinking and doing between experts and workers. Drawn out supply chains mean more organizing along functional departmental lines. It is a misdiagnosed prescription, a drug that provides the lower wages while introducing potentially severe side effects, such as supply chain costs and disruptions to the process of delivering customer value. Unfortunately, the side effects are difficult to see, hidden in the "fine print" of total costs. It's usually a short-term band-aid.

Recently, there has been some return to sanity as nearly a quarter of European and American companies have shortened their supply chain after Japan's Fukushima Daiichi nuclear disaster (March 2011).[5] It took a catastrophic event to expose the problem of extended supply chains, which wrenched managers out of their old thoughtware and badly designed processes of supply. David Hummels of Purdue University and George Schaur of the University of Tennessee estimate a day in transit is equal to a tariff of 0.6 to 2.3% (it's highest in components and parts).[6]

That is a lot of costs piled on top of supposed "cheap" products from overseas. Inditex (Spain), one of the world's two biggest clothes makers (H&M of Sweden is the other), used its main brand, Zara, to conquer the European market. Its horizontal, process-focused business model goes like this. Other fashion firms have their clothes made in China. It's cheap, but managing a long supply chain is costly, in more ways than one. By the time the boat has sailed halfway around the world, the cargo is yesterday's news. Instead, Inditex sources its products locally (Spain, Portugal, and Morocco). On the surface, this appears to cost more, but because the supply chain is short, they can react quickly to new trends in fashion and that gives them a competitive advantage that off-sets any apparent savings in labor costs. Again, it's a cogent process built to constantly adjust itself to changing customer demand (fashion), as opposed to the reliable but slow "boat from China." Instead of betting today on tomorrow's hot look, Zara has a shorter time between ideas and sold, and doesn't get stuck with unwanted inventory. They also sell more products at full price. Since 2001, sales have quadrupled to $19.1 billion.[7] Remember Apple and how it has a shorter supply chain advantage, which can translate into a 1 to 2% value-added for every day a product is not on a shelf somewhere. There are more than a few "pennies" to be gained through the improvement of the distribution and supply chain process.

So, please, if you are a retailer, stop buying everything from China and then complaining that you cannot finance a supply chain that takes months to get goods from 9,000 miles away. And, if you are a manufacturer, look at cycle times, not labor (i.e., irrelevant headcount) as the main source of your cost pressures. ABC Adhesives (Chapter 2) learned this. The essential reward of time compression is cash and unlike our accounting architecture that hides problems, cash does not lie. When management looks exclusively at direct labor costs and not much else, such as slow freight and slow processes, many wrong decisions are made. If we take a different perspective and focus on the horizontal end-to-end process, we will make very different decisions and have a much more efficient and effective supply chain. Manufacturing in North America for goods consumed in North America, when fully accounting for manufacturing costs and not just factory wages, is just as economical if it is a process-focused operation. Labor accounts for only a small portion of a total costs; the bigger cost is elongated supply lines and the associated cash being tied up.

Our history, from Ford to Darwin to Machiavelli, shows that we readily avoid the heavy lifting of process thinking and take the easy way out—at our peril. By 2013, a hundred years after Henry Ford's process thinking, China is neck and neck with America as the world's biggest manufacturer, and 150 years later, Darwin is still right, it is not the strongest of species that survive or even the most intelligent, it's the ones that adapt. Vertical structures are not adaptable, they are dinosaurs.

MORE ROOT CAUSE: NO PROBLEM IS A DANGEROUS PROBLEM

Two of the most important aspects of horizontal organizations include:

1. They require that processes be designed to expose problems (for most, a scary thought).
2. They require that the people who work in the process are willing and able to solve the problems as they are exposed.

This is a markedly different way to operate a business and, yet, as far as I know, it is the only way to increase productivity and outperform the competition.

Every business has a litany of hidden problems and they include, but are not limited to, unreliable machinery, long setup times, erratic flow, poorly trained people, poor quality, poor product development, bad layouts, bad service, bad customer relations, and, of course, inventory. Extra time is waste and it manifests itself in many forms, but inventory may be the most blatant representation of built-in time. It's bad enough that inventory adds to operating costs, increases poor quality, and buffers supply lines, but the bigger problem is the insidious and thieving nature of inventory. Insidious because it hides the treasures inside obstructions to the flow, and thieving because it plunders the most valuable resource of the organization: time. Time is not only hard cash, stealing time shows blatant disrespect for people. Wasted time or time padding is easier to see when in the form of physical inventory; however, wasted time conceals itself well in service industries, in transactional processes and relationship or knowledge processes. In the mid-2000s, as social media made consumer reports on air travel ubiquitous and airline "passengers' rights" drew more attention, the airlines began to pad schedules to protect their reputation and hide the problem—by building in time. In order to be reported as being technically on time, they improved on-time performance by pulling away from the gate and having the customers sit on the tarmac for artificially long periods. It was nothing more than data gaming the metrics. Like physical inventory, the time padding just covered up the real problem: the disruption of flow hidden in customer baggage chaos, ineffective boarding practices, plane cleaning delays, poor gate scheduling, slow maintenance, late crews, and overbooking. Time padding and data gaming, like inventory, hide disruptions to flow and conceal the problems (treasures). The airline looked better on paper despite having done nothing to improve performance and increase customer value. The everyday examples of hiding treasures are endless: queuing up customers in call centers, having more patients in the waiting room than medical clinics can possibly treat, aircraft worth $100 million sitting idle at the gate, wandering around massive big box retailers to find a couple of items. Today, supermarkets and big box stores are adapting to the time issue and providing smaller, faster buying venues to serve more and more customers who are shopping every other day. Instead of buying carts full of groceries and standing in line forever, customers are buying in small batches and saving time. One of the culprits is a call center. For example, when they say, "This call may be monitored for quality purposes," they are not only wasting our time, but insulting the respect for people principle, all the while holding up delivering customer value. And, then there is the big insult when they say, "Your call is important to us ..." and proceed to keep you on hold for 15 minutes. As demonstrated time and again, in most processes, there is about 10 times more disruption to flow than there is actual work and unhindered flow.[8]

Hiding problems gives the warm illusion of no problem; however, no problems are indeed the most dangerous problems of all.

We know this, but continue to create patches and workarounds that hide treasures with poorly thought-out antiprocess-flow practices and techniques, such as departmental incentive policies; ISO certifications of dumb processes; black belt accreditations with no line authority; amortizing waste to pursue unit labor cost while ignoring the greater end-to-end total; cross-functional task forces that go back into their functional silos after being dismissed from the force; month-end, target-obsessive managerial behavior; elongated supply chains; unnecessary complexity; and believing there is a software solution for every problem.

We need to stop trying to make processes useful and start creating useful processes. The fundamental lack of understanding of real process innovation and design is why so many companies spend time and effort on innovation, continuous process improvement, and enabling technology with less than expected results. Management's challenge is to get off the roller-coaster of short-term ups and downs and find what is sustainable because more of the same will just produce more of the same. The title of one of my earlier books is still applicable, *The Future: You Can't Get There from Here,* O.T.I Inc., 2004. I said it then and I say it now: History will repeat itself and the future will continue to look much like the past, unless we change the thoughtware and deal with the root cause problems. The real resistance lies with management and the lack of will to do what it takes to get at process.

CASH FLOW: THE MOTHER OF ALL PROCESSES

In 2008, several major financial institutions collapsed because of the disruptions in the flow of credit to businesses and consumers that were hidden in complex financial structures. From 2004 to 2006, the percentage of new, lower-quality subprime mortgages rose from a historically low 8% to approximately 20% (much higher ratios in parts of the country). U.S. households had become increasingly indebted, with the ratio of debt to disposable personal income rising from 77% in 1990 to 127% at the end of 2007.[9] But none of this was seen in a collective view, the parts were only viewed through the lens of separate agencies and businesses. No one could see the whole process and no one had a clear responsibility to fix the disruption of flow in the financial process. When finally exposed, it was part of a severe global recession. A "no problem" became a toxic disaster; literally, a hidden process too big to fail. Pundits busied themselves affixing different levels of blame to financial institutions, regulators, credit agencies, government housing policies, consumers, and other silos, but the real cause was the mother of all business processes, the macro cash flow process. The problems with, and disruptions to, that flow, such as lower lending standards and higher-risk mortgages (subprime lending), were concealed, until it was too late. The result was no cash flow, delinquencies, bankruptcies, and foreclosures. The problems had been there for some time, but they remained hidden in disparate segments of the process and lost in the white space. The cost, from Wall Street to Main Street, was unprecedented.

I fear our organizations are subject to similar liabilities, unless we shift to designing our enterprises so they are operationally transparent, meaning all employees can clearly see the flow of value to the customer and fix problems in that flow before they reach the customer. By providing such customer value, we create more throughput with less cost (return on sales), and accelerate cash flow (capital turns), and those two data elements create value for the enterprise. Process-focused organization design is just good financial management. It is not about spending the least amount (lowest cost), it is about higher value, the highest percent spending on value-adding activities. The contemptuous and brilliantly perceptive Bill Waddell, a Lean accounting thought-leader, and the most widely read manufacturing blogger on the Internet, incessantly preaches the necessity of process thinking and the end-to-end customer mindset. At the end of the day, he proposes that finance be concerned with one number related to how effective the organization processes are (i.e., how Lean they are)—the percentage of value-adding expenses to total expenses.[10] I have termed this the *cost-to-purpose* ratio that might be measured as the cost-of-work to the total cost-of-work, plus the cost of the things that get in the way of work. For example, how much is of value-adding work (i.e., what the customer perceives to be of value and worth paying for) and how much gets in the way of work (i.e., customer perceives no value and will not pay for—management, supervision, material handling, inspection, fixing broken stuff, sales and marketing, regulatory compliance, administration, etc.)? Remember, the question is not what is of value to the company or what is necessary (i.e., regulatory compliance), but what is of value to the customer. These necessary costs, that add no value in the customer's eyes, but add real costs to the company, do not translate into higher value (i.e., price the customer will pay) because they do not make the deal any more attractive to the customer. Waddell further cautions that this is not a benchmarking tool. The only thing that matters is whether the cost-to-purpose is getting better each and every day (if it is 40% today, can it be 39% tomorrow?). The purpose, of course, is to continually expose and remove waste and only spend money on value-adding efforts. What truly adds value? In most organizations no one knows; therefore, there needs to be a high agreement on this. In Chapter 10, How to Conduct a Treasure Hunt, I provide a method to engage in this type of discussion in a meaningful way.

REFERENCES

1. Rummler, G. A., and A. P. Brache. 1995. *Improving performance: How to manage the white space in the organization.* San Francisco: Jossey Bass Business and Management Series.
2. Perry, M. J. 2011. *Fortune 500 firms in 1955 vs. 2011: 87% are gone.* Carpe Diem Blog for Economics and Finance. Online at: http://mjperry.blogspot.ca/2011/11/fortune-500-firms.
3. *The Economist*, Sept. 7, 2013, The Man Who Showed Why Firms Exist (from print edition, page 13) www.economist.com/news/leaders/21584985
4. Rummler and Brache, *Improving Performance.*
5. Economist.com/blogs/Schumpeter, April 23, 2011, The Case Against Globaloney, www.economist.com/node/18584204
6. Hummels, D. L., and G. Schaur. 2013. Time as a trade barrier. *American Economic Review* (American Economic Association) 103(7):2935–2959.
7. Special Report on Outsourcing and Offshoring. 2013. Home or abroad? Herd instinct. *Economist* (January 19):12.
8. Stalk, G., Jr., and T. E. Hout. 1990. *Competing against time: How time-based competition is reshaping global markets.* New York: Free Press Macmillan, 76.
9. *The Economist*, Nov.22, 2008, The End of the Affair (from print edition, page 21) www.economist.com/node/12637090
10. Waddell, B. 2009. *The Lean ratio.* Evolving Excellence blog, December 16. Online at: http://www.idatix.com/manufacturing-leadership/lean-accounting-just-another-vehicle-for-managing-by-the-numbers/.

5

Process Design and Respect for People

Employees have the right to be successful every time they do their job.

BAD PROCESS, BAD BLOOD

To sum up the discussion thus far on the power of process, I have posited that all enterprises have a business model, explicit or implicit, that represents the way they deliver value to customers, for a profit. Processes provide the operating engine with a circulatory system that deploys the business model, and smart processes enrich the lifeblood of the company and allow its performance to soar, while lousy processes create bad blood and lethargic performance. Process design exposes disruptions to the flow of value to the customer, while creating people who are willing and able to countermeasure those disruptions as they occur, and fix them before they reach the customer. Broken processes hide problems, saddle people with unnecessary stress, and force them underground to create workarounds. Processes can only be healthy and drive performance improvement where there is an intense respect for the people living in the processes.

Respect for people is the belief that *employees have the right to be successful every time they do their job.* The art of doing their job is finding disruptions to flow in the process—what I call treasure hunting—and making improvements. If management truly respects their people, they have an obligation to give them the means to find and solve these disruptions. That requires a clear line of sight of the flow of value to the customer and the information, skills, and authority to remove those disruptions.

Respect for people goes well beyond the vacuous myth of empowerment and other such platitudes and because when contemporary businesses seem to prefer an organization carved into isolated departments, they are not showing respect for people. Respect for people means a true understanding and leveraging of their power and value of experience, creativity, and knowledge. All continuous improvement dogma (i.e., TQM, Baldrige, ISO, Six Sigma, Reengineering, et al.) have no real chance of success without embracing the daily practice of respect for people. When there is respect, people behave as themselves and bring their brilliance to bear without being frustrated by policies and politics, red tape, and bureaucratic organizational mud. Respect for people means people working on things that matter, generously applying their problem-solving skills, creative abilities, and natural energy. This is the secret sauce of process improvement and it only works if it is generously poured over the entire workflow and not just applied in discrete departments. People who understand what the customer values will inevitably use their good judgment to win, regardless of any ill-conceived, cast-in-stone, "we always do it this way" standard operating procedures. In many organizations that I visit, the lack of respect for people is demonstratively flagrant. Lousy processes provide the proof.

The "respect for people" principle demands the creation of usable processes, not processes made to be usable through daily workarounds and other required subversions. It means there is no confusion about the business purpose of the organization's core processes and that customer value is more important than meeting month-end or preparing for a quarterly review. Amazingly, in a 2013 survey by Kelton Global, a Los Angeles-based research firm, 40% of the respondents said they do not understand or have never seen the company's vision.[1]

The power of process is as a self-learning system that will eventually expose the problems and right the ship, but only if those problems are not hidden in the practices and broken processes that require miniheroics by people every day. When the respect for people principle is missing, employees spend inordinate amounts of time on dealing with the things that get in the way of work and the hero is required to tackle the situation in which everything is out of control and quickly impose some type of order. However, in a healthy business process, where respect for people is fundamental, we don't need heroes because every employee is in touch with the process and engaged in making the process better. Heroes create short-term band-aids; respect for people provides long-term, continuous improvement.

STOP RIDING A DEAD HORSE

The tribal wisdom of the Dakota Sioux says that, when you discover you are riding a dead horse, the best strategy is to dismount; it is respectful. However, in today's business world, where respect for employees is not paramount, alternative strategies are often employed:

- Buy a stronger whip (i.e., performance incentives or tighter policy will not improve the broken process).
- Change riders (i.e., getting brilliant people to operate a mediocre process yields mediocre results).
- Threaten the horse with termination (i.e., relocation of a lousy process to a new location maintains a lousy process in a new location).
- Appoint a committee to study the horse (i.e., hire more consultants and specialists as if they know more than the employees who have operated the process for years and years).
- Arrange to visit other sites to see how they ride dead horses (enough said).
- Lower the standards so dead horses can be included (i.e., seek regulatory relief, chase the low-cost spiral).
- Hire outside contractors to ride the dead horse (i.e., outsource to a low-labor country (LLC), preferably offshore with a long supply chain).
- Harness several dead horses together to try and increase speed (i.e., automate the stupid process so as to become more effectively imprudent).
- Declare the dead horse carries less overhead, and therefore, contributes more to the bottom line than other horses (i.e., use creative accounting architecture, build more inventory, and lower the unit cost).
- Provide additional funding to try and improve the dead horse's performance (i.e., get a government subsidy by declaring bankruptcy).

So many well-established practices are dead horses and you cannot increase productivity or improve performance unless, first, you do what a wise man once said, "Get the hell off the dead horse." Without a change in your business processes, you are not eligible for any performance improvement and anything else is arbitrary and doomed to failure.

When I first visit a company, I am often invited to sit in the boardroom and talk, but my response is always the same, "Forget the boardroom.

What happens there is not what I need to know." Then I say, "Let's take a walk through your business." There's an old Chinese saying: "The only truth is what you see." Studies by educational researchers suggest that approximately 83% of human learning occurs visually and the remaining 17% through the other senses: 11% through hearing, 3.5% through smell, 1% through taste, and 1.5% through touch.[2] The brain processes visual images 60,000 times faster than text and 90% of information transmitted to the brain is visual.[3] So, the first thing to do, literally, is walk through the business and look for the process, follow the process, and see where and how it is generating, producing, and delivering customer value, and where it is not. I call this *treasure hunting*, which I cover in Chapter 10. Getting at process is about the power of observation and, to borrow from the vernacular of my skateboarding, snowboarding son, it requires "extreme emersion." You can only know and understand the process by plunging in, by hanging with the people who work in the process and looking for treasure. You have to understand the process and engage the people, and that requires adherence to two principles: direct observation and respect for people.

Not long ago, I was brought in to look at a state-of-the-art, multimillion dollar, 9-million-cubic-meter, 155,000-square-foot distribution center supplying over 1,200 retail outlets. In operation for 18 months and incorporating the latest building design and technology, the center was underperforming in terms of being able to supply all the stores in a timely manner. Daily, it was managing 85 outbound trailers to handle 3,500 orders, or 420,000 separate units (or "eaches"). After we had finished the walk, someone asked me what I thought. I said, "I wouldn't have designed it that way." It was obviously not designed by a process mind. Fortunately, instead of throwing me out, they asked me to explain. My response was, "Let's go back out there and treasure hunt."

SEEING IS BELIEVING

Treasure hunting is to "go look" in the workplace, "go and see for yourself" what the problem is. Get close to it and thoroughly understand it. A good process designer doesn't trust anything other than what he or she sees. This is crucial when you are trying to understand the current state of the process without any reverence for the specific departments or functions it passes through. The value is in the workplace, where you can see the process.

It doesn't matter whether it's an office, a research lab, a fishing trawler, an underground mine, a manufacturing floor, a retail outlet, or a distribution center. Seeing the process allows you to ask the right questions. I have personally gone on over 1,600 treasure hunts in every industry and work environment, from 7,400 feet underground in a nickel mine in Northern Canada to an oil industry forging and heat treatment operation in the jungles of Batam, Indonesia, from call centers in India to chemical refiners in Finland, and from big city law firms to pharmaceutical laboratories and nuclear test facilities. In every case, I have discovered unfound treasures, simple, exquisite opportunities for process improvement that to date had been undetected. These treasures mask themselves in the crevices of white space and are concealed in legacy policy and procedures, ill-conceived information factories, and misaligned measurement systems. Though nearly all of these companies had at least some degree of exposure and deployment to a continuous improvement program, they had not yet embraced the power of process thinking and the underlying principles of direct observation and respect for people. Their continuous improvement efforts had been conducted with their eyes shut, from distant conference rooms and the erroneous maps of Excel® spreadsheets and system data dumps.

LET'S GO FOR A WALK

During that first walk in the distribution warehouse, I identified a simple slice of a process to directly observe: from "collect order pick ticket" to "place assembled order on the delivery trailer." I watched an order selector enter the process. Jane's role was to pick the required products and arrange them on a pallet on a trailer for shipping. First, she took a pick ticket from the warehouse management system, organized her electric pallet truck, headed down the pick face, and began to select the order. At one point, she came up behind another order selector, Brian, who appeared to be slower and was stopped, stuck searching for an item. So, what did Jane do? Did she hop off and help Brian? No, she went around him and headed to the dock with her load. I asked, "Why did she do that?" The supervisor said that, in order to improve productivity, they had put in a policy that had each driver trying to pick 1,350 units per shift. I mused. "Well, that's interesting. Let me ask, 'Is the purpose here to load the trailer or pick material?'" I got a somewhat hesitant reply, "… uh, to load the trailer." This is a critical point, which I will come back to often. It is important, when deeply immersed in a process, to be absolutely clear on what the purpose of that process is. We continued to watch and as Jane arrived on the dock, she dropped her shipment in front of the appropriate loading door because she couldn't put it on the trailer yet. She was out of sequence, ahead of Brian's load, which had to go on the trailer first. When Brian arrived, he couldn't deliver his pallets onto the designated trailer because Jane's shipment was in the way. By the end of the shift, they had over 850 pallets backed up on the dock waiting to be loaded onto the trailer. Stuff sat, stuff waited. Stuff was handled multiple times, checked multiple times, data entered multiple times, and spreadsheets created multiple times; all of it part of guerilla warfare tactics to try and accommodate the ill-conceived policy of 1,350 units per selector per shift. The measure, 1,350, never aligned with the purpose, but never mind, the employees were working hard to hit their pick targets and the department of order selecting prospered. The purpose of the process—load the trailer on time and accurately for the customer— was of no real concern to their domain. Through direct observation and this simple treasure hunt, we discovered some treasure. Hidden in plain sight to the process mind, but concealed from the organization's robust, silo-structure thinking was the misaligned 1,350 units policy. The order selector supervisor, after all, was measured on the number of picks, regardless of the number of trailers loaded or amount of customer (retail stores) demand fulfilled. It became evident that the 1,350 policy disrupted flow rather than facilitated it. The policy created more things to get in the way of work and it did not enhance the work itself. The policy created waste in the process and it certainly had no respect for the order-selecting employees who were head-down obsessed with 1,350, customer be damned. A simple treasure hunt revealed a valuable treasure. And, this is common everywhere I go. Process flow is constantly disrupted by policy, measures, and incentives that concentrate on optimizing a particular part of the process at the expense of providing value to the customer. It creates fiefdoms where people act as if they work for a particular function rather than the customer at the end of the process.

What is most disturbing about these disruptions to flow is that they are self-inflicted; perhaps well intended, but nonetheless detrimental. Not only self-inflicted, but designed to hide the problem. Why was Brian having trouble with this particular order? (In fact, his bar code reader's battery was low, requiring him to read the codes multiple times.) What could be done to countermeasure that problem next time? When Jane bypassed Brian, the problem was ignored and hidden and no containment or preventive actions were taken. The waste was overlooked (as was the root cause, a defective battery charger). Here, the real need was to build a process geared to fulfilling the primary purpose of loading the trailer. Having a pick target was irrelevant and counterproductive. The ideal process would be to *touch it once and load the truck*. Anything else is a variance from the purpose and a problem to be exposed and solved. Now, like our crime laboratory heroes in the popular television series *CSI*, the sooner the evidence is discovered and analyzed, the better chance of solving the problem.

If the work done is what is needed to carry out customers' orders, and only that, then the system is designed on purpose.

Of course, the real purpose of the entire process was to deliver a perfect order to the retail outlet. A perfect order was defined as "on time, complete, as requested, with no overages, no underages, and no breakages." They were not even close and the CEO was receiving a constant stream of phone messages from franchisees complaining about poor service. Ironically, service was supposed to be improved by the new distribution center as they were now supplying more from their own facilities instead of third-party suppliers. This was a change in strategy, but the deployment of the strategy was poorly executed (more about this in the next chapter). Also, the strategy called for opening more retail outlets so the operation had to handle more variety, deliver more products, serve different store types, and add refrigerated and frozen products. The degree of difficulty had increased. At that time, they were delivering a "perfect order" at about a 70% success rate, and using additional third-party logistics firms to manage 20% of the stores they couldn't get to. Of course, I was curious as to why it was only 70% and only 80% of the customer base was being handled out of the center. So we continued the treasure hunt.

THE ENGINEERING CASTLE

The industrial engineering department, living in its own castle, was measured not on value to the customer, but on efficiency gains and cost reduction. For example, the engineers had analyzed the stretch wrapping of pallets and determined that the time it took the order selectors to stop and manually stretch wrap their pallets was about a minute. This calculus was done as a remote analysis, based on theoretical standard times. Following their mandate to reduce costs, they concluded that, if they could get an automated, orbital stretch wrapping machine, the activity of pallet wrapping could be reduced from a little under a minute to about 26 seconds. The savings? Headcount reduction. So, they requisitioned a $90,000 capital expenditure. What did they get? They were rewarded with a five- to seven-minute queue in front of the new palletizing equipment while the drivers waited for their wrapping. What did the drivers do? They hopped off and wrapped it themselves because they weren't about to sit in that line while being measured on the number of picks per shift (to hell with the idea of loading the trailer, the purpose of the process). Instinctively, the drivers knew that workflow was important (the picking flow that they were paid to focus on), so they found a work-around for the wrapping delay. Unfortunately, they were not focused on the right purpose: load the trailer. The outcome exacerbated the problem by adding a resource that wasn't needed and, in the end, encumbered workflow. The engineering department embraced neither the principle of direct observation or respect for people. However, the engineering kingdom prospered because they improved on their mandate to reduce labor costs, albeit, for only one particular resource point in the flow, never mind that it was in no way a constraint to the process. How could it be when there were hundreds of pallets of goods downstream on the loading dock waiting to be loaded onto trailers? The engineering department, like the order selecting department, succeeded in not only creating more disruptions to the flow, but worse, hiding the evidence. At the end of the day, any process is no better than the weakest link in the chain, whether it is processing patients through hospitals or visitors through amusement parks or pallets through distribution centers. The order-selecting silo chose policy (i.e., 1,350 units picked) as its concealment technique and the engineers chose to camouflage their waste as a process enhancement.

Whenever you focus on the resource instead of the workflow, your costs will go up, always. Conversely, whenever you focus on workflow, your costs will go down, always.

The engineers, with their vertical, compartmentalized view, marching to the drumbeat of labor cost reduction, focused on one discrete resource, pallet wrapping, when, in fact, that detached activity adds nothing to improving the flow of value to the customer. It just adds a constraint downstream. The purpose is not to reduce the cost of pallet wrapping any more than the purpose of the process is to select material off the pick face; the purpose of the process is to load the trailer accurately and on time in order to fulfill customer demand.

In treasure hunting, finding one treasure always begets more treasure. We kept hunting in the pick-to-load process. The distribution center was loading 35 trucks per shift because they had 35 docks. They employed a method called wave-picking (i.e., grouping orders to optimize picking). Although it is one of the fastest methods of picking, it is not the best way to load the trailer (i.e., consolidate, sort verify, etc., the purpose of the process). Working with the queue of pallets on the dock, they loaded in sequence (two to five stores per trailer), the front, then the middle, then the back of the trailer. The result? Thirty-five trailers partially loaded. That created more treasures, resulting from optimizing the part (picking) at the expense of the end-to-end process flow. The Chennai Paradox shows up again here in the loading and releasing of one full truckload at a time (i.e., fulfilling some customer demand), which is better than *partially* loading 35 trailers (i.e., fulfilling no customer demand). Inventory shows up again in the form of idle trailers. The incomplete trailers are disruptions to flow (i.e., inventory/time), absorbing lots of labor costs, but triggering no revenue (i.e., receivables). It's a bit like you're working all year, but getting paid only on the last day. That's a tough cash flow model.

COSTS REDUCED 44%, TIME 74%

Today, the distribution center, after redesigning the process by "blowing up" the silos and removing silly policies (i.e., pick targets) and adhering to the flow principle of *touch it once, put it on the trailer,* now loads and releases a truck every 22 minutes. The total elapsed time to pick and load a "medium" order (i.e., a 7 ft. × 30 ft. pallet of 235 items) was reduced from 44 minutes to 35 minutes, a 20% reduction. The cost (hours of paid labor), decreased from 4.56 hours per pick to 2.53 hours, a 44% reduction. The average elapsed time per trailer went from 5.7 hours to 1.46, a reduction of 74%. The number of staged orders (i.e., picked but not available to load until the previous order is complete) went from 72 to 2, a reduction of 97%. Also, side-by-side picking, which is a safety hazard, was eliminated, an improvement of 100%. And, not only is there no longer a mess on the dock, they are cross-docking 40% more; a process that moves material directly from one truck to another as opposed to receiving it, moving it, putting it in inventory, and tracking it. What they did was get off the dead horse. The policymakers stopped riding the dead horse of pick-targets. The engineers stopped riding the dead horse of fixing resources. And, the finance guys got off the dead horse of utilization.

If you go on a treasure hunt of your process and employ the direct observation principle, invaluable treasures will emerge. And, if you practice respect for people, those treasures will be converted from waste to wealth. Chapter 10 sets out the methodology of treasure hunting and it is a methodology that, if adopted, can dramatically improve an organization's operating performance and financial success. It cannot be said too often: Treasure hunting is about extreme emersion in process and it requires the ability to see the process through the eyes of those who live in that process every day, which requires a profound respect for people. It doesn't come from the boardroom or the gleaming tower, it resides in the place where the work happens, in the streets.

Think of the view of the business from the boardroom as the view the tourist has of a city he/she visits as part of the "all-inclusive," prepackaged holiday on a sightseeing bus that never wanders from the trampled trail of proverbial landmarks and tourist traps. The visitor only sees the place from a limited perspective. It's an expected and partial picture. It's not the truth of the city, it's a misconstrued version of reality; an accepted interpretation of what that city is like. It's a simplified view of Chennai. Now, imagine the tourist who rents a bicycle and explores the city, wandering into off-the-beaten-track cafes and out-of-the-way neighborhoods where the reality of the city lives and can be seen and experienced. What if you meandered around and got lost on purpose, letting the unforeseen appear and listened to conversations in coffee shops and chatted with locals in the park? What if you could see and experience the flow and rhythm of the city? You won't be guaranteed of seeing historical landmarks or finding typical souvenirs and you may experience disappointment (e.g., "purse snatching"), but you will have an infinitely greater chance of new discoveries and unique experiences that will prompt new ideas and points of view. It is an experiment that can uncover endless treasures. This analogy goes to the need for the extreme emersion of the treasure hunt, as opposed to the boardroom review of performance as packaged and displayed on Excel or PowerPoint® slides, which cannot be anything more than a superficial (false) tour of the real work itself. The treasure hunter sees the raw truth of the process, warts and all, like the painful workarounds employees finesse every day just to "make it work." Out there, they see one order selector passing another, a queue in front of the orbital wrapper, 35 trailers half-loaded, and they understand the truth. The boardroom sees the target and rationalizes, speculates, and guesses why it is not being met; the treasure hunter sees the capability of the process and knows why the target is not being met and what to do about it.

PROCESS CAPABILITY

The target has absolutely no utility if the process is not capable. The process an archer goes through is illustrative. He or she has a target to hit and an arrow to hit it with and there is an open space between the bow and the target. Once the arrow leaves the bow, the archer has no control over the arrow. The only way to control the outcome is to ensure that the process of delivering the arrow is as good as it can be—either for backyard or Olympic competition. The purpose of the process is to fly the arrow as accurately as possible and hit the bullseye (i.e., send the truck with the perfect order). The business of winning in archery is about having the best bow and arrow possible, learning to be a better archer, training and practicing, studying and adapting to wind velocities and air vacuums, and whatever else goes into the process of delivering the arrow and hitting the target, consistently. The target has absolutely no utility if the process is not capable. The treasure hunter must become submerged in the process to see and understand its capability because that is where and how become the target will be hit.

Golf is another metaphor for process. I cannot tell you how to lower your handicap, but I can tell you that to improve your performance as a golfer, you must improve the process of hitting the ball. The purpose of the process is to hit the ball as accurately as possible. It is not to shoot par or buy the most expensive clubs. We all know how much under-standing of the process is required to hit the golf ball well. The CBS SwingVision camera shows us Tiger Woods' or Phil Mickelson's swing and breaks it down so we can see every fundamental and where there are variances. When we see the process, we begin to understand it and uncover the problems. Only then can we start to experiment, learn, adapt, and gradually produce better and better outcomes. It's continuous improvement at critical points in an overall process, which is aimed at producing better and better performance. It is continuous process improvement by learning to see the process in its granularity, in its raw veracity, authentically without excuse or rationalization. How many times has Tiger broken down his swing (process) to improve it? No matter how good you are—world's no. 1—improving performance comes from improving the process. And, to improve, you must see it; really see it because it is not how you think it is. Great artists paint what they see, not what they think they see.

Once the purpose of the process is understood, the employees' role—their job—is to improve the process. Period. It's not to make widgets, not to pick things, not to field phone calls, not to fill glue buckets. However, this requires an understanding and adherence to the two founding principles of process thinking: direct observation and respect for people. When the distribution center got the people to see and observe the purpose of the process, and created metrics that they could relate to, then improvement was everywhere. And it was manifested in a respect for the people.

THE LINCHPIN: RESPECT FOR PEOPLE—A RIGHT AND A RESPONSIBILITY

Continuous process improvement might not be as old as Machiavelli's theory, but it dates back at least to the nineteenth century when ergonomic practices were employed to make the work easier so that people could be more productive. In fact, respect for people was a cornerstone in the growth of Toyota. Sakichi Toyoda (1867–1930) is often called the father of the Japanese industrial revolution. He started out in the textile trade and invented the automatic power loom and later, in 1935, sold the loom business to start the Toyota car company.[4] Earlier, he had met with Samuel Smiles (1812–1904) who wrote a book, *Self-Help*, that was published the same year as Darwin's *Origin of the Species* and John Stuart Mills' *On Liberty*. Smiles gave the world a seminal work on the ethos of personal responsibility that still inspires people today.[5] It was Smiles' thinking about the human factor that so interested Toyoda. Then his son Kiichiro (1894–1952) and Kiichiro's cousin, Eiji Toyoda (the fifth president of Toyota Motor), embedded Smiles' teachings on "basic respect for people" into their automobile operations. So critical was Smiles' lesson as a foundational element of what evolved as the Toyota Production System (TPS) that a copy of *Self-Help* is under a glass display at the museum that exists on Sakichi Toyoda's birth site. Smiles' message was this: If you tell people what to do, you take ownership and responsibility away from them, so it is critical to give them clear responsibility to create and propose countermeasures to the problems they own. Lean thinking has been mainstream for more than 15 years and there are tens of thousands of people who have been trained and understand Lean principles and, yet, this moral and practical tenet of self-help is rarely, if ever, part of any Lean curriculum.

> Self-help is the root of all genuine growth in the individual; and, exhibited in the lives of many, it constitutes the true source of national vigour and strength. Help from without is often enfeebling in its effects, but help from within invariably invigorates. Whatever is done for men or classes, to a certain extent takes away the stimulus and necessity of doing for themselves; and where men are subjected to over-guidance and over-government, the inevitable tendency is to render them comparatively helpless.[6]

No family of companies has really come close to matching Toyota's stellar performance in building best-in-class business processes (Danaher might be closest). Why not? Because they have been trained on abstract Lean tools and techniques (ie. cellular design, pull systems, standard work, etc.) without the accompanying education or insight on Lean principles which is the essential foundation that Samuel Smiles taught Toyoda: respect people and hold them accountable for finding solutions to problems in their workplace. It's quite astounding. It hasn't happened despite Lean becoming a ubiquitous change management brand; despite the fact Toyota opened its doors to anyone wanting to look under its "Lean hood"; despite vast amounts of knowledge available about Lean through research institutes, popular conferences, articles, publications, benchmarking visits, and industrial tourism; despite any effort to keep the secrets of Lean secret; and despite the fact that nearly 200,000 North American manufacturers—and tens-of-thousands in healthcare and the service industries—claim to be doing "some Lean activities." It's troubling, but not a mystery. When leadership does not embrace and demonstrate the profound power of respect for people, then Lean activity fades away as knowledgeable people attrite over time as operation teams change or short-term priorities become the order of the day.

EMPLOYEE RIGHTS

Respect for people means employees have the right to be successful every time they do their job and that means the custodians of the organization must (1) clearly define the purpose of the process, (2) make the flow of value to the customer visible to employees, and (3) give employees the capability to fix disruptions to that flow.

I have found a canyon-like divide between the oft-heard proclamation, "Of course, we respect our people" and the reality on the ground. I suggest that if you experience the results of a typical treasure hunt, it reveals, consistently, that less than 10% of the activities observed actually add value, which means it is very disrespectful for the people. You are making them do 90% of something that's not worth anything, and they know it. If the customer service center needs to tell the caller they are going to monitor their employees' work because they might screw up (inferred), is that not disrespectful of the call operators? A crucial factor in creating respect for people is giving them a process that works and the only way to give people a process that works is to give them the ability to be part of designing it based on understanding its purpose. It's a valuable quid pro quo. If you respect them, then you will give them *the required information, authority, and skills* to build a better process, and then, and only then, will they give you a continuously improving process.

INFORMATION, AUTHORITY, AND SKILLS

In my first experience as a manager of a manufacturing plant, inheriting that role from a real command-and-control manager, I had, during the early days, a lineup of people at my door asking me a whole variety of questions as to what they should do next. In order to ensure that I applied the respect for people principle, I imagined that each person coming into my office had a monkey on his/her back; the monkey being *the problem*. Their objective was to leave the monkey on my desk and my objective was to have them take the monkey back out and come back with solutions. I applied the rule that if they had *the information, authority, and skills* to solve the problem, then they had to take the monkey with them. If they didn't have those three things, then I owed them whatever they didn't have and they could leave the monkey with me. In concert with this, I have already covered three other things that must be inherent in the organization to engender respect for people: (1) people must have a horizontal view of the business and know where they fit in it, (2) they must have a clear sense of the purpose of the process, and (3) they must have a means to measure variances from the purpose of the process.

Many leaders talk about employee engagement and empowerment, but neither of these labels or the rah-rah, feel-good stuff actually go to continuous improvement because they don't make the intellectual and practical connection between people and process. Extreme emersion goes beyond engagement or empowerment and connects to the principle that all employees have a *right* to be successful every time they do their job. This is the linchpin. Management's responsibility is to provide the best possible means for them to do their job and to convert tangible respect for people into performance improvement. As far as I know, there is no correlation between employee satisfaction or empowerment and output, but—and it's a big but—*there is a correlation between respect for people and output.* For decades companies have said that "people are our most important asset," but they have continually disrespected their people by not understanding how process affects what people do, how they think, and how they perform. Kiichiro and Eiji Toyoda understood. If management wants people to find problems and make improvements, they have an obligation to give them the means to do so. The role of management is to create a process-thinking culture that exposes problems and allows the people to experiment their way to improvement. I delve into the principle of experimentation in Chapter 9. Successful experimentation requires a culture that not only allows failure, it encourages it, teaches it, and preaches it. Those who don't try to avoid failure will find and solve more problems and create more innovation.

I made 5,127 prototypes of my vacuum before I got it right. There were 5,126 failures. But I learned from each one. That's how I came up with a solution. So, I don't mind failure. I've always thought that schoolchildren should be marked by the number of failures they've had. The child who tries strange things and experiences lots of failures to get there is probably more creative.

James Dyson
Creator of the famous Dyson vacuum

Think back to the distribution center where the purpose of the process was to load the trailer because it, in turn, went to the higher purpose of delivering on the customer promise; the perfect order to the franchisee. But, in order for each employee in the distribution center to understand his/her purpose in the process, it was important to get the understanding and thinking down to the individual level and only then could he/she see his/her role in the promise to the customer. The overarching purpose was to build and send the perfect order to the franchisee, but an inherent problem was the fact that the $11/hour warehouse workers (who were far from the customer) didn't relate to that goal. Management needed to provide an understandable and digestible piece of the process and a direction that said, "Your job is to touch it once and put it on the truck." The need is to translate strategy into relevant action and what the person's job is in executing that action. I sometimes make this point with my tongue firmly planted in my cheek and say, "I want you to build a better process. And, by the way, if at the end of the day you have time, then load a few pallets or make a few tubes of adhesives. Anything that gets in the way of that is eligible for problem solving and redesign." I then reassure them that the trailers will get loaded and the tubes will come off the end of the line. And they do. It begins with understanding and commitment from management to redesign the process and then asking the people to build the best possible process. That's the foundation of respect for the people.

A couple of examples include: one on the lack of respect and the other on respect for the people. I did some work in a large call center and one of the real lousy processes we discovered on our treasure hunt was in the complaints department. This was a typical top-down mandated process. I found people working on the telephone with callers, trying to resolve problems when, at one point, a screen would pop up on the computer and prompt: "Don't forget to try and promote." It's called a blue screen and it takes them through a script of what to promote and what to say. It's a bad idea—very bad. It is the antithesis of the first rule in sales: Build a relationship with the customer. And, secondly, it allows no flexibility in the response for the person handling the call. Obviously, it was being "suggested" by persons so far removed from the process that they had no idea what was going on. They had never lived in it, or they were just ignorant of how critical the process is to improving outcomes. The customer service representative is in the middle of handling an irate customer and he/she is now obliged to try and promote something else. That is disrespectful to both the service rep and the customer. Instead of allowing the person living in the process to do what he/she thinks best, the decisions are auto-adjudicated from somewhere outside the reality.

One time, I was running a leadership conference for a company that had a plant in a small town in Indiana, about an hour out of Cincinnati. I flew in on a Sunday, rented a car, and arrived that evening at my hotel, only to find that Murphy's Law had arrived ahead of me. All of my presentation material, workbooks, and simulations, which had been shipped two days earlier, had not arrived. I immediately called the courier, fully expecting to get a recorded message saying something like, "Your business is important to us, but we are closed at this time and …" Or at best, a live person asking some tortuous question like, "What's the shipping number?" We have all been there. But, surprise, I got Jeffery, and Jeffery took over. He found where my stuff was stuck (still in Canada because of new cross-border rules imposed by Homeland Security that my to-date, reliable process had never encountered). He got it to the clearinghouse, flew it to Indianapolis, bused it to Columbus, and put it in a taxi to my location. It was there before 9 a.m. the next morning. That courier company gets it. Jeffery was responding in real time to the problem, not to some policy or up-a-level authority. He had the information, skills, and authority and a clear understanding of what the purpose was and how to deliver customer value, and he did just that. That's respect for the employee and the customer. That's the principle of self-help as Smiles intended it.

Initially, we found considerable disrespect in the processes at ABC Adhesives, where operators on the shop floor knew what was best to do, but no one asked. At ABC, they have what is called a chub line where the sealant is pressed out into "sausages" rather than into cartridges. It's a different process producing higher volumes for contractors as a generic product. The problem was that the chub line, like a sausage line, was finicky and often experienced splits in the skin and the product spilled all over. It caused a mess and fouled up equipment and took a lot of time to clean up. The chub line only ran three shifts a week, so when the people weren't filling the sausages they went and filled other products on other lines (i.e., maximize labor utilization). The mess was left to be cleaned up at the start of the next sausage shift, so when they came back, they spent an excessive amount of time cleaning the equipment. It was like having a pit crew begin to prepare for a tire change after the car pulled into the pits, as opposed to preparing while the car was in the race. What we changed was the real purpose, which was to be ready-to-go as quickly as possible. The equipment needed to be spit-and-polish-clean. We changed the thinking to a pit crew mentality. They started to think like a NASCAR crew. The crew doesn't say, "Oh, here comes Bubba, I'd better go get a tire." No, their work, their value-added, isn't just the 8 or 12 seconds to do that, it's the hours and hours of preparation, honing the process so they can do it in eight seconds. That's process thinking. The job was to be ready when the sausage work came through, so that it didn't take 24 hours (three shifts); it was supposed to take eight (one shift). To achieve that, they needed to be ready, not cleaning and fixing things. So now, when there's no sausage order, their work is to clean up and get it ready to run the next time. Previously, they had been trapped in old thoughtware that dictated that, if they weren't making something, they should go find something else to do. Availability of capacity is more important to the process-focused, horizontal organization, whereas utilization of capacity is more important to a vertical one. Also, as the ABC guys continued to work on problem solving, they discovered that the reason the sausage hose was splitting was because the supplier runs a seam down it in order to make longer pieces and the purchasing department got a better price for longer pieces. The pit crew got involved in purchasing and they negotiated with the vendor to get the same price point for shorter pieces with no seams. The purpose of their process is to be ready to run efficiently at all times. They now produce three days of work in 24 hours of production time as opposed to 42 hours.

CONTINUOUS IMPROVEMENT USUALLY ISN'T

As mentioned, the results of most continuous improvement efforts over the past two decades have been spotty, at best. Not all bad, just well short of what they could have been. Wherever I go, I keep bumping into the same reasons: vertical structure, wrong purpose, wrong measures, and no respect for people. That being said, I do see the pedagogy pendulum swinging more to what I believe is the right approach with new thoughtware. However, it must start at the top with leadership articulating and effectively communicating a clear strategy for the enterprise and, most importantly, an effective process to deploy that strategy.

REFERENCES

1. Kelton Global. 2013. *America's workforce: A revealing account of what U.S. employees really think about today's workplace.* Survey (March). Online at: https://programs. rootinc.com/go/ROOTLEARNING/OnDemandAmericasWorkforce.
2. Parkinson, M. 2012. *The power of visual communication.* Billion Dollar Graphics. Online at: http://www.billiondollargraphics.com/infographics.html
3. Ibid.
4. Magee, D. 2007. *How Toyota became #1: Leadership lessons from the world's greatest car company.* New York: Penguin Group, 9.
5. Butler-Bowdon, T. 2003. *50 self-help classics: 50 inspirational books to transform your life from timeless sages to contemporary gurus.* Referencing *Self-Help*, S. Smiles. 1859. Yarmouth, ME: Nicolas Brealey, 270.
6. Smiles, S. 1882. *Self-help.* London: John Murray, v, 1–3, 5–7, 294.

6

The Primacy of Process: Strategy Deployment and Financial Performance Depend on It

Everyone has a plan 'til they get punched in the mouth.

Mike Tyson

A PLAN IS NOT A STRATEGY

Winston Churchill once said, "We shape our tools and then they shape us." Nowhere is this truer than in conventionally managed organizations where "walled kingdoms" limit our ability to deploy innovative strategic changes and resulting financial performance. It is time to dismantle the disconnected vertiginous towers we have come to accept and to realize that sustained performance improvement only can be achieved by thinking horizontally while living in a vertical world. Like the Chennai Paradox, it can be overwhelming, but the imperative is to learn how to install the requisite business model.

Of course, management wants to start performance improvement with financial review but profit is an outcome, a byproduct of a successfully executed strategy. A better starting point is with the business strategy itself and, specifically, how it delivers customer value. Strategy provides an overriding common purpose for the entire enterprise and, as such, should have no reverence for the organization's departmentalization. Peter Drucker (management consultant and writer) once boiled the definition of a business down to a simple statement: "The purpose of business is to create and keep a customer." It's true, and that is all about the process required to deliver value to the customer and flow full circle to customer fulfillment. I use the term *fulfillment* because it implies more than moment-in-time satisfaction. It denotes long-term customer retention and loyalty. So, process thinking begins with strategy, but perhaps not in the way we would traditionally think.

PROCESS THINKING BEGINS WITH STRATEGY

Strategy is not so much about planning as about execution. A strategic plan is a hypothesis of what will happen in the future, an unpredictable future, and, as such, the plan often proves imprudent as that future unfolds. As Helmut von Moltke, a nineteenth-century German field marshal put it: "No plan survives contact with the enemy." Lawrence Freedman, one of Britain's foremost historians of military strategy, emphasizes this point in his remarkable book *Strategy: A History*.[1] Freedman observes that although it is better to have some kind of strategy than not, unless you are prepared to adapt as circumstances change, it is unlikely to do you much good. His review of what strategy is and how it has evolved, regardless of its application in war, politics, or business, is that there is no end point, it is really about figuring out how to get from one stage to the next, with each stage presenting a new set of problems to be worked out before you can move forward to the next stage.[1] In a recent survey of 300 large companies, CEOs claimed that it is infinitely more difficult to execute strategies than to develop them.[2] Strategy deployment requires execution through processes that are able to learn and adapt in real time; we do not implement a strategy, rather we continuously improve it (Figure 6.1 and Figure 6.2).

In his game-changing book, *Toyota Kata*, Mike Rother peeks behind the curtains at the Toyota Production System (TPS) and explains that,

FIGURE 6.1
Strategic planning: If we think the "uncharted waters" are clear, then we are only in a blind preconceived implementation mode.

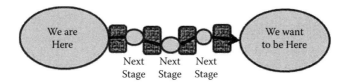

FIGURE 6.2
Strategic deployment: Continuous learning and adaptation toward a new desired state through an unclear and unpredictable territory by being sensitive and responding to actual conditions in the process.

although we have been studying and observing Toyota in some detail and the picture of what it is doing is pretty clear, the actual deployment of process-focused design is very unclear:

> There are perhaps only three things we can and need to know with certainty: where we are, where we want to be, and by what means we should maneuver the unclear territory between here and there. And the rest is somewhat unclear because we cannot see the future! The way from where we are to where we want to be next is a grey zone full of unforeseen obstacles, problems, and issues that can only be discovered along the way.[3]

In other words, as both Rother and Freedman point out, a strategy is not a plan, it must be a deployment tactic. The best we can do is to know the approach, the means we can utilize for dealing with the unclear path to a new desired condition, not what the content and steps of our actions and solutions will be. The only way to find success through deployment then is with a highly disciplined agile process of learning and adapting. The conventional organizational structure is not capable of embracing this approach of flexible discovery. It is not agile enough. Strategy then can best be deployed though smart processes. The way ahead is not through a preconceived implementation plan, as much as through the creation of a deployment process that is open to learning and dealing adequately with the unknown that we run into along the way.

The challenge of strategy is not so much about the planning as it is about deployment. It's about converting strategy into action and making strategy everyone's job, day-to-day, moment-to-moment, as we learn and adapt. For example, if we look at a discount airline like Southwest or its imitators, the strategic plan may be to make a profit by "filling up aircraft by attracting customers with low fares and on-time arrivals." However, this is a statement of "what" is required, and is rather an empty plan without a further discussion on "how." Deployment is all about process. The "how" is the strategic deployment piece, and, in this case, the discount airlines' "how" might be through the process of rapid tarmac turnaround time (i.e., saving time and money). The process of turning the plane faster is the opportunity to execute the strategy of having more passengers on fewer planes (they are in the air more often). Regardless of an employee's role in the operation (i.e., above the wing, below the wing, in the cabin, or part of overall flight operations), success depends on a single process with all functions adhering to the singular purpose of the process: aircraft turn time. Strategic success then is dependent on the effectiveness of the process, where the most significant functions of turn time might include passenger enplaning and deplaning, cargo loading and unloading, airplane fueling, cabin cleaning, galley servicing, and more. And given the infinite amount of external variables (e.g., weather, passenger behavior, mechanical aging), all this requires continual adjustment. Such a herculean effort can only be done where there is absolute allegiance by all functions to the process; where everyone has the same purpose of rapid and safe aircraft turn time. The three core elements of process thinking—purpose, measure, and action—are designed to do just that: set a destination (purpose), and based on the wind and waves (measures) reach that purpose, and, most importantly, constantly trim the sails (action) to reach that purpose. Therein lies the problem. It is next to impossible to make such adjustments in disconnected functional departments, simultaneously, in real time, which leads to poorly implemented strategy, if at all. Only a process-focused business model can successfully execute strategy. Only a process mind is capable of effectively implementing strategy.

I AM NOT A STRATEGY GUY

I am not a strategy guy; I help deploy strategy and transform it into specific actions that improve performance. If the strategy is right, then the degree of success depends on the capacity to execute the strategy across the organization. Process thinking is about the execution of strategy, the arranging, aligning, and deployment of resources, policies, and processes, today, in order to get to the future. According to a recent *Fortune* magazine article, up to 70% of failures are not due to poor strategy or lack of good ideas, but failed execution.[4] That's 70%. The problem is further demonstrated from *Harvard Business Review* statistics: 9 out of 10 organizations fail to execute strategy successfully; specifically, only 5% of the workforce understands the company strategy, only 15% of executive teams spend more than one hour a month discussing strategy, only 25% of managers have incentives linked to strategy, and only 40% of organizations link budget to strategy.[5]

The critical issue is: *How do we translate strategy into action and make strategy everyone's job*? It requires a daily process that reaches across functions and management systems in order to execute strategy; in fact, deploying strategy is more important than the quality of the strategy itself and the success of the deployment is a direct function of the health of the business processes.

THE PRIMACY OF PROCESS

The strategy states the organization's intent on how it will create value and how it will go from a current "as-is situation" to a "want-to-be position." The process is the strategy in action. Without action, there is no execution and, without process, the strategy cannot be well executed and, without execution, there is no strategy. A functional structure is arranged for daily tactics and it does not serve strategy. Again, think about Southwest or its discount imitators executing its strategy at the process level (tarmac turn-around) or Apple positioning for rapid delivery of product with only four days of inventory.

> A smart process is a process that sustainably understands and responds to what matters to the customer.

SKILLS, AUTHORITY, AND INFORMATION

Strategy is deployed through smart processes and strategy deployment institutionalizes the action through the placement of skills, authority, and information at the point where the action can be aligned with strategy. This allows for counteraction to happen in real time, which is the only way to leverage and move the big, cumbersome, elusive strategic boulder through the organization. Of course, an enterprise-wide strategy cannot be executed in an organization made up of piecemeal departments.

The strategy is an attempt, through a process focus, to identify where the blockages to implementation occur, where they are observed, and where they are controlled so as to bring them to a single point of influence inside a common process.

Millions of us buy pizza, whether it's from Pizza Hut or Pizza Pizza or our favorite upscale Italian restaurant. Assuming that the product is to our liking, the rest is about process. The particular process in each pizza business is as different as the pizza toppings and each has a different customer value proposition and strategy. Much of their success hangs on the capability of the process to execute the strategy and meet the promise of the customer-value proposition.

A large takeout-delivery pizza business like Domino's or Pizza Pizza has a strategy based on a promise to deliver to the customer in 30–45 minutes or it's free. What do they have to do? Well, they had better have a world-class (no waste) fulfillment process. When the customer phones, they don't take the time to ask: "How ya' doing?" No. The first question is: "What's your phone number?" Then in a computer-second, your last order comes up. "Same as last time?" Everything is driven toward the hypothesis that, if they deliver in 30–45 minutes, the customer will be satisfied, will give them money, and return as a customer. Now at Pizza Hut, the value proposition and strategy is different; it's about variety, innovation, and a fresh experience. They are always offering a new kind of pizza: crunchy, cheesy crusts, deep dish, thin crust, gluten-free crusts, etc. And they are adding new menu items all the time: calzones, stuffed pizza rollers, chocolate dunkers. To execute this strategy, the process is not about being as operationally fast as Pizza Pizza, it's about having a new product introduction process that can meet an ever-changing demand and convert ideas to pizzas and money, quickly. A third alternative for pizza is a distinctive trattoria where you are served wonderful Italian food and "the best pizza outside Tuscany." These customers are not interested in 30–45 minutes or dessert specials or crunchy crusts that make noise; they want a process that delivers good food, intimacy, personal attention, and excellent service. The only variety they want is in the wine cellar. In other words, there needs to be a clear purpose for the process and that purpose should derive from the strategic direction. As stated, design the process on purpose and on strategy and have a performance measurement system that measures the capability of the process that is delivering the strategy, not simply the strategy or its objectives. The objectives are irrelevant if the process is not capable. We must deploy strategy through process and monitor the process, not the strategy, daily.

WINNING SPORTS REQUIRES A PROCESS MIND

Over the years, I have spent untold hours watching my four children, now grown, playing on the soccer pitch, hockey ice, basketball court, and on field hockey and rugby fields. I always watched—sometimes to my kid's dismay—from a process perspective. Many people have written sports metaphors about how a game mirrors life and I sometimes use a slice of sports to make the point about process. Winning sports teams understand process and they stick their noses in it every game, every play. Ultimately, the objective is to win. The strategy may alter from game to game, be it offensive attack or defense play; however, the process where the strategy is executed requires real-time capability (versus distant target) measures. Coaches often talk about the team's progress over the season as a process. The example I often use is my son Brendan's performance as a starting point guard on the high school basketball team. Here's how he and I measure his performance. We decided that the only thing he focuses on is his assist and turnover ratio. By definition, every assist means two points, which is as good as him scoring the basket. And every turnover he makes means the potential loss of two points. Of course, he has to occasionally shoot or go to the basket, but that is all part of the process-focused measure assist/turnover ratio. He has to go to the basket, not necessarily to score, but to improve his assists. The math is simple. When we looked at the stats, we saw that whenever he made 10 or more assists in a game, they won. And every time he had four times as many assists as turnovers, they won. This gave him something specific to focus on as a process connected to performance measures and the strategy.

Measuring an individual's performance in specific terms can create a focus on specific parts of the overall process of winning a game. If we were talking about the big center, it would be a different set of metrics. His process would be about things like rebounds and second-chance points. Hockey and football have similar analogies. They don't focus on outscoring the competition, even though that is the team's ultimate goal. They focus on the process required to score goals or touchdowns. They know if they can have a better process of doing every little thing that counts—the fundamentals: skate, check, block, tackle—then they will outperform the competition and win. The process of getting the puck out of the corner is crucial to scoring goals. The process of back checking is fundamental to preventing goals. The process of football players blocking in unison so one player can run with the ball is fundamental to scoring. One breakdown in the process—disruption of flow—and the expected performance is not achieved. Every single breakdown permanently eliminated is a marginal improvement in the chances of winning. However, from my experience, organizations rarely place enough focus on these fundamental process capabilities. They may contain a momentary breakdown, but seldom do they apply a preventative intervention. When a factory has a parts shortage, it expedites and contains the occurrence, but does it engage in root-cause problem solving to fix the process so as to eliminate future incidents. When the airline loses a passenger's luggage, does it know what part of the process broke down so it can prevent a repeat occurrence? What about a restaurant order arriving with dressing on the salad, when the order was "on the side"? What about all these everyday disruptions to the process of fulfilling customer demand? All of these elements are about the strategic deployment of the plan and about the organization learning to win (i.e., achieve financial targets) through the development of its processes. Without this focus, no strategy is achievable, never mind sustainable; thus, financial targets are missed. Financial targets are only ensured when specific process improvements (think cost drivers, such as assist-to-turnover ratios) are achieved. Strategic deployment is about defining and implementing these specific process improvements (i.e., improve the assist-to-turnover ratio). In other words, profit is a result of properly managed means and one of its central tenets is a "balanced scorecard" of process improvement indicators.

ONE OF THE MOST INFLUENTIAL BUSINESS IDEAS OF THE TWENTIETH CENTURY

In any business, process improvement is similar. It is about understanding, seeing, practicing, learning, and improving the fundamental parts of the process required to continually alter the strategy to meet the current circumstances. It adds up to the whole organization running more like a bunch of ungainly experiments than the proverbial well-oiled machine. Strategy is deployed through trials and "trystorming." It's counterintuitive, but it's right—if you want significant performance improvement. For more than 1,000 years, the scientific method has formed the basis for technological advancement and despite many more failures than successes, it has always delivered learning to the experimenter. Thomas Edison, the man who had more than 2,000 patents, once said, "I have not failed. I've just found 10,000 ways that won't work."[6] Experience informs conjecture and to do that we form a hypothesis and test to confirm or deny the premise.

In business, strategy plays the part of the hypothesis and the process provides the "test." In their 1996 transformational publication, *The Balanced Scorecard*, Robert Kaplan and David Norton built a framework to provide management a way to complete the experiment by connecting strategy to process through measurements needed to prove success or failure.[7] This has been acclaimed as one of the 75 most influential business ideas of the twentieth century.[8] Their Balanced Scorecard serves as a feedback device—a dashboard—that aligns the business strategy with the performance of the business process and provides a framework for integrating measures derived from strategy. Processes must be built around the strategy so the processes can deliver constant, real-time response on how actions are aligning to strategy. Only a process-focused organization is capable of doing this. Like other artifacts of management science, the successful deployment of the Balanced Scorecard has been severely limited by the functionalized organizations into which it has been shoehorned. As many as two thirds of U.S. companies have reported the adoption of a Balanced Scorecard and, yet, fewer than 20% have been able to drive results.[9] Again the "status quoers" of the functional organization structure have proved to be worthy foes of this proven management concept. The successful implementation of the Balanced Scorecard, like all sound management science, requires a process mind.

By way of illustration, the Balanced Scorecard was originally introduced as a centerpiece in a circular flow (Figure 6.3). However, it is better appreciated as a hierarchical construct (Figure 6.4); as a cause-and-effect linkage where the financial outcome (e.g., profit) is a result of the ability to meet the customer promise, which, in turn, is driven by the "health" of the process (think cost-to-purpose ratio), which, in turn, is driven by the inputs to the process. Specifically, inputs to the process include such things as: continuous process improvement training, appropriate enabling technology, a respect for people, culture, etc.

Note how in cause and effect, a clear hypothesis (i.e., strategy) is created and the core leverage point is the internal process.

Process-focused organizations do not set strategic targets that can only be assessed after the fact (i.e., evaluative). Rather, they set required conditions for getting to the next stage: navigational points that lead to problem solving the way toward, what Rother (*Toyota Kata*) refers to as,

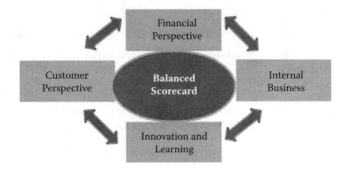

FIGURE 6.3

Generic measures for measuring strategy as introduced by Robert Kaplan and David Norton in their book, *The Balanced Scorecard.*[7]

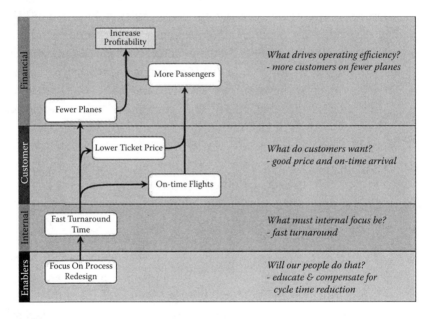

FIGURE 6.4

The Balanced Scorecard as a cause-and-effect framework for communicating the enterprise's strategy.

the succeeding target condition. These required conditions are integrated with, and controlled by, those who work in the process and they are not strategic targets separated from it. The strategy as a plan is what to do; the strategy as deployment is how to implement the plan. In my son's case, the strategy might be to contend for the league championship year after year and, as a team member, his job is to win the game. However, that is out of his control and not integrated with the work. What is within his control are assists and turnovers, and that's what he works on. The process-focused organization works on navigational metrics, variances from the process, not targets and goals. As mentioned, when the arrow leaves the bow, you have no control over the target. Control is in the training, practice, and learning required to master the process of firing the arrow. Target-obsessive management is destructive behavior when the process is not capable of achieving the mark. It creates undue stress. Nothing could be more disrespectful of people than setting a target that the organization's processes are not yet proficient enough to achieve. Lean calls this the *waste of overstressing* (i.e., TPS's *Muri*), and it is most evident at artificial points in time, such as "month end" or when unrealistic project deadlines are set.

It would be more effective to obsess about navigational measures that are designed to help understand and improve the process, thereby, inciting problem-solving action. Consider this. My other son Dylan played hockey. In high school, he was a goaltender and the team traveled a lot. One day he came home with an F in math and, true to my evaluative nature, I judged this as bad. However, my navigational instinct had me look at his hockey schedule and exam schedule and I realized that he wrote the math exam the morning after a road game. Getting off the team bus at 11 p.m. the night before is not a very effective approach for exam writing. So, we looked at when the same situation might occur in the future and put in a countermeasure, which was to stay home and study the previous week-end when such scheduling situations arose. Navigational measures lead to problem solving, evaluative measures lead to judgment without action. Strategy deployment is bottom-up with the process constantly aligning to the environment so as to deliver the strategy. Planning can be top-down, but execution must be bottom-up—through process. The process mind cascades objectives down from the top of the organization in the form of strategic objectives and specific targets, but it requires navigational measures to be developed inside internal processes, which, in turn, are rolled up to the top where the targets reside.

A CEO PERSPECTIVE

Let's step back and briefly talk about the bigger picture, which is germane to understanding the primacy of process from the top down. The Balanced Scorecard provides significant help in creating a horizontal view of the organization and associated process improvement because it recognizes internal business processes as the critical point of leverage in achieving strategy. And it keeps a perspective on both financial goals and customer value while inciting action on the internal processes and future investment requirements in learning and growth. With process thinking, the four perspectives of the Balanced Scorecard are defined as:

1. Financials: Deliver positive cash flow
2. Customers: Deliver on what we promise the customer
3. Process: Design and execute the process to meet customer demand
4. People: Respect employees because they make the process work

Without customers, there is no business. Without cash flow, there is no business. Without the right strategy, there is no success. And, without a process-focused model, there is no successful deployment of strategy (Figure 6.5 and Figure 6.6).

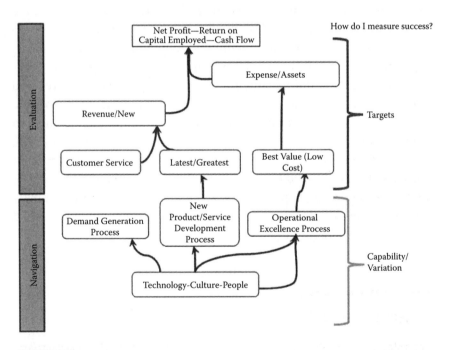

FIGURE 6.5
The Navigational Scorecard measures the capability of the processes to deliver the strategy as measured by the targets.

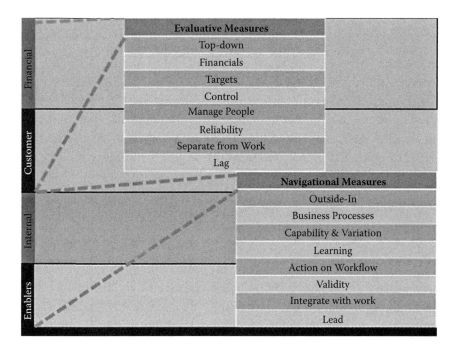

FIGURE 6.6
The essential characteristics of the evaluative measures are at the top of the map and the navigational measures at the bottom.

VALUE CREATION: MANAGE WORKFLOW, NOT RESOURCES

We know the importance of the financials, the customers, and the people, but we too often overlook the critical importance of process to each of these. *Process* is about managing the workflow rather than focusing on the resources in the workflow. Brilliant process management (like Tim Cook designed at Apple) provides the organization with the greatest opportunity to deliver customer value; therefore, as per the cause-and-effect hypothesis structure (Figure 6.5), process management delivers the strategy on the financials, specifically, return on capital employed.

Figure 6.6 shows the essential characteristics of the Scorecard's evaluative measures used for the *customer and financial perspective* (targets). Also shown are the characteristics of the Scorecard's navigational measures used for the *process perspective* (Internal and Enablers). The process mind is primarily interested in the navigational measures.

We know the first concern of most CEOs is financial results, not process, not product, not people. Fair enough. And, they instinctively know that processes deliver results, right through to the return on capital employed (ROCE), but they often do not understand that the health of the processes, more than the products and services, determine their organization's ability to generate wealth and ROCE (Figure 6.7). I never underestimate the focus on making money because without profit (in a for-profit business) there is no survival. Rather, I am talking about how we measure the money and how we act based on those metrics. The critical point here is that ROCE is an outcome of the process, not the purpose of the process. For the moment, let's call the purpose *value creation* where value is what we add when we convert inputs into outputs that our customers value. For them, it is easier (cheaper, convenient) to buy that value than do it themselves (intellectual property is another issue), so the task is to attract and keep the customer—from the competition. The process of generating such profitable demand with less cost, and/or more price, and/or more volume, results in a greater return on sales. The process of fulfilling that demand with less waste increases velocity and employed capital asset turns. At the end of the day, ROCE is a consequence of the health of the core processes, and the opportunity to improve financial performance

Financial Linkage to Process Thoughtware

A process improvement initiative <u>will have no bottom line impact</u> unless it:
1. Increases throughput (revenue)
2. Reduces expenses (resource costs)
3. Reduces investments (working capital, e.g, inventory)

FIGURE 6.7
Return on Capital Employed (ROCE) = Capital Turns × Return on Sales. Capital Turns = Revenue/Capital Employed. Return on Sales = % (Revenue–Costs/Revenue).

is in the design of the process; designing out the enormous amounts of costly waste/disruptions to flow, and changing the 10:1 ratio of things that get in the way of work.

The process has three fundamental drivers of value, which are:

1. the quantity of resources in the process, which is driven by
2. the design of the process that consumes the resources
3. the volume of work demanded of the process

Unless you can control demand ("no thank you" customers, we don't want your business) or control resources (let's hire 1,000 more people), the only real leverage is process innovation, redesign, and improvement. Resources are deployed to create value as commercially measured by revenue, but it is ultimately the health of the process that determines profit and ROCE. Figure 6.8 offers some suggested points of intervention to influence the process.

In Figure 6.9, the ROCE model (in Figure 6.7) is drilled down to illustrate the linkage between value creation and process design. A redesigned process that takes out nonvalue-adding activities reduces the resources required, thus, turns assets faster, provides more capacity, and provides an

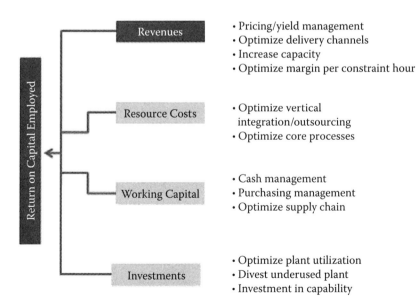

FIGURE 6.8
Potential process improvement opportunities to leverage to increase value creation.

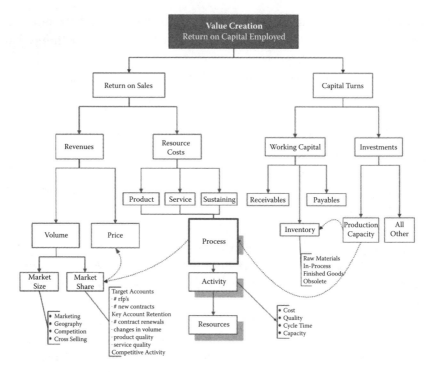

FIGURE 6.9
Driving value creation through process innovation.

increased likelihood of meeting customer demand. It is no accident that process is at the center of any "make lots of money" model.

INVENTORY AND CASH DON'T LIE

The 2007–2009 recession delivered a hard-learned lesson in understanding the liability of traditional accounting architecture when applied to the income statement; however, what has not changed is the reality that cash and inventory do not lie. If we consider that Apple turns its inventory 74 times and RIM wrote down two years' worth of inventory, you know where the cash is tied up. If you want to know the health of a business, you need look no farther than a few things: cash flow, the size of inventory, and things like, for example, the wait-time in processing credit card applications, tarmac turnaround time, or the cycle time in processing insurance claims. These are typical manifestations of the health of processes.

INTERESTED IN A 35% REDUCTION IN LABOR COSTS?

The process thinker is interested in three things related to financial performance. So let me give you three litmus test questions (there are more) of new thoughtware.

1. Throughput: If your process had a 50% increase in throughput, what would it mean?
2. Time: If your process could deliver in half the time, what would it mean?
3. Operating expense: If you could get as much through the "pipeline" with half the expenditure, what would it mean?

Often, in my first discussion with senior executives, I hear that age-old retort, "Yeah, but … our business is different and this doesn't really apply." So, before going too far, I provide some evidence (outstanding results) across a diversity of industries, size of companies, and global locations. Here are some on-average performance numbers achieved by companies with whom I have worked:

- Lead times (cash-to-cash cycle) reduced by 70%
- Asset utilization increased by 60%
- Working capital (inventory) turns increased by 100%
- Cost of quality decreased by 50%
- Productivity (output-per-employee) increased by 65%
- Throughput (same investment base) increased by 83%

However, these results only happen if the operational drivers that influence the financial results are deeply understood. It means understanding the things that drive down costs, such as inventory, as dollars tied up in the time it takes to convert to throughput, shorter cycle times, shorter lead times, and faster-to-market. Throughput is the rate at which the process generates cash through sales and throughput only registers when the service or product is delivered to the customer, in a value-accepting form. The total cost, the real cost—as opposed to silly, contrived specifications like average unit cost—is all the spending the enterprise requires to convert inventory to throughput. From a process mind then, productivity is a ratio of throughput over real cost. Real financial performance comes from eliminating those things that get in the way of work, so the work itself, the value, is delivered faster and with less cost. A way to sum this up is a concept referred to as the Working Capital Productivity Ratio. It is the financial architecture of the process mind.

Working Capital Productivity Ratio

This is important. The three litmus questions above are leverage points that collectively make up the working capital productivity ratio. Its main purpose is to measure improvement in time. The average working capital productivity ratio, as pegged against an average manufacturer in North America, is 20 cents per dollar of revenue.[10] This means you are tying up 20 cents in working capital for every dollar shipped. Further, if you could have the working capital available, it is equal to a 35% advantage in labor productivity.[11]

The three factors of working capital productivity ratio should be dealt with *in sequence*. First, solve throughput; second, solve time; and third, solve cost. If you are a typical manufacturer and in a tough position, the initial reaction is to whack costs, which often starts by cutting head count. That does little or nothing for performance. It's the wrong thinking in the wrong place. It's old thoughtware and the wrong way to start. Because, if you cut expenses first, it starts to cut into bone and you won't be able to get back to throughput. So, if you want a 35% labor productivity advantage, then cut the time it takes you to get throughput and get to market by 50%. This applies to any process.

Post the 2007–2009 recession, domestic banking (i.e., credit cards, mortgages, personal loans, deposit-taking) was (and still is) the bread and butter of every major retail bank. At the time, I was working with a large chartered bank, focusing on the growth of its credit card portfolio, and looking to enhance the growth of this lucrative segment of the business. We applied process thinking to the alignment of strategy, financial performance and process.

They had recently commissioned a major study from a strategic consulting firm. One of the findings was that, for every day they could reduce the time between application for credit cards and the start of spending on the card, there were 10 full basis points of increase on spending for that card. The process was relatively straightforward and designed for a two-day turnaround. The operator entered the application into the system, then it was sent off to the credit bureau for verification, and came back to be approved or denied based on the evaluation of the credit bureau in relation to the risk threshold set by the bank. It was a two-day, auto adjudication. During our initial assessment, we took a sampling of applications and found only 20% were auto adjudicated, the rest were disrupted in their flow. The supervisor suggested we must have taken a misrepresentative sample; however, after monitoring over 200 applications in segments of 10 each, we saw that the best case was 40% auto adjudication and, in some samples, there were none that auto adjudicated. The learning suggested the two days were more like an average of 28 days and there were applications that took 40 or more days. Let's look at a typical sample of what we found.

EXPERIMENTING WITH CREDIT CARDS

This example, Daniel's credit card application, is indicative of what you can see when looking deeply into the process—treasure hunting. First, the application is filled out at a local branch through a secured, outsourced customer service agency called a field marketing representative (FMR), which is commissioned to secure applications in branches, selected retailers, airports, and other high-traffic areas. The applications are collected and forwarded to the FMR central offices for records count, batched up, and then sent by mail at the end of each week to the bank's processing center where they are entered into the system seven days after that. The operation had 30,000 applications in the system at any one time and received about 1 million applications a year. In other words, when every day was worth a potential 10-basis-point increase in the amount spent on the card, this was a free and unnecessary 14 days of waste of waiting and transportation. Also, because the FMRs (there were three companies under contract) were commissioned on the quantity, not quality of applications collected, the clarity and integrity of those applications were always less than ideal. Going back to the contemporary view of the vertical organization, we can see the trap of batch and queue thinking, optimizing efficiency at any point in the process, rather than optimizing the workflow. Remember, the purpose of this process is "spend on card" (Figure 6.10).

The application is received into the system through a scan or optical character reader (OCR), which allows the operator to read and make required changes to the application. It converts the document from a hand-written paper document into an application template in the auto

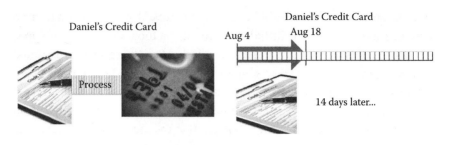

FIGURE 6.10
Daniel's credit card from point of process to 14 days.

adjudication system. This OCR was a somewhat new and expensive system, designed to reduce the time it took the operator to enter the application manually into the system. However, the irony is that the time saved at the value-adding activity of entering the application into the system, actually increased the overall time of the process. Remember, whenever one works on optimizing a discrete resource in the workflow (unless it is a clear point of constraint in the proverbial pipe), the cost goes up. Only by working on the entire workflow (getting to the purpose) will the cost go down. The operator indicated to me, while we were sitting "in the street" at the workstation where the real work takes place, that Daniel's card would bounce at the credit bureau and not auto adjudicate. When I asked why, she explained that the OCR was based on "fuzzy logic," meaning it was accurate only 80% of the time. And, because the FMRs were in such a rush to get their quota of applications, many were poorly filled out (e.g., poor handwriting, missing data points, wrong information in the wrong box, etc.) and, without a quality check, they were likely to get rejected. Operators could make a few adjustments, which ironically took them longer to do than filling out the entire application from scratch, but they could not make changes to critical data points, like names, based on the risk factors set by the chartered bank's fraud department (a separate silo). So, for example, if someone scribbled their name as "S-m-t-h" on an application, the scanner will guess it's a missing letter and add an "i." The problem is it doesn't know for sure; it may well be a "y"—Smyth. Prior to OCR (a capital expenditure that with a bank-wide maintenance contract was in six figures), operators would know to put in the "y" by deciphering the scribble. Now, they simply recognized it would bounce from the credit bureau, and not auto adjudicate, but they were powerless to do anything about it. This is contrary to the principle of *respect for people*. Sure enough, Daniel's credit card bounced because the last name was misread by OCR.

It was then placed in an eight-day fraud queue for correction and returned to the operator. We were now 25 days into the "timeline." With a great sigh, the operator indicated that, on the second trip to the credit bureau, Daniel's card was again going to bounce. She indicated that the address, which was 30 Maitland Street, apartment #401, was listed in its local colloquial speech. She pointed out that all addresses with apartment numbers from this particular jurisdiction bounced (since they read 401-30 Maitland Street, not 30 Maitland Street Apt. #401). Again it would need to go to a fraud queue to be rectified. The two trips to the bureau now had a timeline out to 29 days (Figure 6.11).

While the card was working its way through the fraud queue a second time, a team of operators were working on manually intercepting all applications that would go beyond 35 days in the process. The system had constructed a built-in algorithm that automatically purged any application in the system at 35 days (Figure 6.12), because there was no way it could possibly be dwelling there that long. Sure enough, the application was reissued into the system to give it another 35 days of life.

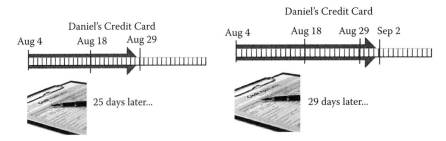

FIGURE 6.11
Daniel's credit card from 15 to 29 days.

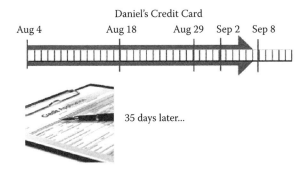

FIGURE 6.12
Daniel's credit card 35 days later.

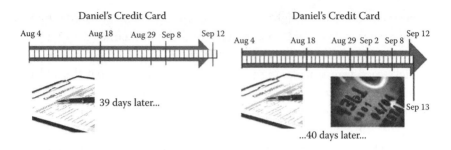

FIGURE 6.13
Daniel's credit card after 40 days.

Ultimately, the card application was approved on the 39th day and the card was issued on the 40th day (Figure 6.13) from the original date of the application.

In the end, we had a total elapsed time of 40 days and only 10 actual minutes of value-adding work. The rest of the process was activities that got in the way of work: waste and disruptions to flow. Ten minutes—the time the operator's fingers touch the keys and type to enter an application into the system. Yet, the bank spent all its effort on reducing the 10 minutes through an OCR application. Surely, a better answer would be to extend the 10 minutes and have the operator enter the application slowly, methodically, correctly the first time, thus, addressing the 40 days, not the 10 minutes. This is a classic example of the paradox of go slow to go fast.

BANKING ON PROCESS THINKING

Today, the bank auto adjudicates over 90% of the applications in two days, thanks to the introduction of process thinking. Through experimentation, a continuous flow processing center was established as a trial. The fraud specialist now sits in the middle of a number of operators, who enter the entire application manually. If they see an obvious discrepancy, an address, a name, or a data point that would indicate a likelihood of not being read at the credit bureau, they call the fraud specialist over and discuss the action. Once approved for change, on the spot, within the established risk tolerances, the change is made and the application issued. A simple white board in the middle of the operation is used to document each variance and when they are deemed to be chronic, and not an episodic event, the authority is placed back in the operators' hands to make changes. The OCR is unplugged and the operators are much more engaged in the process. The experiment was run for 90 days, the new process was documented as standard work, and we now have 11 such processing centers in place. The results are remarkable. The end-to-end document processing and control process has been reduced by 83%, while productivity has been enhanced 400% without employees working any harder. Employees are fully engaged and now empowered to make decisions affecting their process.

As touched on earlier, I often berate management who still operate on old thoughtware by thinking that if they go to China or other places offshore and get, say, a 35% labor productivity advantage, they will improve performance. As I pointed out earlier, when all costs are considered, they should have stayed home and figured out how to reduce production time from six weeks to three weeks and achieved the same thing. The kicker? Every dollar of freed-up working capital is a one-time boost in earnings and a permanent increase in return on capital employed. If you understand that 80 to 90% of what is being done in your process is waste, then it is axiomatic that achieving even a 50% improvement should be a slam-dunk. It is. That's why I can "guarantee" a 50% improvement—at a minimum.

Absent a change in process design, the organization is not entitled to improve productivity. Any other method of leveraging improvement is arbitrary and doomed to a low probability of success.

IT'S NOT A MATTER OF TECHNOLOGY

I find companies continually turning to technology for a solution, thinking that if they just automate, do things faster, and create reliable systems, they will improve performance. Most of the time it doesn't work. Instead, they could get more capacity by taking waste out of the process, thereby, increasing throughput. More throughput, less time, less waste, less cost. Too many companies waste a Brink's truck full of money by going out and raising a capital appropriation to increase capacity without doing the easy fix first. I say, "If the appropriation is for capacity, rip it up. Conversely, if the appropriation is for increased capability, then take it through due process." The process mind understands the difference between capacity and capability.

Process thinking should be a part of all cost saving and capacity thinking. I can't tell you how many times I have heard management say things like: "We have to have a new enterprise-wide firmware software system" (e.g., Enterprise Resource Planning (ERP)). What I don't hear is: What for? At what cost? ERP makes sense if the process is stable, repetitive, and unchanging, and you are trying to make it reliable. If not, it solves nothing. The Meta Group conducted a survey of 63 companies, covering a wide spectrum of size and industries that installed an ERP system. They analyzed the total cost of ownership, including professional services, software and hardware costs, from initial installation through two years. The range of costs was dramatic, ranging from a low of $400,000 to a high of $300 million. That averaged out to $15 million and the average cost for each user in a firm was $53,320.[12] As one would expect, the cost of ERP deployment increased with the size of the company and number of users. Total ERP costs often run about 0.5 to 1% of revenue.[13] None of that focused on continuous process improvement. These reliability-oriented management systems may well be vital to any large organization, but they are no panacea (Figure 6.14). As Roger Martin points out in *Design of Business*, "An ERP system can provide real-time data to track whether resources are being used efficiently, but it cannot generate a robust strategy."[14]

I often hear, "I wish you had been here a year ago because we just spent a lot of money trying to improve capacity." In one case, a company had built a warehouse that, after we reduced their inventories, they no longer needed.

2011 ERP Costs		
Type of cost	**Amount**	**%**
License fees	$150,000	24%
Maintenance fees	$81,000	13%
External consulting fees and customization	$180,000	29%
Infrastructure upgrade costs	$40,000	6%
Internal costs	$180,000	29%
Total	**$631,000**	**100%**

FIGURE 6.14

The enormous costs of enterprise firmware software with no clear business case for performance improvement impact. (From Michael Burns, *CA Magazine*, August 2011.)

In another, process thinking saved a company from building a plant. And, in another, a paint line. Capacity is all about process.

The question I leave with senior management is this: Why not look deeper into this process issue? The barrier is not a lack of evidence of success—there's plenty of that, it's a lack of will to understand the primacy of process and its direct impact on strategy deployment and resulting financial return as measured by ROCE. In the following three chapters, I dig into the details of how to become a process-focused organization through the Purpose–Measure–Actions model.

REFERENCES

1. Freedman, L. 2013. *Strategy: A history*. New York: Oxford University Press, xi.
2. Foundation for the Malcolm Baldrige National Quality Award. 1998. *The nation's CEOs look to the future*. Survey/study no. 818407, July.
3. Rother, M. 2012. *Toyota kata: Managing people for improvement, adaptiveness, and superior results*. New York: McGraw-Hill, 8.
4. Charan, R., and G. Colvin. 1999. Why CEOS fail. *Fortune* (June).
5. Niven, P. R. 2002. *Balanced Scorecard Step by Step: Maximizing Performance and Maintaining Results*. New York: John Wiley & Sons, 9.
6. From an ad for GPU Nuclear Corporation, in *Black Enterprise* magazine Vol. 16, No. 11 (June 1986) p. 79
7. Kaplan, R. S., and D. P. Norton. 1996. *The balanced scorecard*. Boston: Harvard Business School Press.
8. Niven, P. R. 2002. *Balanced Scorecard Step-by-Step: Maximizing Performance and Maintaining Results*. John Wiley & Sons, New York, 2002.
9. Bunting, J. 2010. *The unvarnished truth: Why balanced scorecards & performance management efforts fail. The glue*. A blog about making strategy stick. Online at: http://www.strategyexecutionblog.com/2010/06/why-balanced-scorecards-performance-management-efforts-fail.html.
10. Stalk, G., Jr., and T. E. Hout. 1990. *Competing against time: How time-based competition is reshaping global markets*. New York: Free Press/Macmillan, 5.
11. Ibid., p. 31.
12. Site administrator post. 2010, November 16. *What does ERP really cost*? From Axis Global Partners. Online at: http://www.axisgp.com/2010/11/what-does-erp-really-cost/
13. Wailgum, T. 2010. *ERP costs: 3 signs companies are wasting less costs*. I.T. World. Online at: http://www.itworld.com/software/95577/erp-costs-3-signs-companies-are-wasting-less-money
14. Martin, R. 2009. *The design of business*. Boston: Harvard Business Press, 42.

7

Performance on Purpose

If you can't describe what you are doing as a process, you don't know what you are doing, and you have not designed the process on purpose.

THREE CRITICAL ELEMENTS

Purpose, measure, and action are distinct parts of the greater organizational whole and critical pieces in building business processes that maximize the generation and fulfillment of customer demand. Together, these three elements are the basics of the operating system or organization's thoughtware, and the driving force in deploying the business strategy.

Wherever there is an exchange of information, there is a process and, wherever there is a process, there must be these three components: a **purpose** to fulfill customer demand, a **measure** to better understand and improve the process, and **action** derived from the measure to incite action on the process. This is the model that we will discuss in the next three chapters (Figure 7.1).

Operating model description: The measure informs us of the distance (variance) from the purpose, which, in turn, incites action (an experiment). The measure then validates the experiment's hypothesis (did it get us closer to the purpose?).

To move to a process-focused organization, we need to understand the relationship between purpose, measure, and action. Note that I am referring to the operating system that enables the business model and not just

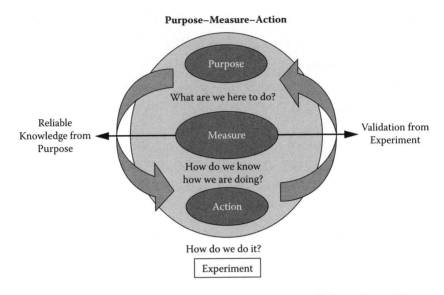

Purpose–Measure–Action

FIGURE 7.1
Purpose–Measure–Action.

a continuous process improvement tool or technique. As in the examples I have cited, designing an effective process always starts with the purpose.

The purpose of a process is to design against demand and it is the primary determinant of performance. Understanding the purpose of the process, and thus being able to see all the activities that get in the way of delivering that purpose, is the most important thing to be learned about performance improvement. It changes everything about how we see the organization. Designing a high-performance process starts with articulating and communicating the purpose of the process and then designing that *process on purpose*. Optimally designed, the process only contains activities that contribute to the purpose, thereby, running at minimum cost. This is called the *entitlement* point of the process meaning the process is eligible to run at a certain performance level (i.e., cost-to-purpose ratio), given the current level of investment committed to the process (i.e., human, structural and financial capital). The majority of processes operate at less than half their entitled performance level, which means there is a 50% improvement readily attainable without additional capital investment, if the process is designed on purpose. This makes a lot of sense when considering the process has more waste than value, but the waste can only become visible when value (purpose) is clearly defined.

ENTITLING YOUR BUSINESS PROCESS

A process is a series of activities that consumes resources (cost) in the work required to convert inputs into outputs (into purpose). The activities determine the resource levels the process requires, which in turn determine the cost to convert inputs into outputs. Because the design of the process determines the activity level, process design is the main influence on performance. Obviously, fewer activities consume fewer resources and provide for less cost. However, reducing activities indiscriminately may well undermine the purpose of the process, unless we are certain the activities being decreased are not limiting the ability of the process to deliver its purpose. We must be *entitled* to eliminate activities. Often, in a valiant effort to quantify product cost, organizations approach the challenge as an accounting problem and attempt to accurately trace overhead costs to products and functions. That approach is an attempt to figure out how to spread the waste rather than eliminating it. The process mind has no need to chase product costs, rather it is focused on organizing processes and operations to reduce and eliminate overhead costs. No need for complex accounting input and control here; all the information required is embedded in the process and it is either adding value or it is not.

Let's take the process of changing a tire. The activities required to change a tire include: stop, jack up the car, take off the old tire, put on a new tire, jack down the car, and drive on. This series of activities (i.e., the process) takes a professional racecar pit crew a few seconds. A Formula 1 crew of 20 completes the task of changing four tires in less than 3 seconds (the current record is 2.3 seconds). This same process for changing one tire takes the average driver perhaps 20 to 30 minutes. Our elongated process time is produced by all the additional activities we perform (e.g., reading the instruction book, moving stuff in the trunk, searching for the tools). So, which process is better? Which one has a better cost-to-purpose ratio? We can only answer the question by evaluating the performance level of these processes in the context of their purpose. More importantly, we can only increase performance by understanding the purpose.

The Formula 1 pit crew's purpose is to win the race; therefore, they design the process so all the additional activities that do not contribute to the process are executed "offline." Looking for tools and equipment is done outside the critical path of the process, thus, reducing the time required to change the tire. Of course, the cost (resource level of 20 crew) is set in relation to the purpose. You and I might achieve a multisecond tire change, but would need to carry a professionally trained crew in the back seat, a compressor and air hose in the trunk, and frequently let the team practice. This is ludicrous of course, but only because we have a different purpose; therefore, we set our activities accordingly. We do not need to achieve a best-of-class process since it gives us no competitive advantage. Our competition cannot do a 2.3-second tire change nor are our customers willing to pay for a 2.3-second tire change. Given the Formula 1 investment and the willingness of the customer to pay for it (i.e., a winning purse), they are entitled to a less than 3-second tire change. For the professional driver, a second saved in the pits is directly related to time saved on the track as well as positioning (i.e., competitive advantage). Nevertheless, we can redesign our layperson's tire-changing process so it is also an entitled process, so its performance is 50% better without any additional capital outlay. This means we design it on purpose to get to our destination in a timely and cost-effective manner. How might we do that?

We could do some offline process improvement work; open the instruction manual one leisurely Saturday morning, read the section on how to change a tire, and then have a couple of dry runs in the driveway. Then, arrange our trunk so our golf clubs, gym bag, and accumulated junk are not in the way, and become familiar with the tools required and the location of the spare tire. Perhaps next time the 20 to 30 minutes becomes 10 or 15. In this case, we could cut the process time by 50% and improve the cost-to-purpose ratio by cutting our costs (i.e., resources). The pit crew is entitled to a less than 3-second tire change, you and I are entitled to 10 to 15 minutes. However, if our current performance is 30 minutes, we have a lot of continuous process design improvement to do to get to entitlement. The journey to an entitled process is to continuously expose and remove activities that do not contribute to the purpose. Even for the professional crew, continuous improvement is critical. The crew has taken at least a second out of a pit stop in the last few years due to improvements (i.e., the Ferrari crews train with high-performance coaches from the Olympic team). Like all processes that flow across multiple functions, departments, and resources, there needs to be strong coordination of people: twenty people in the pit working on one car with one common purpose even though each function has a specific role key to overall success. All business processes, which nearly always cross multiple people, functions, and departments, first and foremost, need a laser-focused, mutual purpose that is abundantly clear to all constituents in the process.

Value can only be defined by the customer.

THE CUSTOMER DEFINES THE PURPOSE OF THE PROCESS

Without a clear and collective focus on customer value, there is no opportunity to design a high-performance business process. Therefore, meeting customer demand becomes the single-minded, nonnegotiable requirement in the designing process. That means eliminating all activities that do not contribute to that purpose and, if the work being done is needed to meet customer demand, then the process will be high performing. It will be an entitled process. Added value is only defined by the customer. For example, customers decide whether they are willing to pay for a business or economy ticket, overnight delivery or two-day delivery, the premium cost of a craft bakery or the low cost of a supermarket.

Designing the process on purpose is in strong contrast to the conventional "labor cost is everything" business model where cost reduction through resource reduction (i.e., headcount or low-labor-rate countries) is the primary method to address performance improvement. Resource reduction is immediate and, at least in the short term, appears to provide a cost reduction. However, the improvement is specious, in that it does not say anything about the cost-to-purpose ratio. Taking resources out without reducing the activities that do not contribute to the purpose usually provides no performance improvement. Any alleged performance improvement can be attributed to calibrating that improvement against a contrived purpose. A contrived purpose (i.e., one that is not defined by the customer) would be: "meet the budget" or "reduce the cost of labor" or "reduce the average unit cost." None of these purposes are of value through the customer's eyes, unless they lead to customer value, like a price reduction. Otherwise, meeting the budget is not derived from customer demand and provides no value. "Meet the budget" means each department in the process needs to "make their numbers" and the easy way to do this is by off-loading costs on upstream and downstream departments, other segments in the process. Think how the distribution center moved the cost downstream when they focused on a pick target for order selectors or a headcount reduction target for wrapping pallets. The budget process incurs all types of activities the customer is not interested in paying for; activities such as meetings to explain budget variances.

CUSTOMER DEMAND DEFINES CUSTOMER VALUE

Demand can and should be well defined, not vague. It needs to be precise, even mathematical. For example, we might define demand in terms of the number of items created (e.g., number of widgets, phone calls, trailer deliveries, people served, new ideas, lines of code, sales calls, purchase requests, laboratory tests, applications, patients, orders, and so on). Then if we divide this number by the time available, we can determine at what rate the number of items being created need to flow through the process. In this way, the obligation of the entire process is driven by customer demand. For example, in the distribution center referenced in Chapter 5, the customer demand compiled from 1,250 customer outlets was 21,678,733 units (discrete items to be selected) on 179,000 orders per year. Given the 24/7 nature of the business, this translated to 59,393 units over 490 orders per day. If a trailer could carry about 700 units, the center will have to load 85 trailers each day. Therefore, to design on purpose, we would need to entitle—with existing resources—our process to be able to load and release a trailer every 17 minutes (Figure 7.2).

Recognize that the demand is from the customer's perspective and does not consider the capacity of the process: resource requirements or process capability (e.g., cycle time through the pick-to-load process). However, the process designer now has an equation with two variables to solve for: (1) how long to complete the process? and (2) how many resources

Demand Analysis				
How many trailers are required each day?	☐ ☐	59,393 units / 700 units per trailer	☐ ☐	84.85
What is the cadence with which trailers have to be loaded?	☐ ☐	1440 working minutes per day / 85 trailers required per day	☐ ☐	16.94

FIGURE 7.2

Demand analysis. It is important to find a common unit of measure for the demand. In this case trailers were used.

are required? In this case, it took seven people two hours to load a trailer; therefore, the process needs to be designed to that specification. Process improvement comes from redesigning the process so it takes either less than 2 hours and/or less than 7 people. However any change cannot violate the 17-minute demand.

The key to determining the purpose, as defined by customer demand arithmetic, is to treat the purpose as measurable and to subordinate all other siloized objectives to that purpose. The critical question is: Does this action help get us closer to a 17-minute trailer load/release capability? Thechallenge is to overcome—in a Machiavellian sense—the functional disciples of the vertical business model. We need a strict adherence to the purpose of the process, a single-minded determination and a collective focus on the purpose of the process. To achieve this, there is no room for departmental goals getting in the way. For example, picking 1,350 units per order selector per shift does not facilitate the demand of one trailer every 17 minutes, because it would be better to build a perfectly linear process and pick 2,470 units per hour (as a team); any more would cause a bottleneck downstream if the 17-minute cadence was to be maintained; any less and we would starve the downstream operations.

Recall how the engineering silo at the distribution center reduced the actual pallet wrapping time by 60% and saved on one operator in exchange for a $90,000 capital investment (i.e., the system required no operator and could wrap a pallet in one third the time). However, the order selector had to queue for up to 11 minutes (average 7 minutes) waiting for access to the new equipment, which added manpower requirements to the end-to-end operation. This functional objective of reducing the pallet wrapping time by 60%+ detracted rather than added to the purpose. This additional elapsed time was hidden in the siloized process as everyone kept on picking and loading, and having more pallets queued up. Cost reduction at any discreet resource in the process that is not a constraint to output is a contrived purpose because it is concentrating on the function, not the workflow. The engineering department got credit for headcount reduction and yet, never asked the basic question: How will this investment improve the process to achieve its purpose—a 17-minute trailer pull?

Figure 7.3 illustrates the distribution center in its original functional structure, while the Figure 7.4 shows the new structure redesigned into three horizontal processes of value, or value chains (ambient product, frozen product, and refrigerated product), all with the purpose of loading the trailer at a 17-minute cadence. Note the horizontal structure

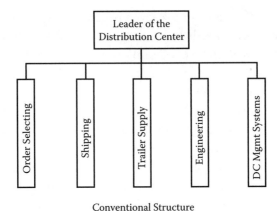

Conventional Structure

FIGURE 7.3

The original functional structure of the distribution center.

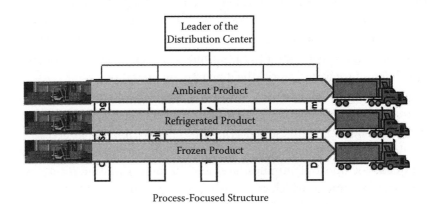

Process-Focused Structure

FIGURE 7.4

The process-focused structure of the distribution center.

has covered up the vertical functions (e.g., order selectors, engineering, shipping, etc.) because they have shifted their allegiance outward to the customer—load the trailer.

A process is a series of actions directed toward a specific purpose and these workflows have activities that either (1) contribute to the purpose or (2) do not contribute. To reference the tire-changing metaphor, jacking the car up is an activity that is of value to the purpose of winning the race or getting to our destination in a timely manner. It is the work. Rummaging around the trunk, removing all the stuff, preventing access to the spare tire, does not contribute to the purpose; it gets in the way of work.

The challenge is to eliminate the latter and do more of the former. Without a clear understanding of purpose, the ability to distinguish and act appropriately on these two types of activities is not possible.

THE CULTURE OF PROCESS

In previous examples, the focus was on the purpose of the process: In the mid-1990s, Southwest Airlines collectively focused on 10-minute tarmac turnaround time; the distribution center focused on loading the trailer at 17-minute intervals; the back office acquisition people focused on a two-day, card approval rate; and ABC Adhesives focused on 60 pallets per shift. Their continuous improvement actions were always based on a hypothesis that such action would move them closer to the purpose.

The idea of common purpose is not new; in fact, it is analogous to common sense. Companies with a clear sense of purpose do better than those without. Organizations that focus their energies on customer-defined purpose beyond pure profit, do better than those without such a culture of purpose. A survey by Deloitte (professional services organization) found 90% of people who believe their organization has a strong sense of purpose also report a strong financial showing over the past year.[1] When all members of an enterprise, regardless of the size, have a mutual interest and a well-communicated strategy that concentrates resources on the purpose of the process, the results can be astonishing.

In 1941, war preparations were tentatively moving forward in America when Germany invaded Russia and Japan attacked the U.S. naval base at Pearl Harbor, Hawaii. What then emerged was an energized American workshop with a fanatical focus on purpose—win the war—by supplying the customer (allies) with the equipment needed. By the end of 1942, America's output of war material exceeded the Axis Powers (Germany, Italy, and Japan) and, by 1944, its factories built an airplane every five minutes while its shipyards launched 50 merchant ships a day and 8 aircraft carriers a month. These big enterprises (Lockheed, Bechtel-McClone, Chrysler, Boeing, General Electric) did not succeed just on their own, they had help from small businesses. The Boeing B-29 bomber, for example, had over 40,000 different parts supplied by 1,400 subcontractors.[2] Given the infinite interfaces and staggering logistics of such an undertaking, the only plausible way to succeed was to adopt an obsessive focus on the purpose of the process, to concentrate on the complete horizontal flow to the customer (i.e., allies), and eliminate suboptimal functions. It was a powerful, unfettered, and relentless customer-centric process.

The lethargic nature of a vertical organization, combined with a contrived purpose, is simply too sluggish to achieve the requisite purpose. Those orthodox structures can't see the purpose of the process for the forest of functional subpriorities, departmental incest, managerial hubris, and meaningless, misaligned measures.

BACK TO THE FUTURE

During the war, to meet customer demand of the war theatre, Boeing designed its process on purpose. It used the arithmetic of customer demand (the number of aircraft divided by the time available to build them). Boeing displayed the mathematical imperative to all employees using visual signals to pull its product through U-shaped flow cells at a set cadence (Figure 7.5). Boeing built high-quality airplanes at the rate of 17 a day, that's one every 1.3 hours, while reducing the cost by 51% ($242,000 to $140,000).[3] However, once the war ended the collective purpose appeared to disappear and things returned to "normal," vertical departments.

FIGURE 7.5
The process mind assembling B-17S for the Allies in WWII in the Boeing Plant 2, in Seattle, Washington. (Associated Press file photo. *Denver Post*. September 15, 2010).

Boeing, like most manufacturers, abandoned the process-focused model and adopted, in the late 1950s and early 1960s, a results-oriented production mentality. Its operating creed was "Manufacturing Resource Planning." The new church was discrete scheduling (i.e., optimize the parts, not the whole) and the deity was "Material Requirements Planning," which pushes materials based on forecasts (schedules) rather than pull to customer demand (as mathematically determined). Like most manufacturers, from 1960 forward, Boeing became a disciple of the conventional illusion of Material Requirements Planning and blindly accepted its inherent transactional waste, feeding the complex beast, tracking work orders and jobs in all sorts of stages of completion, and creating inventory and massive amounts of paper work. The truth and tangible evidence about flow, simple flow, was forgotten. Boeing, of course, was just an example of how nearly all manufacturers operated since the post-war period (batch and queue), and still do today.

HOW WE GOT HERE

Material Requirements Planning and its ever more complex offspring Manufacturing Resource Planning and ERP (Enterprise Resource Planning) were built based on the design of functional plant layouts of the 1960s. They attempted to take advantage of the growth in high-speed random-access computing power. Material Requirements Planning logic directed process designers away from the true purpose of the end-to-end process and reinforced with iron girders the optimization of the departments and functions. Material Requirements Planning logic was not just contained in the manufacturing and logistics world, but the same mindset was adopted by the service industry. Think of all the handoffs in back office processing for insurance claims, purchase orders, or account applications, or the bouncing of a customer from one operator to another when dealing with a call center. Still, today, this old thoughtware is pervasive and insidious.

The Material Requirements Planning logic was conceived early in the 1960s when Joe Orlicky installed the first Material Requirements Planning at J. I. Case, in Racine, Wisconsin. Ollie White at Stanley Tool in Connecticut soon followed and they joined forces in 1967 to sell the Material Requirements Planning crusade to APICS,[4] which at the time billed itself as the American Production and Inventory Control Society and was the brand name for operations excellence for most of the ensuing

45 years—a period when long lead times, marginal quality, big batch sizes, low variety, and deep bills of materials all existed. Adding insult to injury—from a process perspective—in the 1980s and 1990s, APICS added accounting (Manufacturing Resource Planning) and other business functions (ERP). Today, ERP is at the forefront of Supply Chain Management thinking, which is still based on 1960s logic. The only change to the thinking is an update in the APICS acronym to refer to Advancing Productivity, Innovation, and Competitive Success. We continue to install this algorithmic nightmare, even though it contains no inherent method for process improvement. ERP is hopelessly underequipped to handle today's Lean operations. Fundamentally, ERP is designed to conceal, not expose, disruptions to flow; it is master scheduling that makes sure there is enough water (waste) in the river to cover the rocks (problems). ERP is not based on the current reality of high variety and speed to market, where short cycle times do not allow for the luxury of pushing work into the business processes. To the process mind, time is of the essence and we need to pull work through the process and expose the rocks (problems) so we can see them and remove them. The main difference between 1960s functional thinking and today is the assumption that automated information management is good, and all possible automated information is best.

FORTY YEARS LATER

Fortunately, some 40 years later, Boeing and others were enlightened enough to attempt to return to a horizontal workflow model and attempted to install a leaner operating system. In 1996, they engaged Chihiro Nakao, a renowned Japanese Lean sensei with Shingijutsu Co. LTD. He was an original architect of the Toyota Production System. When he arrived at Boeing, he stated, "Your grandparents were making airplanes a lot better than you (referring to the Boeing of 1944)."[5] He saw that the previously focused purpose of fulfilling wartime customers had been replaced with contrived purposes and short-term financial targets. There were flaws everywhere. Targets were set for shipped goods (i.e., contrived purpose, because the customer only finds value in his particular order), which focused on keeping the plant moving. Workers were aware that the rework department would fix anything. Assembly workers, who had the most important job, were seen as least important, and schedulers and inspectors were held in higher esteem.

In the 1940s, success depended on the operators building the planes to a set cadence, whereas postwar measured success on meeting the schedules. The schedulers, located well away from the production trenches, turned to their information factories to create schedule-driven environments. They used forecasts and economic order quantity (EOQ) batches to optimize cost. Meeting schedules is another example of a contrived purpose. The same was true of quality, where inspectors were the new quality experts, not the people who built 17 planes in a day. Why build quality in when it could be inspected in later? Better to just keep the plant moving and allow it to hit shipping targets based on forecasts and batch size optimization. None of it had anything to do with the real purpose of customer value.

It is hard to care about a customer in a system that does not encourage you to do so. Only when the purpose is expressed as "serve the customer" can process design be understood in customer terms.

Target-obsessive management behavior may be the greatest barrier to improving financial performance.

Where the true purpose of fulfilling customer demand is replaced by contrived purposes, the organization is seduced into focusing on discrete resources at the expense of the collective whole. A simple illustration can be extracted in almost any organization. In an engineering office, the contrived purpose might be "billable hours" or, in a service call center, "average call handling time" or, in a manufacturer, "equipment utilization." Upon reflection, one can discover numerous examples of "normal" business activities that are not based on purpose, but merely add costs to support contrived purposes. Experience suggests there is no correlation between billable hours and on-time, on-specification project delivery. And average call-handling time does not encourage first-time-right problem resolution. Machine utilization is useless if that machine is not a constraint to meeting customer demand. Machine availability better correlates to the purpose of the process. The Formula 1 pit crew is only utilized for a total of three to six seconds (of the 7200 seconds of the race), but their availability is critical to accomplishing the purpose of winning the race. Certainly, it would be silly to have someone drive your car continuously around the block while you read this book so that your vehicle is better "utilized." Contrived purposes in functional, suboptimized processes are no less absurd. No doubt the mother of all contrived purpose is "month-end syndrome," driven by quarterly shareholder value targets. In turn, this artificial milestone forces employees to be run ragged in meeting month-end numbers (i.e., regularly shipping more product in week four than in week one). I would be a rich man if I had a dollar for every business who initially insisted that "no continuous process improvement work could be done the last week of the month" because all resources must be fully occupied to close the books. More batch thinking, I guess. Why not close the books every day?

REAL DEMAND VS. FORECASTING

What Chihiro Nakao brought to Boeing was a "back-to-the-future" perspective, through the lessons of TPS, like don't change the shop floor process to accommodate the idiosyncrasies of MRP-type scheduling algorithms (e.g., ERP). He entered a Boeing world, which was representative of how mass production had worked to date in nearly all businesses. They create processes full of waste through "cast in stone" equipment scheduling and material planning procedures requiring absurd amounts of extra inventory to accommodate the "schedule risk" of the individual operations. The Shingijutsu folks began to lead Boeing (and others) back to their grandparents' thinking with a clear purpose—meet customer demand. And, they did it by viewing the entire value chain and building to real demand with simple visual control and problem-solving tools, as opposed to a multimillion-dollar ERP installation. About the most complex type of factory is one like Toyota that makes thousands of cars with hundreds of permutations per day, and it does it with no ERP-type shop floor control (ERP/MRP is used for capacity planning and financial costs, but shop floor control is pure manual pull, based on the actual demand of the customer). Of course, this rule of building to actual demand instead of educated guessing (forecasts) applies equally to all processes including service industries. This concept is articulated in John Seddon's incredibly fresh and intensely profound book, Freedom from Command and Control, where he urges us to rethink how we manage service industries and move from focusing on activity-related measures like budgets and targets to focusing on purpose. He suggests we think of it as "customers pulling value from the system."[6]

In designing the process so that it's capable of meeting demand there are only two variables we can leverage to solve the equation: (1) resources working in the process, and (2) the design of the process. A business process has three fundamental elements: (1) The quantity (Q) of resources in the process, which is driven by ... (2) the design of the process (P) that consumes the resources and ... (3) the volume of work demanded (D) of the process.

The volume of work demanded by the process represents the purpose of the process and as such is not a variable; it is a fixed element that can be mathematically represented. It is the equivalence for which we must solve. Therefore, the other two elements are variables: quantity of resources and the design of the process ($D = Q \times P$). Because the quantity of resources represents a cost to the process and the customer demand cannot be fulfilled if that quantity reaches an unsustainable threshold (i.e., costs too high to stay in business) and then no customer demand will be met. So, within a threshold tolerance, the only way to solve the equation is through the redesign of the process. Think about the service you encounter in stores, on the phone, at the airport, in the doctor's office, at the fitness center, in the restaurant. If the organization can design and operate a process in a sustained way that understands and responds to what matters to you, then it's a well-designed process.

SHAREHOLDER VALUE IS A CONTRIVED PURPOSE

By suggesting shareholder value is a contrived purpose in relation to designing high-performance business processes, I am not in any way diminishing the right or need of the investor to get a return on financial speculation. What I have said is that shareholder value does not guarantee customer value, while a focus on customer value will provide shareholder value. If shareholder value is a process specification, then lousy share price is a symptom of bad process.

We need to remind ourselves that time-based tactics are the essence of good process design. Removing time is not doing the work faster, it is removing the things that get in the way of work. A sprinter covers 100 meters in less time than the hurdler. The challenge is not to run faster, but to remove the hurdles. The roofer does not cover the gable top sooner by hammering faster, but by having the next shingle and nail readily available. Time consumed, but not spent on purpose, is manifested in many forms: waiting, transporting, searching, doing the same thing over because of a defect, making more than the purpose needs, (i.e., more patients queued in the wait room than the dentist can handle; it's inventory). Yet, for all of this, the shareholder value model, which simply assesses whether there was a profit relative to the assets it took to generate the profit, reigns supreme and defines inventory as an asset. (The shareholder value model never really equates "waste" —like inventory— to "cost".) This is an absurd perspective to the process thinker. Of course, if you pull inventory out of this shareholder value model, the model collapses. Perhaps the number one consumption of time, not spent on attaining purpose, is procedural complexity. Processes are really quite simple; you make something, preferably one at a time and move it out of the operation as quickly as possible. Once you remove the inventory and focus on the velocity of the single unit, you begin to realize how much of that complexity is due to not having an unwavering focus on the purpose. Even a slight shift away from the purpose of fulfilling customer demand (e.g., placing the enterprise on a contrived purpose like average unit cost) will automatically wrench the process through excessive delays and abnormal variations and result in not only failing the purpose of the process, but increasing total (real) cost.

Remember, both Henry Ford and Toyota knew that inventory is not an asset. However, since General Motors introduced the DuPont financial model in the 1920s, declaring inventory to be a financial asset, the world of continuous process flow was effectively rendered obsolete. The vertical organization, worshipping at the altar of shareholder value with department managers as high priests, became the business model for 90 plus years; customer value be damned. The modern Ford Motor Company, Delphi, General Electric, Boeing, IBM, and virtually every other publicly traded American manufacturer, regards inventory as an asset. Fortunately, Toyota stayed the course with continuous flow and defined inventory, in operational terms, as waste. The problem here is the classic trap of a contrived purpose. The DuPont model works perfectly for increasing shareholder value through an increased return on investment by leveraging the remarkable fact that the cost of production (cost of goods sold) can go down while inventory is growing. This conventional trickery is part of the smoke and mirrors of classical "economic order quantity (EOQ) theory" and its offsprings: unit labor cost and machine utilization. Economies of scale are really a way of saving a little bit of cost through a whole lot of inventory growth. Therefore, designing a process on purpose becomes subservient to the contrived purpose of shareholder value. It is not by chance that the high-performance businesses (e.g., Apple, Danaher, and McDonald's) have processes built on speed (high inventory turns) and, coincidently, their shareholders seem to be satisfied. These companies, by virtue of designing the processes on purpose, have driven down inventories. They recognize that cash and inventory do not lie. The DuPont model (initially used by the DuPont Corporation in the 1920s and little changed since) assumed inventory as an asset on the premise it could be converted to cash at any time; however, today, where product and service variety are ubiquitous and the life cycle of many products is measured in months (smartphones, anyone?), inventory can only be recognized as an asset when it is converted to revenue (i.e., throughput is converting inventory to revenue). High inventories are liabilities because they risk being obsolete prior to conversion to revenue. Inventory turns or any inventory/time comparable measures, such as tarmac turnaround time, are a critical manifestation of the health of the business process. Therefore, nothing can be as important a manifestation of process health as time-to-purpose (e.g., inventory turns). Simply put, the shorter the time that customer demand dwells in the process before being fulfilled, the less the cost.

So, why are more companies not singing this process-focused business model song? Probably because, when you have a contrived purpose like shareholder value, there is no managerial will to tell Wall Street that you are going to take a massive, one-time profit hit by writing off the accumulated overhead costs embedded in inventory and then pronounce that inventory will no longer be a hidden reservoir for excess costs in the future. This is the equivalent of the "too big to fail" enigma central banks and governments were faced with in the recent great recession. This also is true in the service business. Moving a service call center from an "average call handling time" to "solve the customer's problem," risks increasing costs in the short term because calls take longer and might require more resources. However, in the long term, they dramatically reduce repeat calls because problems are now prevented, not just contained. However, taking this longer-term view and committing to it is a rigorous "carrot diet" (see Chapter 12) that many CEOs just won't swallow. Shareholder value is so ingrained in the business psyche of the corner office that most of its occupants are convinced that it is the *only way* to quantify the business.

THE DANGERS OF EOQ THINKING

The critical process drivers (in order of importance) of the customer-centric, process-focused business model are: (1) throughput (i.e., revenue generated), (2) time-to-deliver the purpose (i.e., inventory), and

(3) elimination of activities that get in the way of work or disruptions to flow (i.e., operating costs). One of the problems is that this process-fixated thinking initially appears to the legacy thinker to threaten costs. In a vertical world, it is difficult to see how costs are associated with disruptions to flow. The EOQ theory is based on the belief that low cost is attributable to scale and cost targets; therefore, larger batches translate into lower costs. This might even approach the truth if there was no variety in the offerings of the enterprise; if all demand was the same with no variation. Building 10 instead of 1 (where demand is for 1) in order to lower average unit cost, may *increase* the total operating cost of the process. The other 9 may never be converted to revenue, thus representing a liability, not an asset. What if the next smartphone is released before the previous smartphone inventory is converted to revenue? The old thoughtware of shareholder value assumes moving from providing service A or product A to providing service B or product B requires a time-consuming and costly changeover (i.e., the effort and activity required to provide a substitution or switch in product or service). Based on the prevailing mantra of unit cost, it assumes that building 10 allows for the amortization of that changeover across the number of widgets produced. The thinking is that making 10 instead of 1 from that one-time changeover will drive down the unit cost and, because inventory is an asset, all is good with the other 9. Remember, 60% of Apple's revenues are generated by products that are less than four years old.[7] The point here is that we do not have time to build 10 when 1 is needed; we need to build 1 at the same cost point as the 10.

Conversely, process thoughtware designed on economies of flow will adjust the design of the process ($D = Q \times P$) by exposing and eliminating those things that get in the way of the flow. The idea of reducing the changeover or wait time is a fundamental starting point for any process being redesigned on purpose. For example, assume you are lining up at a quick service restaurant at the cashier station to complete a transaction. As the queue gets longer (inventory builds), perhaps another cashier window may open or a triage process is set up to sort the line by customer demand type. Perhaps the customer that only wants hot coffee and not a complete lunch order can go to a select cashier. This becomes even more critical in a world where variety is the norm and each transaction is not 100% predicable. A hospital emergency ward provides a case in point. The Great Ormond Street Hospital for Children in the United Kingdom was experiencing a very high mortality rate for congenital heart surgery. They found that the journey from the operating room to intensive care unit (ICU) was high risk for the patients (their inventory). They had problems with handovers from the operating room to ICU. This handover was not well documented, so they videotaped their internal process, collaborated with a Ferrari F1 pit crew, and developed new handover protocol. This included the documentation of standard work to improve the handoff of information, better procedures, and better coordination of the medical teams. They also established better definitions of staff's roles. For example, the anesthetist had overall responsibility for coordinating the team, similar to the Formula 1 crews "lollipop" man. The lollipop man is the guy who holds up the pit sign (looks like a big lollipop) that tells the driver where to stop and when to take off. He is responsible for the safe release of the car after the tires have been changed. Before the new procedures at Great Ormond Street, 30% of patient errors occurred in technical and information errors. After the changes, it was down to 10%[8]. Only by managing the end-to-end flow will cost (in this case, error) go down in a sustainable manner. If you don't deal with the process, you just won't get better.

STOP MAKING PROCESSES USABLE
AND START MAKING USABLE PROCESSES

Imagine for a moment, you are sitting in a fancy restaurant and your steak is the best you have ever had. But, now it's time to leave and it's taking forever to pay your bill. If only the restaurant would focus less on giving you a better steak and more on giving you the steak better. Of course, the steak (product) has to be excellent, but value (i.e., lost customers) is being jeopardized by poor process. Consider electronic devices, like smartphones. Most of us have them and because they are basically all the same, one would think companies would differentiate on their customer service process. But, they don't. Instead, they try and differentiate on "bundles" and "plans" and "deals," which are complicated and confuse the customer. That, certainly, is not the purpose of the process, although the CEO of Telecom, New Zealand, publicly admitted that telecom companies used "confusion as a marketing tool."[9] Their products, bundles, and deals are so complicated that people who threaten to switch carriers generally stay put because switching is just too much hassle. Besides, they get the same treatment from the competitor. However, to be fair, these people are not customers, they are hostages. *The Wall Street Journal* reports, "In effect …

wireless plans … have become like the Hotel California. Subscribers occasionally try to check out, but they almost never leave." According to *The Wall Street Journal*, the four major carriers in the United States offer 700 combinations of smartphone plans.[10] Usually the mere mention of cell phone bills or cable service guarantees another horror story. Not long ago, I was preparing to leave for Australia on a speaking tour covering five cities in two weeks. Just before heading out the door, my smartphone crashed and I wound up in a hopelessly complex interaction—a waste-filled process. When I phoned for help and blindly accepted the mandatory "on hold" waste of waiting (inventory) message, I was told, and I quote, "Just find the serial number on the back of your device and type that into the space provided along with your IP address and the exact wording of the error message you encountered." What? They might as well have asked me to solve a sudoku puzzle. Regardless of the brilliance of their product, the process failed me—and the company and the industry. But, they get away with it because they are all the same—bad. That's an opportunity for someone to break out and change the playing field and gain a significant competitive advantage by creating a very useable process.

BUILDING VARIETY INTO THE PROCESS

In today's tumultuous world, the most vital reason to design business processes on purpose is to effectively accommodate an ever-increasing variety in customer demand. In 2012, global industrial output was 57 times greater than in 1900,[11] faster than the growth of the overall economy, mainly because businesses kept getting smarter. They are leveraging technologies, electronics, biotechnology, and the Internet. Most remarkable is the ever-growing variety of products and services. There are about 10 billion different products being produced each year, more than the population of the planet. Globally, production is rooted in vast supply chain ecosystems and these ecosystems require process thinking that allows anyone to hook up to any global supply chain. It's about designing the widget in one country, assembling it in another, using components from dozens of other countries, and designing a business model for agility and speed in order to ultimately meet customer demand. The traditional business model was designed on the premise that cost goes down (by about 15% per unit) every time volume doubles; therefore, set up once and run campaigns. Now, we have learned that cost goes up by 20 to 35% per unit every time variety doubles,[12] so it creates a need to set up as often as variety dictates and process one at a time. The fact that the 2013 Global Electronics Forum in Shanghai featured 22,000 new products[13] means today's businesses need to be built to handle ever-increasing variety. We can no longer compete with old thoughtware based on an industrial age that operated on an each-discrete-function, efficiency-is-paramount model.

There is a widening chasm between what our current management models can solve and what they need to solve, especially when we don't know what we don't know. A prime example of a vertical versus a contemporary horizontal model is software development (Figure 7.6). The traditional business model for software development can be defined by the waterfall model: one group defines the product, another builds mock-ups, and then engineers build it to specifications. This is a long, arduous process with numerous handoffs from function to function and hardly effective in modern-day production where software life cycle is measured in months. The more effective approach to software development, deeply rooted in process thinking is "agile." Agile software development is the ability to add and iterate quickly, throughout the product life cycle, and it follows the precepts of the Agile Manifesto, a 2001 document written by a group of developers who preferred individuals and interactions over project management and tools.

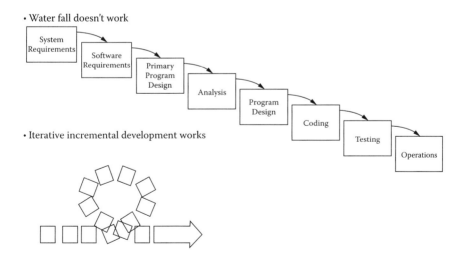

FIGURE 7.6
Agile development takes place in rapid cycles of test-code-test code (iterative), as opposed to test-test-test-test-code (waterfall).

RELIABILITY VERSUS VALIDITY

Since the days of the highly skilled master craftsmen, who meticulously created one-of-a-kind, high-quality, customized artifacts using simple tools and enormous labor costs (i.e., hours), we have, for the most part, chosen to design business processes to reduce labor costs even at the expense of high quality and customization. We have reduced the labor costs through building the process for the purpose of performance *reliability* (high command and control for flawless repetition to achieve predictability). We have done this chiefly at the expense of building processes for the purposes of meeting changing demand. Process reliability is the wrong design, it is exactly what prohibits a 50% performance improvement. If you are interested in performance improvement, you need to be cautious of those promoting process reliability, disguised as ISO (International Organization for Standardization) auditors, Six Sigma black belts, ERP suppliers, and standard cost accountants who still preach the virtues of EOQ. Hiding problems with reliability never allows for ultimate resolution. It's appropriate to cite the age-old cliché for this age-old thinking: "out of sight, out of mind."

Of course, where the volume is high and the variety is low, reliability works fine. However, fine is not enough, unless you are a true commodity provider. As mentioned, the retail banking industry recognizes it makes 80% of its revenue from 20% of its customers. (In fact, this Pareto rule lives in nearly all processes.) The bank drives the 80% to a low-cost option, like an automated teller machine (ATM). The value of the ATM is in its reliability and predictability. But, when it comes to competing for the high-margin customer demand, like a mortgage, a line of credit, or investment options, the need is for a customized and cogent-persuasive process to meet the customized, individualized, one-of-a-kind customer purpose. For these products and services, the retail bank needs a relationship process. The cogent-persuasive process is iterative and exploratory in nature; it seeks out distinctive demand and designs a solution within some predefined parameters (Figure 7.7).

TARGETS VERSUS CAPABILITY

The other bane of designing the business on purpose is a target. Targets are a staple of the traditional organization and are nearly always financially

Craft	Mass	Process-focused
Highly Skilled Workforce	Narrow Skills	Multi-skilled Workforce
Simple, Flexible Tools	Single Purpose Activities/Processes	Highly Flexible Activities/Processes
Customized to Each Individual	Intolerant to Customization	Accommodates Mass customization
One at a Time	Batches	One at a Time
High Cost	Low Cost	Low Cost
Low Volume	High Volume	High Volume
High Variety	Low Variety	High Variety

FIGURE 7.7

Process-focused organization design adopts the best elements of craft and mass production.

defined, which distracts the process from its true purpose of customer value. A target has no utility if the process is not capable of hitting the target. In designing a process on purpose, targets need to be replaced with capability or, more precisely, variances from the capability (i.e., meeting the purpose). The marketplace is so dynamic that processes are, by definition, in flux and like the weather, not predictable beyond a few hours or a day or two. As visibility of the future declines, targets become difficult to see, irrelevant, and a major source of stress, because they appear unattainable. And target-obsessive organizations create performance measurement and management systems that lead away from performance-on-purpose design. They are measuring the wrong thing.

Changing the way we measure the business is the most effective way to create a high-performance process. The measure helps understand and improve the capability to deliver the purpose of the process and it provokes direct action on the process. The next chapter demonstrates the imperative of measurement and its link to purpose.

REFERENCES

1. Schwartz, A. 2013. Businesses with a strong sense of purpose are more successful. *Fast Company* May 31.
2. Herman, A. 2012. *Freedoms forge: How American business produced victory in World War II*. New York: Random House, 336.
3. Ibid pg. 338.
4. Ptak, C., and C. Smith. 2008. *Beyond MRP: Meeting the current materials synchronization challenge*. Paper presented at the APICS International Conference, Kansas City, MO. September 15. Online at: http://replenishmentplus.com/pdf/Beyond%20MRP.pdf.

5. Jenkins, M. 2002. Getting Lean: Across the enterprise Boeing is attacking waste and streamlining process. The goal? Cost competitiveness. *Boeing Frontiers Magazine* cover story, August.

6. Seddon, J. 2005. *Freedom from command and control: Rethinking management for Lean service.* New York: Productivity Press, 46.

7. Economist.com/blogs/schumpeter, November 23, 2013; *Management Thinkers Disagree On How to Manage Complexity*, (Print Edition pg. 68), www.economist.com/news/business/21590341

8. Butler, J. 2009. *What a Hospital learned from F1*; www.rdasia.com/what-a-hospital-learned-from F1. Readers Digest. Asia

9. Telecom Confusion Comments Criticized; May 9, 2006, onenews, tvnz/content/712017/425823.xhtml.

10. Gryta, T. 2013. Inside the phone-plan pricing puzzle. *The Wall Street Journal,* July 31. Online at: http://online.wsj.com/news/articles/SB10001424127887324110404578630110732955422.

11. *Are we Better Off Now than in 1900?*, March 13, 2014; Article Posted By Paper, Cool International, coolintl.com/are-we-better-off-now-than-in-1900.

12. Stalk, G. Jr. and T. E. Hout. 1990. *Competing Against Time: How Time based Competition is Reshaping Global Markets.* New York: Free Press Macmillian, pg. 46.

13. Economist.com/blogs/schumpeter, November 23, 2013; Management Thinkers *Disagree On How to Manage Complexity*, (Print Edition pg. 68), www.economist.com/news/business/21590341.

8

Measure What Matters, Not What Is Easy

Sometimes what counts can't be counted and what can be counted doesn't count.

Albert Einstein

IT ISN'T WEATHER FORECASTING

I once asked an audience why we have target-based business measurement systems that project monthly, quarterly, and even fiscal year-end numbers. One despondent voice in the back called out, "In order to make weather forecasters look good." The point is well made, particularly if you add the humorous claim that being a meteorologist is the only job where you get paid despite being wrong half the time. However, the scientific method used to predict tomorrow's weather, however inaccurate, is still more valuable to the customer than revealing yesterday's weather with 100% certainty. The challenge is to continually improve the process used to foretell future conditions so as to be continually more accurate.

If we are to improve performance, then what and how we measure is critical and it must be rooted in the theory that measuring the capability of a process is as important, if not more so, than simply measuring whether we hit yesterday's target or not. We need to run the business with leading indicators, not just *lagging* metrics. We need to measure the current condition and its ability to predict the future condition, as opposed to relying on the past. Over time, I have discovered there is an inherent danger in relying too much on historical metrics. Einstein's quote above is referring to physics, but I am sure he would agree that, if this is true in a scientific discipline, it is also true in business, even though business is more of an art than a science. I adhere to the idea that because we can't measure future conditions with perfect accuracy does not mean we ought not to try—and that it cannot be done. A somewhat indicative measure of the future (e.g., weather) is better than a perfectly accurate measure of the past. After all, a precise measure of that which does not matter is inferior to revealing an imprecise measure of what is critical to the future. That, at least, is the view of the process mind. The process requires direction and navigational instruments that allow the organization to chart its future, in real time. The process needs leading indicators and points of reference, signposts along the way, and a way to interpret what these leading indicators mean. These are navigational measures. This does not mean ignore evaluative measures completely, organizations need both to evaluate the past and chart the future. I refer to this requirement as a Navigational Scorecard.

THE NAVIGATIONAL SCORECARD

The Navigational Scorecard tries to achieve a better balance between drivers of performance and performance outcomes. The strengths of performance drivers are that they are predictive and allow the organization to adjust behaviors for performance; however, while they are based on a hypothesis (i.e., experimental action), the supporting data are difficult to collect. Performance outcome measures are usually objective and easily captured, but they reflect success in the past, and thus, are evaluative. In a process-focused organization, we are trying to shift emphasis from evaluative measures to navigational measures. Evaluative measures generally tend to be used as a "weapon" (good vs. bad) and are often irrelevant, too general, arrive too late, and don't start with a customer-in-mind measure. Navigational measures are more about process drivers that start with customer demand (i.e., purpose) and measure transformation from input to output. There are three points where we can measure a process (Figure 8.1): inputs (lead indicators), transformation (process indicators), and outputs (lag indicators). Let's say the output of a skills development process is "certified employees" because

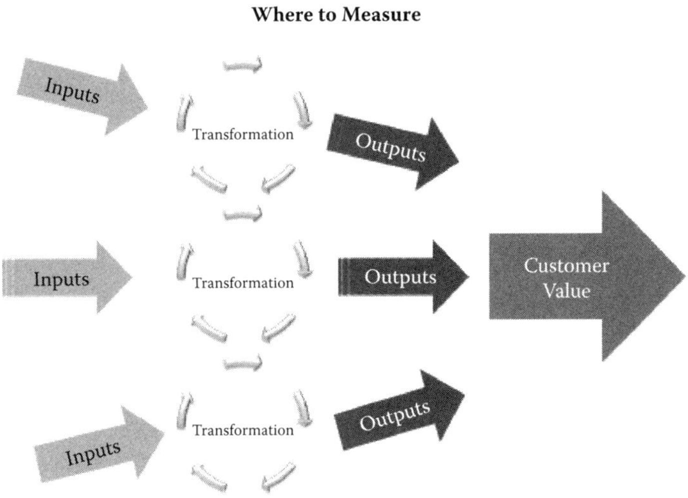

Where to Measure

FIGURE 8.1
Process inputs, the process itself, and process outputs.

> Any measure may be a lead (navigational) measure for one strategic
> objective and a lag (evaluative) indicator for another–example:
> - **Objective #1:** Increase employee productivity
>   - Lag measure: output per employee
>   - Lead measure: # multi-skilled/cross-trained employees
> - **Objective #2:** Attract & retain qualified employees
>   - Lag measure: # multi-skilled/cross-trained employees
>   - Lead measure: # departments with certification (skills
>   matrix) programs
> - **Objective #3:** Create certification program for customer
>   service
>   - Lag measure: number of customer service employees certified
>   - Lead measure: certification skills matrix program created

FIGURE 8.2
Lead (navigational) measures and lag (evaluative) measures.

we hypothesize that trained employees are a measure of productivity
improvement.

Any measure, in fact, may be a lead measure for one part of the process
and a lag indictor for another. Examples can be seen in Figure 8.2. where
Objective # 1 or output (increased employee productivity) comes from
the input (attract and retain qualified employees) which, in turn, comes
from the input (create certification program). In this way, the measures
provide a compass, a navigational framework, to continuously improve
the process.

Measures: Lead and Lag

Another way of looking at navigational measures is to calibrate them against these three rules:

1. The measures encourage the desired behavior from frontline troops.
2. The measures provide the information management needs to make effective decisions.
3. Rule #1 takes precedence over Rule #2.

Purpose–Measure–Action Model

Measuring Purpose

It is no accident that Measure resides at the center of the Purpose–Measure–Action (PMA) model and forms the essence of the Navigational Scorecard. To reiterate: All value is the result of some process and a process must have a Purpose, a Measure, and an Action (Figure 8.3). In this context, a measure has two purposes: (1) to evaluate (reliable knowledge from the *purpose*) and (2) to navigate (validation from the experiment). The measure evaluates how well we are doing against the purpose and helps navigate our journey toward that purpose by feeding back information from the actions we take

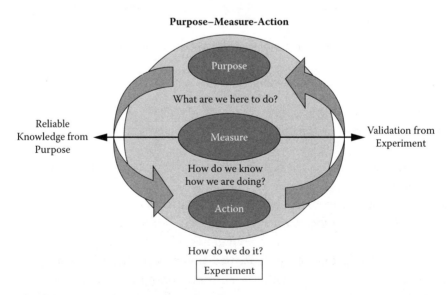

FIGURE 8.3
Purpose–Measure–Action (PMA) model.

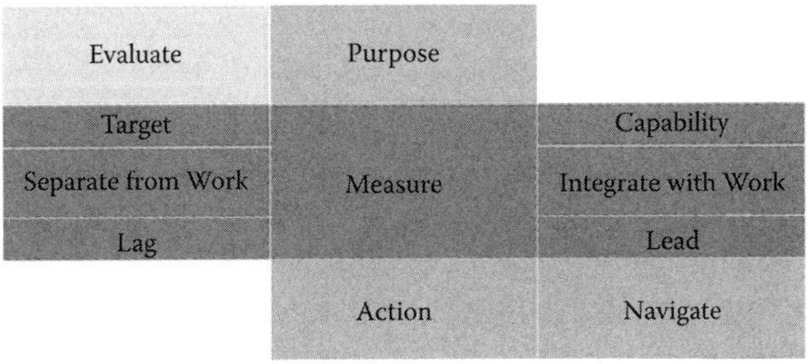

Evaluate	Purpose	
Target		Capability
Separate from Work	Measure	Integrate with Work
Lag		Lead
	Action	Navigate

FIGURE 8.4
Measures evaluate our position relative to the purpose of the process and help select the action required to move closer to the purpose.

to improve the process (i.e., experiments). Referring back to the Balanced Scorecard Model that we discussed in Chapter 6, evaluative measures calibrate our performance against financial goals and customer demand, while navigational measures allow us to make midcourse corrections based on the results of ongoing experiments. In addition, the evaluative measures point us in the direction of where our next experiment should be in order to enable future improvement. Navigational measures are integrated with work—as opposed to residing in an abstract information factory—and are predictive, not just a recording of the past. Most important, they incite action; to do something about the process as directed by the measure (Figure 8.4).

Measures: Evaluation and Navigation

Evaluative measures are of only limited use to the process mind. The measure as an evaluative tool is based on a reference to the target (usually financial budgets), collected in an abstract information system well away from where the activity influencing the result occurred (financial statements) and is available well after (lags) the actions causing the result have happened (last month's performance). Navigational measures are about the health of the process. The measure as a navigational tool is based on the variance in the capability of the process to deliver the purpose. The navigational measure is observed and controlled where the action influencing it occurs, and is an early predictor of the potential impact on the purpose. Remember, we are trying to allow employees to see the flow of value to the customer and fix disruptions in the flow prior to impacting that purpose. For example, from an evaluative measure in the distribution center example described in Chapter 5, we might reference yesterday's perfect order performance, but it is still yesterday's news and we can only read about it after the report is produced. The historical perfect order data of about 70% does not tell us anything about the capability of our process. (Remember the "load the trailer process.") The process is designed to touch it once and put it on the trailer, therefore, a good navigational measure would be the number of times we touched the item more than once and put it on the trailer. We do not need an information factory to do that, we need some direct observation from the people living in the process. That is a navigational measure leading to action. Nor is yesterday's news integrated with the work. A good navigational measure is visible moment-to-moment. The distribution center now measures how many pallets are staged at the loading dock at the end of the shift, but not on the trailer. If it is fewer than yesterday, that is good; if it is more, not so good. All experiments (actions) are designed to improve the process as revealed by the number of pallets left at shift's end. The measure is visible and integrated with the work. When plotted on a Navigational Scorecard—borrowing from the Balanced Scorecard Framework—the plotting of navigational and evaluative measures might look like those in Figure 8.5. Evaluative measures are more about

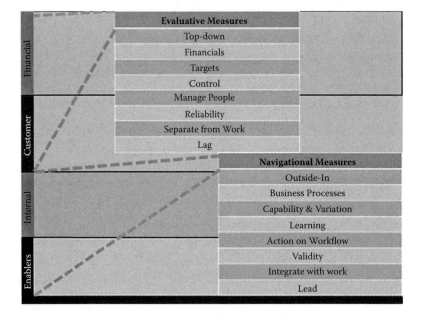

FIGURE 8.5
Navigational Scorecard: Characteristics of evaluative measures for "what" (customer and financial perspectives) and characteristics of navigational measures for "how" (internal process and future enabling perspectives).

"achieving targets" while navigational measures are more about "learning and adapting" and making mid-course adjustments.

The evaluative measures tell us the results of what we are trying to achieve (e.g., customer value and financial performance) and the navigational measures assess how well our processes are performing and how well our experiments are succeeding. Let's look at each of these elements.

Consider Southwest Airlines or any discount airline strategy of focusing their purpose (i.e., on time, low cost) by leveraging the core process of tarmac turnaround. In terms of a Navigational Scorecard, it might look like Figure 8.6, where the primary weighting of each purpose (bubbles) suggests fast ground turn time as the most important focus and it will be measured by the time from on-ground, or on-gate until release from gate, or in the air. Now, all actions focus on impacting that process.

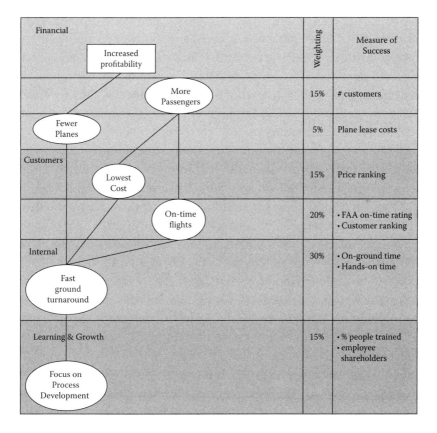

FIGURE 8.6

A generic Navigational Scorecard for a discount airline depicting an operating strategy and associated measures to improve tarmac turnaround.

Conventional organizations do not tend to prioritize process-focused measures as they are based on cause-and-effect hypotheses, and are therefore difficult hypotheses on which to collect supporting data. However, given that we are looking to fulfill customer demand, *only* navigational measures can provide the motivation, learning, and evaluation elements needed for success. These measures, in the hands of the operators living in the process, allow them to understand what they have to do to fulfill the purpose, drive the right behavior, and implement the proper actions. Flight attendants, gate agents, ground crews, etc. can all focus on the process capability measure of tarmac turn time, rather than fret about a distant target measure of "increased profitability," knowing the former done well will result in the latter being achieved.

Navigating the Future

From a navigational perspective, we are measuring variances in the process. Evaluative measures are traditionally top-down and invariably used in functional silos with little consideration given to how they impact other groups' performance or, more specifically, the process as a whole. The procurement department serves as an example. The department focuses on cost reduction (e.g., infrequent large volume buys to get a better price), while the manufacturing department is measured on just-in-time material delivery as manifested in raw material inventory turns (i.e., ship smaller amounts more often). These vertical allegiances do not lend themselves to enhancing customer value. Evaluative measures are typically in the language of financial targets, often crafted in three-month increments working toward the next earnings release. They are driven by the stock market, particularly the New York Stock Exchange, which is shorter-term than ever, primarily driven by investor activists aggressively looking for short-term gains and playing the expectations game the analysts set. Those measures are real, but often at the expense of the R&D, innovation, and market development goals established over the longer term. As mentioned earlier, that is one of the reasons Michael Dell took his company private so he could focus the firm on more, long-term innovation. Ironically, it is next to impossible to influence the short-term quarterly numbers, but it is possible to guide the longer-term strategy, which, as discussed in Chapter 6, is influenced by the health of the process deploying the strategy. Evaluative measures focus on outside-in measures because navigational measures are internal feedback mechanisms.

The conventional organization tends to incorporate only evaluative measures that are easily counted; however, counting only these makes us prisoners of our past, which makes it impossible to create a future that would be different than an extrapolated past. But, and this is important, future information must be more than a "wild guess," it must be palatable to the orthodox, MBA-influenced manager, who relies on facts, such as accounting reports. After the fact evaluation of yesterday's performance is of marginal use to the process mind. Accurate though it may be, it does not help the employee understand and improve the process. It may be silly to bake and time cookies with a smoke alarm or wait until you run out of gas to get a refill, but there you have it, the information is accurate, though useless. Instead, the process-focused organization collects factual information about what works and what does not work. It's similar to the canary in the coal mine where early detection was paramount. Let me be clear, navigational measures are not about predicting the future because, as far as I know, no one can do that. Rather they are designed to deliver information from actions and provide learning on how to make required midcourse corrections to better achieve the purpose of the process. Proverbially, navigational measures trim the sails *now*, based on the current wind and wave conditions, not based on yesterday's weather. As mentioned earlier, I determined that one predictor of my son's performance in math class was whether he wrote exams the morning after he played a hockey game. This is the critical distinction between an evaluative measure and a navigational measure. The evaluative measure of his poor math grade is based on a bad/good scale. His mark was bad. However, it does not lead to any problem-solving action. Looked at as a navigational measure, his mark incites action and an experiment to stay home and study the weekend before. Only upon completion of the experiment (stay home on the weekend to study) will the hypothesis be verified against the impact on the purpose (improve math mark). In business, evaluative performance measures things, such as revenue growth, volume shipped, budget met, conferences attended, website hits, etc.; whereas, a navigational measure is predicative in that it results from an experiment that can be designed to predict the likelihood of achieving the purpose. As such, good measures should calibrate the gap between the current condition and the purpose and provide information from the experiment to allow for ongoing adjustments. If my son stays home to study the weekend before the exam–game situation occurs, does his math grade improve? We don't know until the experiment is completed and the results are measured.

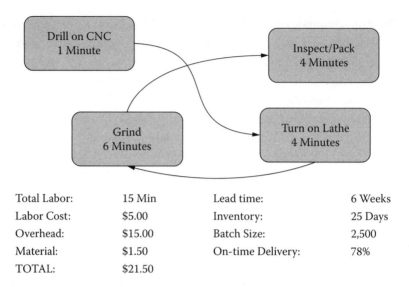

Total Labor:	15 Min	Lead time:	6 Weeks
Labor Cost:	$5.00	Inventory:	25 Days
Overhead:	$15.00	Batch Size:	2,500
Material:	$1.50	On-time Delivery:	78%
TOTAL:	$21.50		

FIGURE 8.7
Siloed structure before experiment.

Consider this experiment deployed to see if we are getting closer to the purpose of fulfilling customer demand. In Figure 8.7, we have a traditional structure where a widget is being made based on evaluative measures derived from the accounting architecture. The unit cost of the widget is $21.50 (information separate from the work). (This example is drawn from the literature on Lean accounting, particularly the remarkably insightful teachings of Brian Maskell.[1])

Now, we run our experiment and redesign the operation into a continuous process flow (Figure 8.8):

- Co-locating the equipment into a sequenced flow
- Replacing the CNC (computer numerical control) machine with a low-cost, quick-change drill press
- Reducing the batch size from 2,500 to 250
- Reducing the lead time from 6 weeks to 2 days
- Lowering the inventory from 25 days to 5 days
- Improving capacity
- Freeing up the CNC for other work

The results are as follows: The unit cost of the widget has gone up by nearly 20% to $25.50.

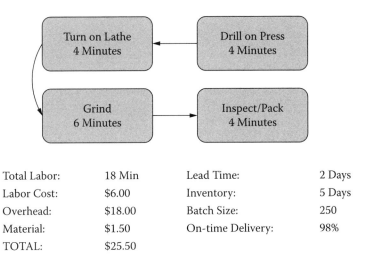

Total Labor:	18 Min	Lead Time:	2 Days
Labor Cost:	$6.00	Inventory:	5 Days
Overhead:	$18.00	Batch Size:	250
Material:	$1.50	On-time Delivery:	98%
TOTAL:	$25.50		

FIGURE 8.8
Process-focused structure after experiment.

Based on the feedback from this experiment, what should be done? The purpose of fulfilling customer demand has been significantly enhanced if we apply what we learned from the experiment: shorter lead times and improved on-time performance. And, if inventory is a manifestation of the health of the process, improvements have been made there as well. The traditional accounting architecture tells us the costs have gone up; therefore, the experiment tells us we should not continue with the process-focused design. Actually, the experiment is operationally and financially successful, but the measures are misleading. The decrease in inventory is good for the customer because it shortens the delivery time and it is good for the shareholder because it releases cash that can be used elsewhere. However, the accounting architecture (remember the DuPont model in Chapter 7) suggests a decrease in inventory reduces the amount of operating expense that can be capitalized for that accounting period and is, therefore, a bad thing. Inventory from this measurement perspective is an asset and, yet, to the process-focused thinker, it is waste. Likewise, the reduction in space, increase in capacity, and improved layout will not directly translate into lower costs, unless we put more through the pipe or reduce some headcount.

Furthermore, in this example, labor costs have apparently increased, even though production has moved from an expensive—and expensive to keep running—CNC process to a simple drill press. The overhead rate,

	Process-Focused Thoughtware	Evaluative Accounting Architecture
A	Increase in inventory is waste & lengthens the order-to-cash cycle	Increase in inventory capitalizes expense & "improves" bottom line
B	Process design: reduction in cell space, reduces waste (motion, staging, conveyance...)	If there is no reduction in spending, there is NO bottom-line impact
C	Labor: +20% ☑ Setup: −80% ☑ Inventory: −90% ☑ Freed capacity (CNC)	- BAD - Somewhere in overhead? - BAD: Loss of overhead absorbed - BAD: Unabsorbed overhead

FIGURE 8.9
Process thinking and traditional evaluative (accounting) at odds.

which approximates costs, should be lower on the manual machine, but isn't in our traditional measurement system because overhead continued to be allocated on labor, not on overall assets. Remember, the process mind attempts to eliminate overhead, not allocate it (Figure 8.9).

Financial measures have no navigational value.

Does the Measure Incite Action on the Process?

Two key questions to ask about your measures:

1. Does the measure indicate whether you are getting closer or farther away from the purpose?
2. Does the measure help incite action on the process that will remove waste?

Once again, the lesson is: Measure what matters, not what is easy and what matters is the purpose of the process. A measure matters if it helps employees understand how activities impact the ability of the processes to achieve the purpose. It further matters if it stimulates your organization to action that leads to problem solving.

We have been comfortable using financials as a measurement because they often provide the CEO with decisive information, but they have no navigational value. They say nothing about business realities like the culture of innovation and the ideas of people or supplier relationships. They give no early indication of customer problems because they are looking in a rear view mirror, reinforcing functional silos (e.g., departmental budgets), and sacrificing longer-term thinking. Let me repeat, *financial measures have no navigational value.*

A test of a good measure can be recognized by answering "yes" to these four questions:

1. Does the measure help in understanding and improving the performance of the process?
2. Does the measure relate to the purpose of the process?
3. Is the measure in the hands of the people doing the work?
4. Does the measure incite action on the process?

If the purpose of the two types of measures (to navigate and to evaluate) are in conflict, we must defer to the navigational purpose over the evaluative. And, yet, in nearly all instances, we defer to the evaluative. I have found that in survey after survey of senior management there is a consistent dissatisfaction with the current measurement system, in that it is not seen to be an effective performance measurement system. I suggest that is because, when the organization encounters a navigational versus evaluative conflict, everyone defers to the evaluative measure. And, yet, the cost-to-purpose ratio is the only real measure of financial performance because that ratio is a navigational measure. Only with a picture of the entire workflow can we create navigational measures that are meaningful. A simple rule of thumb is that all measures should start with the customer in mind.

A measure has utility if it is in context of the purpose. Without context, measures have no perspective. I enjoy illustrating this point with a story I heard about a man in a hot-air balloon, floating above the countryside. He was lost. As he hovered over the 9th green of a golf course, he hollered down to the golfer lining up a putt and shouted, "Excuse me, I am lost, could you tell me where I am?" The golfer looked up and said, "Yes, of course, you are directly over the 9th green." Then he went back to putting. The irritated balloonist hollered back. "You must be an accountant because the information, although totally accurate, is completely useless to me." Context is critical. Figure 8.10 exemplifies the principle that information out of context can be misleading.

If we get what we measure, isn't it time to start measuring what we want to become?

Perspective drives action and perspective
is driven by measures.

It is only with a total process perspective
that we can properly create the evaluative and navigational
measures required to achieve the purpose.

FIGURE 8.10
Which road leads north (north being our purpose)?

A THOUGHTFUL EXERCISE

Think about your business and ask which navigational indicators would you want to look at on a daily basis so as to determine if you were on purpose and fulfilling customer demand profitably. The traditional evaluative lagging indicators, such as profit, cost, repeat customers, and so on, cannot help employees understand how they can influence performance on a day-to-day basis. Consider a crucial process like recruiting and staffing. How would recruiters' behavior change (and be directed toward when and where to improve the recruiting process) as a result of learning about last month's sales per store numbers? It wouldn't. What recruiters need are leading indicators of performance. I was once brought into a large retail conglomerate, which was amalgamating a number of different business units (i.e., clothing, hardware, etc.) and putting together a central service so that they had a common process for things like staffing. They called it a shared services model that brought together retail, human resources, and financial operations. We knew staffing would be difficult to solve, so instead of trying to bring all the different staffing processes from the different business units together, we took the best of each and built a world-class staffing operation using process thinking. We started with identifying the purpose of the staffing process of course, then identified the critical measures required to inform the process while directing employees to undertake the proper actions (experiments).

First, we picked three measures (from the customer's perspective): one of quality, one of cost, one of time. By the way, asking the process designer in any business to pick these three measures (one in each of these categories) helps them begin to see their process. These were the measures they selected.

1. Cost Measure: External cost per hire
2. Time Measure: The external time-to-fill a request
3. Quality Measure: The 90-day turnover rate (i.e., how many people lasted beyond 90 days).

We worked on redesigning the "on-boarding process" (i.e. the purpose was not just to recruit but have productive employees within three months of hiring), process flow and reliable methods. We provided input into the action plans and applied tools to the daily staffing work. After 18 months, the results were in:

- On 90-day turnover, they went from 16.6% to 8.4%
- On the external time to fill, they went from 88 days to 53 days (40%)
- On cost per external hire they went from $1,482 to $977 (34%)

None of the three indicators would ever show up on a financial statement but, as the company has learned by testing the theory, they have a predictive correlation with profits.

If we get what we measure, isn't it time to start measuring what we want to become? This is not to imply that we need to eliminate evaluative hard data, rather that we do not allow measurement myopia—and mania—to crowd out the all-important soft judgment based on navigational information. Because management itself cannot be measured, we have to rely on judgment, and we can use soft judgments to check hard facts.

One of the first steps toward the creation of a high-performance, process-focused organization, after the purpose is clearly set, is to create a Navigational Scorecard to measure the success of each action and the ability of that action to move us closer to the purpose. To create navigational measures, here are some basic guidelines:

- The test of a good measure is to ask if the measure helps in understanding and improving performance.
- The purpose of measures is to develop knowledge through action on the system.
- Navigational measures move away from managing people to having them understand and act on the system; act to remove causes in performance variation.
- Navigational measures help see waste and causes of waste.
- Rather than be constrained by measures, the people who do the work should use measures (and actions) that enable them to control the work.
- Understand the linkage between purpose, measures, and actions.

WHAT AND HOW ARE WE DOING?

A Navigational Scorecard is a management concept that attempts to align the organization's purpose and strategy with the work people do every day. If the purpose answers the question: "What are we here to do?" then the measure answers the question: "How do we know how we are doing?" The primary focus of the Navigational Scorecard is to help understand and improve performance, not in terms of classic units of production, but in terms of flow of value to the customer and in terms of the health of our process. The design of the scorecard is based on the ability to learn and adapt, as opposed to targets met, and the guiding principle is experimentation. The scorecard measures, then lead to actions on the workflow. Most importantly, these measures are in the hands of the employees and usually reside in the process.

In summary, when it comes to measurements, we need to move from target measures to capability measures, focusing on increasing the knowledge of how work is worked on and how to make it better. We need to stop being obsessed with financial information and targets and

FIGURE 8.11
The purpose of measurement is to develop knowledge through action on the system.

understand that the power is in the process. By removing the traditional results measures, employees are freed from the tyranny of target-obsessive management and can experiment with the best way and apply the learning. Think of it somewhat like a pilot in the cockpit, having navigational measures, in real time, and taking action to constantly improve the process (Figure 8.11).

The challenge now is for the employees of the process to read the measure from the navigational scorecard and create actions and experiments to improve the ability to achieve the purpose. I cover this in Chapter 9.

REFERENCE

1. Maskell, B. 1991. *Performance Measurement for World Class Manufacturing.* Cambridge, Mass. Productivity Press.

9

Action: Experimentation and the Scientific Method

Action is an intimate conversation with the situation by committed and knowledgeable people in search of improvement.

Don Schuon, learning guru

STOP BUMPING AND THINK

To put the above quote less politely, performance improvement might just come from smart people making stuff up as they go along and getting some of that stuff right. Process-focused experimentation is like that; it trusts people who work in the process know most about the process. And, if the people have a good problem-solving methodology, including information, skills, and authority to execute those methods, then leave them to learn and adapt the process until it is able to consistently achieve the purpose.

There is a wonderful excerpt from A. A. Milne's *Winnie-the-Pooh* series where Christopher Robin is dragging his best toy friend, Edward the Bear, down the stairs by the ear, *bump, bump, bump.* Edward the Bear thinks, as far as he knows, it is the only way of coming down the stairs, but sometimes he feels that there must be a better way, if only he could stop bumping for a moment and think of it. The Action component of Purpose–Measure–Action is about stopping and thinking about a better way. It requires experimentation, and the way to do it is through what I call treasure hunting which is action to seek out, find, and recover treasures in the process, treasures that improve the performance of the process. First, let's look closer at how action is incited.

I am not a gambler, far from it, but I often use dice to explain the power of experimentation. After we have completed a walk-through of one of the company's business processes (i.e., treasure hunting) and are back in the conference room, I bring out the dice. I tell the group, "There is no better way to demonstrate the principle of experiment, learn, and adapt and how it exposes process than with a little gambling—and a little wager."

I take one die and make the following proposition to them (Figure 9.1). If you ante up $100 to wager and I offer to pay you $450 if you guess the right number on one roll of the die, what are the odds of winning? Obviously, it's one in six. When I ask if they like those odds, most do not. Then, I take them through a probability exercise. With 1-in-6 odds, the probability of picking the winning side is slightly better than 16%. They get $450 if they are right, but there is a 5-in-6 chance (83%) of getting nothing, plus losing the wager. Without overly dissecting the math, they are, statistically, going to be losing $25 per roll (i.e., [(1/6) (450)] + [(5/6) (0)] = –$25). In a business situation, if you add a few zeroes to those numbers, not many managers would like the odds.

Then I make it more interesting. I ask, "What if the die was loaded and two thirds of the time it would come up six?" (I have replaced the one with an extra six). I add a caveat. "But you don't know that yet." So, you are no farther ahead in deciding how much to bet because of that lack

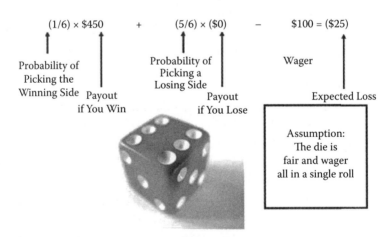

FIGURE 9.1
The probability of picking a winner is slightly better than 16%.

of knowledge. In other words, the die is not fair—like most tough business decisions—but you still don't know enough to make a better, safer bet. One side has a likelihood of coming up one third of the time and the remaining sides a probability of two fifteenths. Even though the die is loaded, without the knowledge that it's loaded, it's still not a good betting situation (Figure 9.2). When I do this with executives, a couple of guys get six, but most don't. Then I ask, "What if you knew the die was loaded for six?" Now, you know which number has a likelihood of coming up one third of the time, therefore, you are going to bet it exclusively. And, by betting on it exclusively, you are going to win, statistically, $50 instead of losing $25. It is a journey of experiments and every time we bet, we learn. However, it's important that we never stop experimenting. We need to keep it going and reinvest the learning because once we stop, we must be assuming we have a *best of class* process and we fall into the mindset that this is it, this is the best we can get and then no continuous process improvement is possible. If we don't continually certify, through constant experimentation, that the process is the best it can be, we can be certain it soon will not be.

Knowledge comes from experimentation.

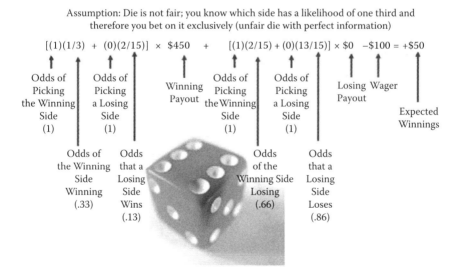

FIGURE 9.2
What if you knew the die was loaded for six?

So *knowing* that the die is loaded, what would the wagering strategy be in order to discover if there is a best side to bet (i.e., a better way) and capitalize on the knowledge we learn as the rolls increase? I ask them: "How would you change the game from one in which you are likely to lose to one you have better odds at winning?" Most people immediately realize that the only way they can do that is by gaining the knowledge that it's loaded. And, the only way to do that is *play as many rolls as possible while losing as little as possible.* So, instead of betting $100, they bet $1 at a time and discover the six coming up more often. By the time they have dropped $10, they have a much better knowledge of how it works and can then make better bets (i.e., decisions). It's about developing knowledge through experimentation. After discussion, it becomes clear that, rather than stake a lot on a few big changes, it's better to stake a little on many rolls (i.e., small experiments) and observe the outcomes. The assumption is that there is no big bang or blanket solution and that a series of experiments offers far less risk and far better odds. The opportunity is to design the process on purpose through ongoing experimentation. Only by a series of small wagers, measured on how much we learn—not how much we improved—will we ultimately get the performance improvement we are seeking. Action then is many small initiatives in the form of experiments. I sometimes call this "trystorming" because the goal is to develop a deeper understanding of the process and improve it from that perspective. Any experiment is an action designed to learn how to continuously improve the process to create more value with less waste.

Learning requires failure.

THE SCIENTIFIC METHOD

The fundamentals of experimental thinking are rooted in the scientific method, but the scientific method is *not* rooted in traditional business thinking. It is counterintuitive for most management because learning through experimentation and discovery is foreign to the business practitioner who is steeped in thoughtware that is based on acting on "a sure thing." And, yet, so much of business is uncertain that the idea of testing hypotheses should be standard procedure. The essence of experimentation is to see the phenomena through direct observation.

I repeat: If we can't see the process, we can't do anything about it, and, if we can't describe what we are doing as a process, we don't know what we are doing. Observation is at the core of experimentation, so we need to look at how the process performs against whatever standards there are and if we don't know the standards, then we don't know what the purpose of the process is and, yet, that is the foundation of the Purpose–Measure–Action methodology (see Chapter 8). We must formulate a prediction for the hypothesis (i.e., increase throughput of the number of pallets of adhesive per shift) and confirm that if, in fact, the focus shifts to the output of the process (i.e., pallets of product) rather than input (i.e., labor efficiency of mixing pounds of adhesives), then perfor-mance, as measured by throughput, time, and cost, will improve. The experiment is planned, where the goals, deliverables, responsibilities, and metrics of the experiment are established, and then a trial is imple-mented (countermeasures to eliminate and remove waste). It can be for a few days, a month, or even 90 days, after which a reflection period is taken to check the effects of the trial. After review, either the hypothesis is refined or another experiment is run. Or, the new way is documented as *standard work* and the rest of the organization is taught the new way, and then, if required, it can be rolled out across the organization. In this way, a small bet (the experiment) is made prior to committing to an across-the-board implementation, thus acting safely to eliminate waste and create value while learning and adapting. Then do it again and again. By standard work, we can establish precise procedures for doing things in the best way possible, as proven through the experiment. The stan-dard work provides a baseline for continuous improvement and a con-stant condition with which to experiment from. If everyone did the work differently, there would be too many variables and no conditions for a proper scientific experiment.

FEAR OF FAILURE IS THE ENEMY

The fundamental principle of the scientific method is that *the experiment informs the hypothesis*. In rolling the die, the hypothesis is that one num-ber might come up more often than others and the experiment sets out to prove, or disprove, that. In business terms, the hypothesis could be lower costs, faster turnaround, better quality—whatever you are trying to achieve, and the best way to achieve that is to experiment your way toward it, one small, investigative action at a time. Unfortunately, the main barrier to the application of this scientific principle is the inherent fear of failure embedded in organizations, and management's psyche—the thoughtware—thereby, creating an avoidance of perceived risk in experimentation as a legitimate action plan (i.e., the die could be wrong). Fear of failure is the enemy of innovation and ingenuity and it gets in the way of experimentation. Action on the process to remove waste and create value through experimentation is only effective when the experimenter accepts that the purpose of the experiment (the action) is to learn and then, based on the learnings, to adapt. Growth comes from doing things for which the outcomes cannot be predicted, which in turn, come from experimentation (think research and testing), which leads to learning. The sticking point is that learning requires failing. After all, a true hypothesis can only be tested through experiment if it is possible to refute it. However, the prospect of failure, for all kinds of psychological and sociological reasons, is not part of the business organization's DNA. And yet, to build a process-focused organization through the Purpose–Measure–Action model, failure must be acceptable; in fact, celebrated. Part of the mantra of a process-focused organization and the action it takes is failure. Fail fast and fail effectively through lots of experimentation. It is about incremental, low-risk improvement. Conventional organizations do not have the requisite thoughtware for developing a process of discovery, learning, reflection, and adaption and, yet, in the twenty-first century, it is imperative in order to make faster, more informed, better decisions. Ironically, the majority of our processes are not easily and readily adaptable to change despite the fact that western civilization has been built on this scientific principle. Adaptive and evolutionary systems by their very nature involve experimentation. Continuous process improvement in business requires us to learn and adapt through constant observation, assessment, trialing, and evaluation of the processes.

The process needs to be designed so that the people are willing and able to repetitively run a series of experiments and problem solve, every day. They need to think and breathe process. They need a process mind. They need to understand that they are not making shirts, picking parts, filling buckets, they are solving problems to meet the purpose, which is, in the end, to fulfill customer demand. They know how their part of the process relates to that. The only method that I know that achieves this is the scientific method: Run an experiment and see if the experiment moves you closer to an answer. Like in rolling the dice. Process thinking and action based on a hypothesis is fundamentally different from functional thinking and actions based on historical facts. The former uses more set-base decision making, while the latter uses more point-based decision making. In set-based thinking, you begin measuring the set, the process, and, as you get closer, you refine the targets. For example, if I ask you: "Can we meet Monday at 3 p.m.?" You will likely say, "No, I'm busy. How about Tuesday at five?" And I say, "No, I'm tied up." Then the following day you are going out of town and I'm out of town the next week. Conversely, if I said to you: "Are you available to meet next month?" the odds are that I will get a "yes." It's not point-based; it's set-based. Once we decide it's the next month, we have eliminated the other 11 months and we can focus on a week in the month. It's a process working a clear condition (a meeting), but with a grey territory to be traversed to get there. Let's do it in a series of sets: month, week, day, and hour. It's as Rother defines in his book, *Toyota Kata*,[1] we are establishing a target condition (i.e., month), then another target condition (i.e., week), until we secure a one-hour meeting between us. Action through experimentation is a daily habit of the process mind.

The scientific method is measuring the validity of one particular variance, a problem, against the purpose of the process (e.g., to load the trailer), which allows us to see what is working and what is not. It's incremental and iterative. When a CEO asks, "Where do I start?" I say, "Do the simplest thing that works and experiment your way there." Then, as you get feedback from that simple thing, learn, adapt, and expand. Simplicity is about not trying to increase performance by 40% overnight, rather doing it incrementally until reaching 40%. For example, Figure 9.3 represents an accounts payable process (illustrated in 41 slides) where each slide is one discrete activity in the process. By looking at the process with this granularity (achieved through a 90-minute Treasure Hunt), we will come to understand that only 3 (of the 41) activities represent value (work) in the customer's eyes, while the rest of the activities are waste (i.e. things getting in the way of work). This means 93% of the activities are impeding, rather than facilitating, the flow of value to fulfilling the purpose of the process (i.e. to fulfill the customer's need of receiving payment). Put another way, those three steps represent only 2 hours in the entire lapsed time of 3 days required to complete all 41 steps (7% value-adding process, by activity, and less than 3%, by time). By eliminating, combining, sequencing, or otherwise simplifying some of these "wasteful" activities an immediate incremental improvement in the process can be realized. Further experimentation may eventually result in a better process closer to its true value of 2 hours as opposed to 3 days.

Treasure Hunt of Accounts Payable Process in Pictures	 Overnight envelope with original invoice is received	 Open Envelope and Extract Contents
 Log on to e-mail	 Open e-mail from Vendor	 Launch e-mail attachment (invoice) into Excel
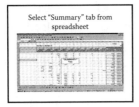 Select "Summary" tab from spreadsheet	 Add totals for "Service1" and "Service 2"	 Open second spreadsheet
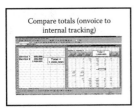 Compare totals (onvoice to internal tracking)	 Confirm numbers match (if not perform research and reconciliation steps)	 Print copy of second spreadsheet

FIGURE 9.3

This series of slides demonstrates the 41 discrete activities required to pay an invoice. In this example, of 41 activities, 3 were work (value) and the rest were things that got in the way of work (waste). The process took three business days, but only required two hours of time, which is a cost-to-purpose ratio of 99.97%. In other words, value to the customer was only added .027% of the time the invoice resided in the process. The rest was waste.

Place hardcopy of internal tracking spreadsheet with invoice

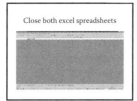
Close both excel spreadsheets

Compose new e-mail to distribution indicating invoice has reconciled

Address and send out confirmation e-mail to 4 individuals

Print hardcopy of e-mail

Put hardcopy of e-mail with original copy of invoice and reconciliation spreadsheet

Staple three sheets together

Initial and date invoice

Walk documents to finance

Stage documents at finance

Open on line reconciliation database

Locate report for the month of the invoice

Locate column for invoice data

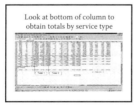
Look at bottom of column to obtain totals by service type

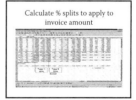
Calculate % splits to apply to invoice amount

FIGURE 9.3 (*Continued*)

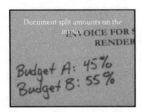

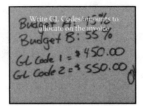

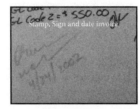

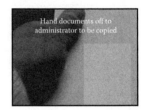

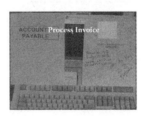

FIGURE 9.3 (Continued)

THE CORNERSTONE OF CONTINUOUS IMPROVEMENT

Experimentation anchors continuous improvement because continuous improvement comes from constant experimentation. The experiment is always successful because we learn more about how we can continuously improve the process and performance. *The purpose is to improve the process.* That's it. Sounds simple, but it's not easy. It's trial and error that constantly validates the process. It's about understanding that by tomorrow you have to be better and do differently than today. Remember, you are not trying to increase the bottom line by 20% by Tuesday, you are trying to build a sustainable process that exposes problems, therefore, allowing you to outperform the competition. Sometimes I take management onto the floor and put them in an area for 30 minutes to observe, and, with a flip chart, come up with a minimum of 10 (often up to 30) opportunities for experimentation. The question they are looking to answer is: What is stopping the process from working to the documented standard? Often, one of the key observations is that there is no standard. Yet, without a standard there can be no basis for improvement and, without that, there can be no foundation for an experiment. We are looking for variances from what they think the standard is. Then, in the next 30 minutes, they spend the time creating a countermeasure to one of the variances that they saw. Right away, this creates a bias toward action. It demonstrates that if you give smart people the right information and trust them to make good decisions, they will do it. Standard work not only establishes precise procedures for each employee's work, it is critical as a baseline for problem solving and improving activities. Standard work is not just documentation, it is about teaching, measuring, and improving the process.

Action is about creating a problem-solving environment and that comes from having a clear purpose and navigational measures. We are looking to create people to "run to the fire" and understand what caused the fire because root cause problem solving is a core competency of the process-focused organization. By setting up resources of people and increasing their creative knowledge for problem solving, we can lower overall costs. It is about leveraging the power of the people to act so that they remove complexity from the flow.

If you want to build a ship, don't drum up men to gather wood, divide the work, and give orders. Instead, teach them to yearn for the vast and endless sea.

Antoine de Saint-Exupēry
French writer and World War II pioneering aviator

We were working with the financial services unit of a large company who had morphed its back-office credit card processing into part of a retail banking operation which, in a further effort to differentiate its credit card offering, had developed an auto service club and roadside assistance service for cardholders. The competition for credit cards has become vicious, as retail bankers have recognized the power of incentives and differentiators like loyalty programs as important marketing tools for acquiring new customers. Customers who might be resistant to switching banks may sign up for a second bank's credit card if the rewards are attractive enough. In this case, roadside assistance is an example of the benefits of holding a particular card. More and more luxury car companies, and some midrange car companies, are providing GPS packages that include roadside assistance. However, the car companies need a service-level agreement (SLA) with a roadside assistance provider to deliver the service. Huge call centers have taken such SLAs as this on. A call center I worked with did its own credit card service-level agreements. Contracts are awarded to service providers based on the cost-per-claim and the customer service response rate. For this company, the cost-per-claims was about 10% above the required rate to be competitive in the bid for these contracts.

We began with a demand analysis in order to determine what the demand on the process was. Process redesign always starts with understanding customer demand because every process has three vital components: (1) the demand, (2) the resources to deliver the demand, and (3) the process that uses those resources to deliver the demand. If you can't change demand (i.e., we don't want your business), or if you can't change the resources (i.e., we can't afford more costs), then your only alternative is process redesign. The third option, process redesign, is about solving for "demand" within the resource constraint. The purpose of the process is to meet demand, thus the need to design the process on purpose. The demand analysis showed that there was considerable variety in calls that didn't fit "the blue screen." The blue screen is a predisposed algorithm that calls up a screen with a set of standard work instructions for the operator, which allows him/her to ask the right questions and give the answers needed to optimally solve the problem. That is, send Joe's tow truck from 5th Street to Elm Street because that's the optimal, customer value, cost-effective response. In most cases, the decision is straightforward, but there are many variations to the type of calls received; too many to create blue screens for all variations. For example, a customer could have a break-down in a remote area and the help has to travel a distance greater than the norm and the costs are potentially prohibitive. So, we began to think of any call outside a certain norm, in other words, an abnormal variation, as an outlier. There were standard and repeat calls, let's call them normal variations, and there were these outliers that could potentially create bigger problems or, conversely, create high customer satisfaction and value if properly solved. For example, a breakdown in a remote location, far from a service station might best be solved by sending a professional to fix the problem (e.g. flat tire, mechanical failure, etc.) on-site rather than incurring a prohibitive towing charge. These were not normal blue screen problems. We placed these outliers into a problem-solving process value chain that was not encumbered by functional structure or standard metrics, such as average-handle-time or blue-screen-accuracy or call-wait-time. In these outlier cases, the response team was there to solve the problem. Once these exceptions to the rule were solved and measured individually, the average cost dropped under the 10% delta required. By getting inside the process, we were able to identify major variances that were impacting costs and then changed the measuring methods to reflect the reality and take action.

When the primacy of process is recognized and then enacted through the Purpose–Measure–Action model, process improvement and overall performance increases, significantly. The starting point is extreme emersion in a Treasure Hunt, which I cover in the next two chapters.

REFERENCE

1. Rother, M. 2012. *Toyota kata: Managing people for improvement, adaptiveness, and superior results*. New York: McGraw-Hill.

10

How to Conduct a Treasure Hunt

A problem is not a crisis; it is a treasure.

ECONOMISTS HIDE PROBLEMS

Have you ever had a burning desire to go somewhere and dig up hidden treasure? Most of us have treasure hunted in some form, whether taking a cruise to exotic locations, wandering through a museum, or the more mundane weekend activity of rummaging through garage sales. Even buying a lottery ticket is a type of treasure hunting. Humans are natural treasure hunters.

I am a professional treasure hunter, constantly helping organizations to uncover the treasure that allows them to dramatically increase performance. However, it hasn't always been so. The truth is, I am a reformed treasure *hider,* a recovering concealer of treasures. In fact, I used to be a serial hider of problems. I was formally trained and educated as an economist, a labor economist, but I am all better now. As a recovering economist, I struggle to expose waste rather than amortize it (read *conceal*). My cure started when I discovered there were three types of economists, those who can count and those who can't.

An economist is the antithesis of a treasure hunter. Economists love to hide problems in processes and create fancy names for them, like amortization. Amortization can technically be defined as payback, but amortization is actually economist-speak for "hiding waste," just like "quantitative easing" is an economist's code word for printing money. I like to say that if you actually understand these complex, euphemistic economic terms, you are not paying attention and, worse, you are avoiding problems.

A problem is not a crisis, it is a treasure. It's a deviation from expected standards or results and it is a good thing—a discovery. As treasure hunters, we want to always look for, find, and resolve problems, never bury them. The purpose of the treasure hunt, and its simplicity, is to observe, discover, and learn in the real place where work happens. There is no simpler or more powerful approach to creating a process-focused organization than treasure hunting.

GETTING STARTED

As I described earlier, a treasure hunt starts by gathering some people together who work inside the process, are customers of—or suppliers to—the process or perhaps support the process in some way (e.g. support functions like: information technology, procurement, customer service, etc.) A well-conducted treasure hunt on a healthy process will reveal more disruptions to flow than sitting in a classroom mapping a lousy process. The treasure hunt team observe, learn, and document the process by asking key questions: *What? Who? Where? When? Why? How?* Ultimately, treasure hunters are looking to investigate "why," explore "what if," and determine "how." From this, they identify the value-added and non-value-added activities and take that learning to develop a compelling story of "what is" and "what could be." It starts with a team of three to eight people (ideally five to six) who identify a piece of the process and begin to walk it, step-by-step, from beginning to end. They collect and analyze data and the information they gather is real and relevant. The exercise is based on daily, but difficult to see, operational optics. The team's objectives are to:

- understand the flow of information, products/materials, and people required to complete a customer requirement by experiencing it;
- examine and document the current process flow and understand where people must go, who they must talk to, and what data sources they must access to get information to do their job;
- identify areas of waste, problems, and opportunities; and
- collect and analyze process data in preparation for process improvement.

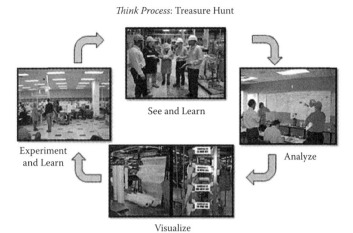

FIGURE 10.1
The fours steps of a treasure hunt.

The treasure hunt consists of four steps (Figure 10.1):

1. See and learn the process.
2. Analyze the current condition.
3. Visualize the target condition.
4. Experiment and learn.

Step 1: See and Learn the Process (Figure 10.2)

A: Select the Process

There are treasures in every process and you approach the process through direct observation. It begins with some initial analysis on where to start. Do not get in the classic trap of analysis paralysis, rather focus on being "about right." There are some guiding questions that can be used in selecting a process.

- What is the problem?
- Where is it observed?
- What area is it in?
- What do your current measures tell you?
- What process is it in?

A critical point is time. If conducting the treasure hunt takes longer than 90 to 120 minutes, it means the selected process is too large and requires

Step 1: See and Learn the Process

A. Select process
B. Prepare for treasure hunt
C. Conduct treasure hunt

FIGURE 10.2
Treasure hunting.

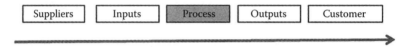

FIGURE 10.3
Documenting the scope of the treasure hunt (SIPOC).

additional treasure hunts. Trying to look too wide prevents treasure hunters from looking deep enough and observing with the intensity and discipline required to reveal treasure. Remember, you are not going to find $20 bills; they probably have been discovered. You are looking for $20s worth of pennies—and there's plenty of them. You are riding a bicycle through the city streets, not sitting in an air-conditioned, tinted-window, tour bus.

A useful method in defining the scope of the process is the completion of a supplier–inputs–process–outputs–customer (SIPOC) form (Figure 10.3).

The SIPOC is an initial step in helping shift focus from a narrow, functional perspective to an end-to-end horizontal perspective, from a discrete activity to the end-to-end process focused on output. For example, instead of thinking of a purchasing department (i.e., specialized function), think of its output; material availability. When you think output, you are looking at things from the customer's perspective and then you can work upstream to frame the process that fulfills the demand. The discipline of completing this exercise is that it allows the team to do some quality thinking around the process including: if the process even exists, how it is measured, what information systems are currently used to enable it, how many resources are involved, what preliminary opportunities for improvement might be available, etc.? Eventually, it allows the team to identify the actual scope of the treasure hunt and begin preparing for it (Figure 10.4).

In this example (Figure 10.5), the scope has been selected, called *place* and *chase,* and it covers a scope of process from the placement of a purchase order (PO) for a particular piece of equipment to the receipt of that piece of equipment. Often it is useful to identify a specific PO and a precise piece of equipment that has already been purchased and then reenact the process. In this case, the team chose to follow the journey of large freezers that were being bought centrally for restaurants that were located across the country. By opting for a specific example, the team avoids the anticipated "noise" created by the inevitable "what if" questions and "depends on" replies. Now, the answer can be a specific PO and a specific piece of equipment and the journey it took. Although there will be the predictable comments suggesting that this particular example does not represent what normally happens, do not believe it. In all cases, a treasure hunt will reveal 80% of the truth and inevitably at least one great treasure will be unearthed. It is not the precision of the selected process that matters, it's the act of observing, seeing, and learning that matters. If you find no waste, either you have not learned to look and listen, or you just hit incredible odds—go buy a lottery ticket. We are now wandering the backstreet of Chennai, not gazing out the modern and insulated office tower window.

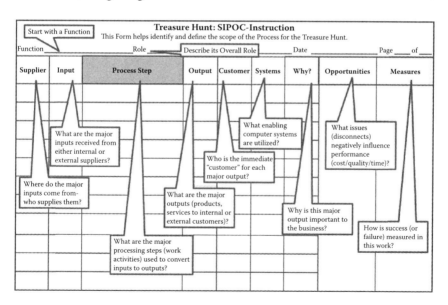

FIGURE 10.4
Instructions for documenting the scope of the treasure hunt.

Treasure Hunt: SIPOC-Example

This Form helps identify and define the scope of the Process for the Treasure Hunt.

Function_Equipment Purchasing_Role_ source all equip for all stores   Date_   Page_   of_

Supplier	Input	Process Step	Output	Customer	Systems	Why?	Opportunities	Measures
Eng'eers	Drawings	Create Template	Schedule A	Operations	T-Tracker	Mgmt sign off	• Sort requests by type • Reduce handling • Merge complaints dept with central • 75% of volume in Q4 • Impact of green demands • 50% non standard-too much variation • Multiple spreadsheets • Siloized • Checkers checking the checkers	• Lead times • Pricing • Equip costs
Project plan	New equip required	Select Product/Vendor	Quotes			List of new items		
Quote	P.O.	Place & Chase	Receive equip		SAP	Buy new equip		
Supply chain	Min/Max Trigger	Create PO	Buy New equip					
		Customer service	Repair, supplier, invoice,			Solve customer issues		

FIGURE 10.5

Example of a completed SIPOC form.

B: Prepare for the Treasure Hunt and Assign Roles

It is important that each member of the treasure hunt be assigned and trained on at least one specific role. Although the participants have a common objective, they are bringing a unique set of eyes and focus to the process. As more treasure hunts are conducted, you will discover other roles and responsibilities that are indigenous to your business, but as a starting point, these are the key roles required. They include:

- Tour guide
- Scribe
- Mapmaker
- Archeologist/pacer
- Wasteologist
- Process router

Tour Guide

This is the subject matter expert and the curator of the process who escorts the team through the scope. If the scope covers more than one area of expertise then the tour guide and another role can swap positions at the appropriate point. The tour guide's responsibility is to provide team members with an excursion that exposes the daily reality of the process so that, in a structured way, questions about the process are answered, from each role, whether mapmaker or wasteologist:

- What do we do? What are the steps involved?
- Who does it? Who is responsible for the steps?
- Where do we do it? Where do we go to do the steps?
- When do we do it? How long do the steps take to do?
- How do we do it? What are the steps that are followed?
- What is value added? What will our customers pay for?
- What is necessary? What is waste?

No one knows more about that process than the tour guide because he/she has worked inside it on a daily basis for a long time.

Scribe

This person documents the sequence of activities and other data on the Treasure Hunt Worksheet (Figure 10.6), completing the description of

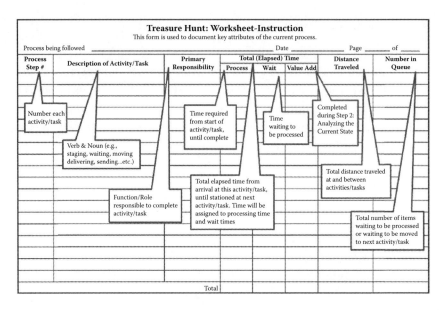

FIGURE 10.6

Instructions for documenting the treasure hunt in real time.

each processing step, the person or group with primary responsibility for that step, the total time of the process, the meters/feet or paces traveled between activities, the number of items in queue, etc. Note that many of these data points are provided by other members of the treasure hunt team; however, the scribe is accountable for their proper documentation. As with all roles, there are instruction sheets with callouts and examples for ease of training.

In the example, notice the granularity of the process steps (Figure 10.7); small enough to define if it is "work" or that "which gets in the way of work." Discrete enough to be able to see the waste: waiting, excessive motion, multiple data entry points, communication gaps, pointless meanings, rework, poor planning, etc. You are learning to look carefully so as to be able to see the treasures for which you are seeking. Sometimes you need to look very closely to see Waldo. That is why the treasure hunt team has multiple members, each looking from a different perspective. The scribe is tasked with journalizing as much of this expedition as possible. Of particular interest are the wait times, when nothing appears to be happening to the specific artifact being followed. The team should think of itself in a very *Zen*-like manner as "being" the PO document or "being" the physical part as it flows through the process, often sitting in an in-basket

Treasure Hunt: Worksheet-Example

This form is used to document key attributes of the current process

Process being followed _____ Date _____ Page ___ of ___

Process Step#	Description of Activity/Task	Primary Responsibility	Process	Wait	Value Add	Distance Travelled	Number in Queue
			Total (Elapsed) Time				
1	Open envelope	Receptionist	4 hours	1 min			27
2	Extract contents	Receptionist					
3	Log onto e-mail	AP clerk		2 min			16
4	Open e-mail from vendor	AP clerk		1 min			
5	Select summary tab from spreadsheet	AP clerk		1 min			
6	Add totals for service 1 and service 2	AP clerk		5 min			
7	Open second spread sheet	AP clerk		1 min			
8	Compare totals	AP clerk		5 min			
9	Print copy of second spread sheet	AP clerk		1 min			
10	Walk to printer & return	AP clerk		6 min		180m	
11	Compose email re: reconciliation			10 min			
12	Print 4 copies of email	AP clerk					
13	Walk to printer & return					180m	
14	Put invoice, reconcile & email in envelope						
15	Walk to finance	Mail				630	
16	Stage documents at finance	Accounts Mgr	3 days	1 min			5
17	Move to Controllers office for sign off	Controller				120	7
18							

FIGURE 10.7

First page of a completed treasure hunt on an accounts payable process.

(e.g., email), or idling in a storage area or tucked away on a spreadsheet. By following a document while it gets printed, copied, and filed, or a widget as it gets moved, staged, moved again, and staged again, the team will see the buried treasure in plain sight as in the Accounts Payable Process example.

Mapmaker

Nothing visually represents flow, or lack thereof, like a geographical map. The mapmaker traces the flow of material, parts, information, products, and people, then draws the path of each using colored pens to identify different flows (e.g., material flow–blue, product flow–green, information flow–red, people flow–black). The layout is a topographical drawing of the work area, which indicates workstations, equipment, storage, and staging locations. The drawing shows where people must go and the path of raw materials, work-in-process, and finished goods. The team often calls it their Spaghetti Map (Figure 10.8).

Treasure hunting an electronic process is no different. The map connects all the legacy systems, standalone spreadsheets, and personal computing devices required to complete the process. The electronic process is no different than the pencil and paper approach, except it is much faster and cheaper, thus, allowing information to be managed closer to real time,

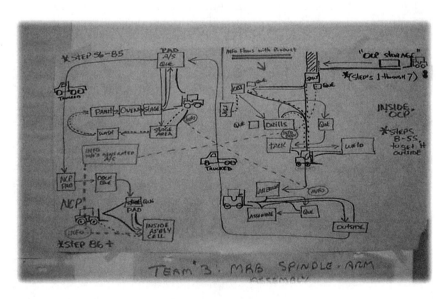

FIGURE 10.8
Completed topographical (Spaghetti) Map.

because massive amounts of data can be crunched at the push of a button. The execution of the process requiring the information being calculated still needs to be done and it is still part of the process. Enabling technologies represent processes; they are not processes themselves. Once, when working for a large pharmaceutical company, I spent significant time at its beautiful headquarters' campus, composed of numerous buildings, laboratories, employee recreational facilities, classrooms, offices, common areas, stores, meeting rooms, restaurants—none of which were connected in the original construction. Only after months and months of observation (as to where people trampled between buildings as demonstrated by the packed-down paths), were formal sidewalks and bordering foliage installed. I often marvel at the power of applying technology to enable the natural process rather than forcing the people to adapt to the technology (i.e., sidewalks arbitrarily installed with the best intentions of architects well removed from the daily activity as opposed to being designed by those who do the activity daily). Mapping a flow of information connecting technologies requires seeing the true process, not one the IT experts designed and installed. The mapmaker needs to be vigilant when mapping information flow, regardless of the technology enabling it. Recall the illustration of Daniel's credit card (Chapter 6). In that case, the map created was a series of screen prints, linked together based on the physical location of the specific operator (e.g., Field Marketing Representative, Data Entry Operator, OCR, Fraud Specialist, or Credit Bureau). Although each role sat in a different silo, all of the information was passed along electronically.

Figure 10.9 is a map from the treasure hunt of an information flow process. (i.e., transactional). The Post-it® notes represent where data are moved: from spreadsheet to firmware software, from spreadsheet to manual, from spreadsheet to spreadsheet, from manual to enterprise firmware, etc. In each case, there is an indication of duplication of information.

Archeologist/Pacer

This role is somewhat flexible, and depends on the type of process selected by the treasure hunters. In a logistics or transactional process, it is critical to measure distances traveled between each step and report distance to the scribe. Also, it is important to document and count the work in process at each staging and storage point. For example, how much work is in an in-basket or staged in front of a machine? Or how many purchase requests are in a system or calls stacked up waiting to be answered? Recall, in the claims process in Chennai, when doing batches of 50, there would, at any

FIGURE 10.9
Treasure hunt team documentation of the flow of information from order entry to production order.

point in time, be 49 claims staged (i.e., either completed and waiting to go out or not yet done and waiting to come in because the operator was always working on one claim at any particular moment). In doing one-piece flow, there would be no waiting. In a transactional process, as well as a relationship or knowledge process, it is critical to collect artifacts, such as screen prints or spreadsheets, and software application screens, including the number of fields where data are entered and number of screens accessed per process (Figure 10.10).

Wasteologists

It is critical to identify all the disruptions to flow and it is the wasteologist who, based on observations and input from other team members, identifies and documents sources of waste on the Waste Chart (Figure 10.11). It is useful to have two wasteologists, one with a camera and one documenting the sightings (Figure 10.12). The team can accommodate more treasure hunters by adding wasteologists as spotters. The spotters are looking for flow improvements, bottleneck operations, changes needed in workplace layout, and they should use generous amounts of What, Who, When, Where,

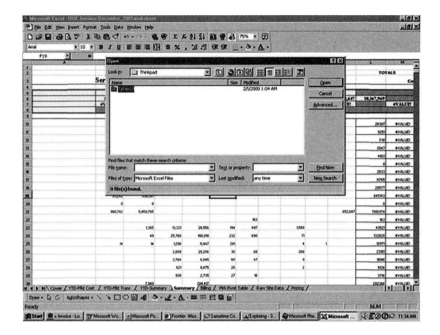

FIGURE 10.10
Screen print captured by the archeologist during the treasure hunt in an accounts payable process.

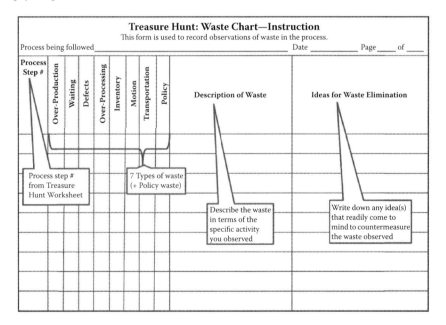

FIGURE 10.11
Instructions used to capture waste during the treasure hunt.

FIGURE 10.12
Picture of waste taken during the treasure hunt by the wasteologist: transactions waiting for processing.

How, and Why. When finished, the cameraperson should be able to put a photo storyboard together of the treasure hunt—without any photos of people, because people are not waste, even though their activities might be.

Note the types of waste listed on the chart (Figure 10.13). These are the classic seven wastes described by Lean thinkers as activities that consume resources, but create no value for the customer. There is also a waste classification called *policy*. From my personal experience, on 1,600+ treasure hunts, policy waste represents upward of 80% of all waste in most transactional, relationship, and knowledge transfer processes. For example, the distribution center that set a target for each order selector to pick 1,350 units per shift is a good example of policy waste. It is a policy not aligned with the overall purpose of the process (load the trailer). Policy waste is nearly always detrimental to fulfilling customer demand. I have set out some waste definitions at the end of this chapter that will assist the wasteologist.

Process Router

As the treasure hunting team members physically walk the flow of the process, they use a real order/router (Figure 10.14) that is indicative of the standard process flow. A router is a document that describes the sequence

Treasure Hunt: Waste Chart-Example

This form is used to record observations of waste in the process

Process being followed   Date   Page   of

Process Step #	Over-Production	Waiting	Defects	Over-Processing	Inventory	Motion	Transportation	Policy	Description of Waste	Ideas for Waste Elimination
5						×			Walking around cart lifting boxes looking for summary tags	Set a standard for how and where to place tags on cart
14						×			Walking around cart looking for first store	Training of fillers on arranging stores on cart properly
15						×			Having to rotate and move box in order to see label	Need reliable method for labeling and loading
18			×						Rearranging poorly placed product on cart	Need to stack efficiently every time-training
20			×						Filler not putting a number of pieces on summary tag	Complete summary tag with pieces and ID#
20			×						No way for consolidator to check for tag verification	Create visual markings for location of carts for easy consolidation
24		×							No set standard of where to take empty carts (go to demag?) lined up?	Visual marking of where cart should go and who should move
27		×			×				Pails for filling are the wrong size and in the way	Set up min/max system for line side stocking of pails

FIGURE 10.13

Completed page of Waste Chart in a product assembly process.

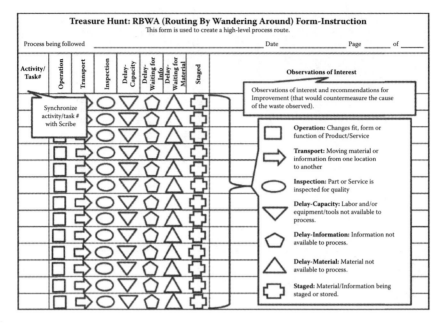

FIGURE 10.14
Instructions for completing the RBWA form during the treasure hunt.

of operations the process goes through to complete its journey. The process router is assigned to create that routing document. While walking the process, use the Routing-By-Wandering-Around (RBWA) form (Figure 10.15) to categorize what is going on at each step that the scribe records. It is important that this role, and all roles, follow the tour guide and move at the pace of the scribe.

C: Conduct the Treasure Hunt

As always, respect for people is of the highest priority. When treasure hunting, you are encroaching, albeit, with permission, in the special places where people go every day so they can feed their families, contribute to society, and develop personally, so treat their space with reverence and follow the protocol for entering and exiting people's areas. You are in their home; act accordingly. Communicate with the right people: manager, supervisor, coach, and the people you are observing and interviewing. Be courteous and nonjudgmental, and ensure the team sticks together. No sidebar discussions or group cliques. You should think of the treasure hunt as three critical elements: go see, ask why, and show respect.

Treasure Hunt: RBWA (Routing By Wandering Around) Form-Example								

This form is used to create a high level process route.

Process being followed _____ Date _____ Page _____ of _____

Activity/ Task#	Operation	Transport	Inspection	Delay-Capacity	Delay-Waiting for Info	Delay-Waiting for Material	Staged	Observations of Interest
	■	⇨	◯	▽	⬠	△	✚	Hard to find what items to buy
	□	⬛	◯	▽	⬠	△	✚	Multiple photocopying-back and forth to printer
	□	⇨	◯	▼	⬠	△	✚	Only reviewed on Fridays
	□	⇨	●	▽	⬠	△	✚	Budgets are decentralized
	□	⬛	◯	▽	⬠	△	✚	Getting signatures
	□	⇨	◯	▽	⬟	△	✚	Waiting approvals
	□	⇨	◯	▽	⬠	△	✚	
	□	⇨	◯	▽	⬠	△	✚	
	□	⇨	◯	▽	⬠	△	✚	
	□	⇨	◯	▽	⬠	△	✚	
	□	⇨	◯	▽	⬠	△	✚	
	□	⇨	◯	▽	⬠	△	✚	
	□	⇨	◯	▽	⬠	△	✚	

FIGURE 10.15
Partially completed "routing by wandering around" form.

Step 2: Analyze the Current Condition

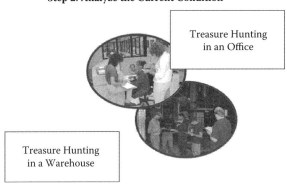

Treasure Hunting in an Office

Treasure Hunting in a Warehouse

FIGURE 10.16
Treasure hunters in action.

Step 2: Analyze the Current Condition (Figure 10.16)

In Figure 10.17, the treasure hunt team is discussing the points of possible drill sites, where rich amounts of waste have been identified. This is being done by depicting value-adding activities in different colors. This process flow chart, created from the documents completed during the hunt,

Step 2: Analyze Your Current Condition

A. Process flow chart

B. Spaghetti map

C. Snake chart

D. Process scorecard

E. Treasures

F. Storyboard

FIGURE 10.17
Treasure hunt team analyzing the treasures found on a recently completed treasure hunt.

describes the highest-level view of the end-to-end process. The team now has the ability to see the current situation as it really is down in the streets, as the extreme immersion tourists might see in a city.

Once the treasure hunt has been completed, the team returns to a room with sufficient wall space, lots of Post-it notes (at least three colors), flip-chart paper, masking tape, and plenty of colored markers. It is time to analyze the treasures they have collected. The task is to create a report covering all of the six critical chapters (A through F in Figure 10.17). Each part of the report is to be done on flipchart paper so that it can be posted and seen by all (Figure 10.17). The information needs to be tactile, visible, and in real time. Computers are not needed, no PowerPoint® or Excel® spreadsheets. Pretty doesn't count. This is about presenting the hard-core, messy truth.

Treasure Hunt Findings Report

A: Process Flow Chart

The team creates a Process Flow Chart (Figure 10.18) of all the discrete tasks identified on the scribe's worksheet (left-hand column). The tasks are designated with a different colored Post-it note, based on whether they are classified by the team as things getting in the way of work (disruptions to flow) or work (value, things the customer would pay for). Each Post-it note has a verb and a noun to describe the task/activity (e.g., move pail, enter address, pick item, copy document), using the discrete step number (top left of note); the time required to complete the task (bottom right of note); and the position/function responsible for the task (e.g., machine operator,

Step 2: Analyze Your Current Condition

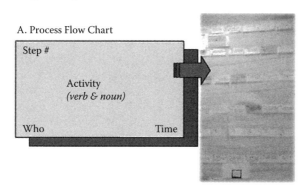

A. Process Flow Chart

FIGURE 10.18
Are the "activities" observed during the treasure hunt facilitating or disrupting flow?

data entry clerk, business analyst, software tester, attending nurse, order selector, etc.). It is important for the team, when determining the classification of the task as to its value, to make this decision through the eyes of the customer, which may best be calibrated by asking:

- Does the action change the fit, form, or function?
- Is the customer willing to pay for the action?

Write the activities/steps onto Post-it® notes (the router can help here) and place and sequence Post-it notes on flipchart paper.

- Use one color for value-added steps.
- Use a different color for non-value-added steps.
- Use a different color for staging or waiting steps.

B: Spaghetti Chart (Figure 10.19)

From the map created by the mapmaker, transfer the movement of product, information, and materials to flipchart paper. Indicate the different flows using different color markers and number each step—using the same numbers as the Process Flow Chart. Once the topographical map is recreated, it is not difficult to see why it is called a Spaghetti Chart. Just as the Process Flow Chart created with the Post-it notes provides a view of where the treasures are, the Spaghetti Chart begins to lay out a ground route into the areas where disruptions to flow exist. So, be very thoughtful in your discussions about value; it must be seen from the eyes of

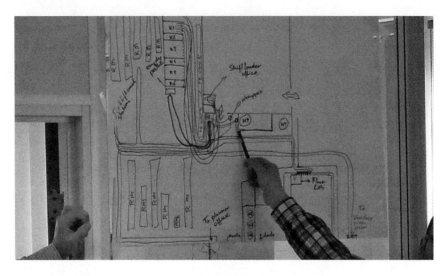

FIGURE 10.19
Topographical map showing where all the *treasure rich* areas reside.

the customer. If not, the treasures will be difficult to see. It is intellectually lazy to indicate an activity as value when it is really only of value to the company or deemed "necessary" because regulators say so. Think about the purpose of the process and what the real indicators of success say. The Spaghetti Chart helps reassure your assessment of work versus things that get in the way of work, assuring you are not rationalizing or perhaps being defensive. Never forget that the process has powerful impetus and clings to the status quo, so be sure to fight back and challenge the activities in the process, always calibrating them against the common purpose.

C: Snake Chart

Often referred to as the Information or Material Flow Chart, the Snake Chart (Figure 10.20) illustrates the numerous times the treasure hunt team crossed functional silos from one department or function to another (Figure 10.21). Each time there is a crossing, there is a hand-off and, each time there is a hand-off, there is a liability. Even if every hand-off was flawless 99% of the time, if we assume 10 hand-offs, the process is less than 90% reliable. The Snake Chart reveals opportunities to redesign a process-focused organization simply by eliminating all the hand-offs. With no hand-offs (i.e., no white space), the place where the disruption to flow is observed, where it originates, and where it is controlled, can be located in the chain of value under the one point of influence—the customer—as

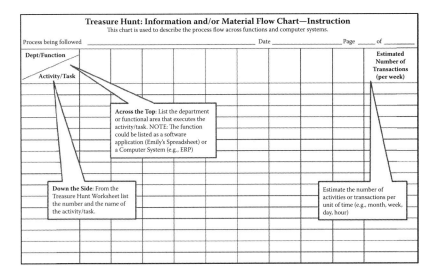

FIGURE 10.20
Instructions for illustrating where the "silo walls" impede flow of value to the customer.

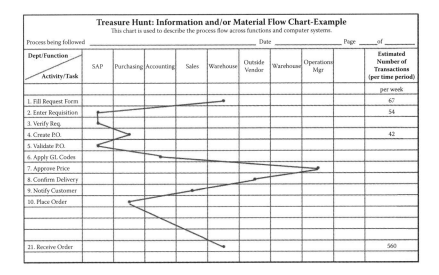

FIGURE 10.21
Completed chart illustrating where the blockages to flow reside.

opposed to multiple "masters" by referring to the Snake Chart. Be sure to include legacy systems (i.e., CRM, ERP, HRMS, etc., or any home-grown, patched-together scheduling system, order tracker, knowledge bases, master schedules, etc.) as well as departments and functions identified on the horizontal axis (Figure 10.22). They could be receiving, holding, and

Step 2: Analyze Current Condition

C. Part/Information Flow (Snake) Chart

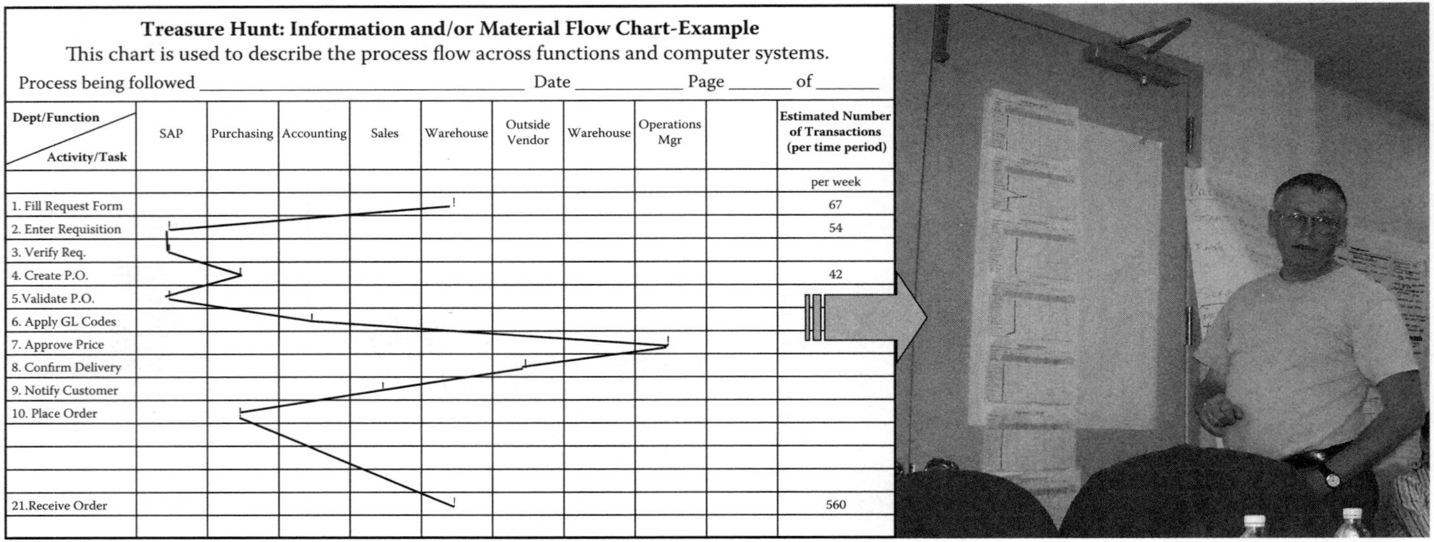

Treasure Hunt: Information and/or Material Flow Chart-Example

This chart is used to describe the process flow across functions and computer systems.

Process being followed _____ Date _____ Page _____ of _____

Dept/Function Activity/Task	SAP	Purchasing	Accounting	Sales	Warehouse	Outside Vendor	Warehouse	Operations Mgr	Estimated Number of Transactions (per time period)
									per week
1. Fill Request Form									67
2. Enter Requisition									54
3. Verify Req.									
4. Create P.O.									42
5. Validate P.O.									
6. Apply GL Codes									
7. Approve Price									
8. Confirm Delivery									
9. Notify Customer									
10. Place Order									
21. Receive Order									560

FIGURE 10.22

Treasure hunter presenting the depth and breadth of the organization's structural barriers to flow.

releasing information critical to the health of the process and you need to know how much "the system" ensnares the process with silly policies that command new workarounds. You want to be able to see them in your analysis.

D: Process Scorecard

When properly conducted, the treasure hunt reveals some interesting information, specifically, some data points that can be converted into a Scorecard. The elements of the Scorecard are operational data points that can be understood and impacted by actions from the people who live in the process. The Scorecard does not consist of abstract and distant metrics, rather they are real, tactile, meaningful measures that help understand and improve the process. They are navigational in that they help understand and improve the process by leading to problem-solving actions on the process. Here are the fundamental measures that are common to most processes; however, the treasure hunt team may want to add or delete some to suit their particular hunting area. The team should develop a summary sheet on a flipchart collecting the following data (Figure 10.23 and Figure 10.24):

- Number of activities/tasks/steps—from the worksheet
- Number of value-added tasks—from the worksheet
- Percent of value-added—calculation of first two steps
- Distance traveled

Step 2: Analyze Your Current Condition

D. Process Scorecard

- # of activities/tasks
- # of value-added tasks
- % value-added
- Distance traveled
- # of screens accessed
- # of fields entered
- total process time
- total value-time
- % of value-added time
- # of checking tasks
- # of handoffs
- # of queues
- # of items in queue

FIGURE 10.23
Treasure hunter presenting the quantifiable value of the treasure found on their hunt.

Measures	Current Condition	Target Condition	Change
Treasure Hunt: Process Scorecard Template Template to create Scorecard on a Flipchart for both the Current Condition and Target Condition NOTE: Some Measures may not apply (e.g., distance traveled when process is 100% electronic)			
	Treasure Hunt	Vision	Improvement
1. # of Activities/Tasks			
2. # Value-Added Tasks			
3. % Value-Added Tasks			
4. Distance Traveled			
5. # Screens Accessed			
6. # Entry Fields			
7. Total Elapsed/Process Time			
8. Total Value-Added Time			
9. % Value-Added			
10. # Storage Points			
11. # of Checking Steps			
12. # of Handoffs			
13. # of Staging Steps			
14. # in Queue (all staging steps)			
15.			
16.			

FIGURE 10.24

Sample scorecard template: the measurement categories can be modified, added to, or deleted based on the nature of the treasure hunt.

- Number of screens accessed
- Number of fields entered
- Total process time; how long would the process have taken?
- Total value time; how much time spent on value-added steps?
- Percent of value-added time—calculation
- Number of storage tasks
- Number of checking tasks
- Number of hand-offs (including manual to computer)
- Number of queues (stages, delays, nonflow, etc.)
- Number of items in queue (pieces, units, orders, requests, etc.)

Remember, the natural linkage between Purpose–Measure–Action. We are collecting navigational information about the process, information embedded in, not extrapolated from, the process. These will be the metrics that guide the experiment. They are for the benefit of the treasure hunt team, not external eyes filtering the data through dollar signs. The leadership team is always accountable to assure linkage of the experiment to the strategy (i.e., Strategic Navigational Chart as discussed in Chapter 8).

E: Treasure Chest

Once again, on a flipchart, the team will record all the treasures revealed, including the disruptions to flow, the problems, ideas, and, of course, waste discovered (Figure 10.25). This flipchart is the first effort to identify improvement opportunities; preliminary ideas captured while in the heat of the hunt. Where possible, the waste and type of waste (as defined at the end of this chapter), as well as the activity number (i.e., from the scribe's worksheet), should be registered. The activities designated as waste can now be considered eligible for elimination or reduction or perhaps combined with other activities or resequenced to create improved flow (Figure 10.26). You are beginning to determine what excavating equipment, what information and what resources will be required to follow the topographical map (Spaghetti Map) into the areas the Process Flow Map is indicating as performance improvement opportunities.

F: Storyboard

Never has the maxim, "A picture is worth a thousand words," been more appropriate than on a treasure hunt because we learn through direct observations (Figure 10.27). As mentioned earlier, 83% of what we learn

Treasure Hunt: Waste, Problems & Ideas (Treasures) Template Use this Template on a Flipchart to identify Treasures. NOTE: This is the first step in identifying waste elimination opportunities.			
Activity/ Task #	Waste Observed	Type of Waste	Improvement Opportunity

FIGURE 10.25
The Treasure Chest: begin to form ideas on opportunities to eliminate disruptions to flow.

Step 2: Analyze Your Current Condition

E. Treasures (waste, problems, ideas)

• Reduce

• Eliminate

• Combine

• Re-sequence

FIGURE 10.26

Documenting ideas to eliminate, combine, reduce and/or re-sequence activities to improve the flow of value to the customer.

Step 2: Analyze Your Current Condition

F. Storyboard

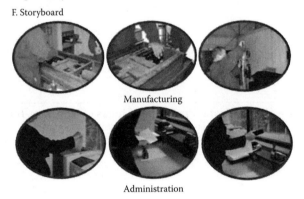

Manufacturing

Administration

FIGURE 10.27

A picture really does reveal the wastes!

is through the visual sense, 90% of information to the brain is visual, and it is processed 60,000 times faster than text.[1] This is another reason that flipcharts and colored markers are used instead of spreadsheets and word documents in treasure hunt report-outs. The cameraperson will have taken a series of photos, which are now edited into a story of the treasure hunt. This is presented with as much creativity as the team wants because it is telling a powerful, emotional, and often humorous story. Sometimes the photos are of silly things or a series of "workarounds" or perhaps a photo of each of the examples of waste and, as illustrated in Figure 10.27, it is a series of shots of the activities, in sequence, required to complete the process.

As a final note on Step 2, Analyzing the Current Condition, it is valuable to bring a few people into the room who were not part of the treasure hunt and share with them a report of your six elements of discovery. It is powerful to do two or three treasure hunts simultaneously and have each team report to each other. It makes for a very compelling story as it brings reality to life. In preparation for the report, assign a team member to each part and follow this agenda:

A. Linear Process Flow Chart (including screen prints)
    a. Focus on silly things
    b. Focus on value-added steps and why
B. Spaghetti Map (topographical)
C. Snake Chart (part Information/flow chart)
    a. Focus on hand-offs
    b. Focus on reverse flow
D. Process Scorecard
E. Treasure Chest (Identified wastes /problems and ideas to eliminate)
F. Storyboard (pictures)

Step 3: Visualize the Target (Future) Condition (Figure 10.28)

The team now turns from the current condition to the desired future state of the process. The purpose of this exercise is to describe the future condition of the same process as it might look if all the disruptions to flow were removed. Keep in mind, *it must be designed without spending any*

Step 3: Visualize Your Target Condition

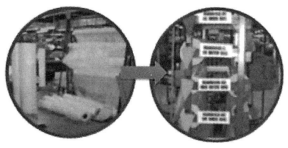

A. Vision statement(s)   D. Layout/distance for new vision
B. New process flow   E. Issues and challenges
C. Data analysis   F. Actions & resources

FIGURE 10.28
Imagine the process without waste.

additional money. The challenge is to create a better process with brains, not bucks, and to state the possibilities without waste, and ultimately design and experiment toward implementing the new process.

Making a Difference

Visualizing the future condition helps to keep a focus on where the organization is going, not simply where it is. It allows for a focus on the right and positive things and creates enthusiasm, energy, and passion. It helps the team recognize the difference they can make rather than focus on what they cannot do (Figure 10.29). With so much accessible opportunity discovered in the treasure hunt and the truth of the direct observations, the team is positioned for success and feels confident about what can be achieved. It begins with high-level vision statements and drills down into specific, immediate, and simple actions or experiments the team can do to remove the disruptions to the flow.

A: Vision Statement(s)

Now the team begins to develop a story of how they can create a process that is faster (time), better (quality), more productive (cost effective), and simpler (more reliable) (Figure 10.30). These statements are triggered from the Treasure Hunt Report and may include: declarations around the operating metrics collected; less hand-offs, higher value-adding ratios, less time, fewer checking steps, less distance traveled, enter information

FIGURE 10.29
Treasure hunt team designing the future condition.

Step 3: Visualize Your Target Condition

A. Write Vision Statement

Focus on:

• Business objectives
• What's important
• People, not money
• What's achievable
• Process

FIGURE 10.30

The treasure hunt team's vision for the new waste free layout.

only once, reduce the batch size, etc. The vision statement from the distribution center was "touch it once and put it on the trailer" (i.e., Action) and "achieve a 17-minute time to load the trailer" (i.e., Purpose), as measured by the "number of pallets on the loading dock, but not on the trailer" (i.e., navigational measure), and the "variance from 17 minutes" (i.e., evaluative measure). The back-office credit card applications team envisioned a two-day turnaround and the adhesives team wanted to eliminate and sustain a condition with no backlog and a five-day lead time. These possibilities were not just distant dreams, but real possibilities based on the enormous amount of opportunity discovered from their treasure hunts. They are not only doable, but there is energy behind them. Time-based vision statements are powerful because time is universally understood and it can be reduced to the elimination of those activities that get in the way of work. Time recognizes not the redundancy of people, but the redundancy of the activities in which they are engaged. As such, it is liberating; it says, let's get rid of the "stupid and sillies." And people are gung-ho to do that. Time reduction is empowering and accessible, whereas, cost-based language is threatening and coated with a negative sense of job loss and belt tightening.

B: Design the New Process Flow

First, describe the new process as it will look in the future, including details regarding time and operation. Then repeat the process used to map the flow of the current process, including a re-creation of both the Process Flow Chart and the Snake Chart (Figure 10.31). It is important to put as much control

Step 3: Visualize Your Target Condition

B. Design New Process Flow

(deleted steps tagged)

FIGURE 10.31

Creating statements describing the process as we want it to be.

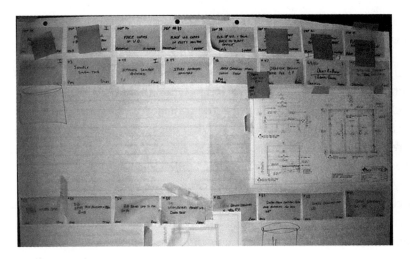

FIGURE 10.32

Square Post-it notes cover the waste that will be eliminated in the new process.

of the process inside the process owner's function as possible by reducing or eliminating all hand-offs as illustrated in the current state Snake Chart. The actual conducting of the experiment (discussed in the next chapter) usually requires the creation of a discrete stream of value through to the customer, such that those who work in the process can see the flow. This step identifies that stream of value, where it starts, where it ends, and who works inside it. Eventually, the process is designed without the disruptions to flow.

As illustrated in Figure 10.32, for every non-value-adding activity removed (i.e., square Post-it note) from the original Process Flow Chart, there must be an action created. This will become part of the action plan (section F below).

C: Data Analysis

To quantify the change in performance, analyze the results of the new process in the same way that the current process was analyzed. Compare these numbers to the current process and record them on the same flip-chart page created for the current process (Figure 10.33). This provides a measure of improvement in the process based on navigational metrics that represent an improvement in operational performance. For example, a reduction in the number of wasteful activities, which reduces the time it takes to complete the process, and any time reduction in the process is a reduction in the cost of operating the process. In turn, this can be an increase in inventory turns and an increase in throughput, all at the same investment point. Resist the temptation to quantify the numbers in any excruciating detail; they are directionally correct and about right. They are close enough because they are measuring the process itself and assessing its health. Whether 2 or 4% of the activities are value-adding is not important, the story of the data is that there is not 70 or 80% that are value-adding. The story is that the 10:1 ratio of waste to value exists in the process. If there is not a general belief that a dramatic reduction in time can be achieved through the elimination of those disruptions to flow—as manifested by increased throughput, higher inventory turns, or a reduction in waiting time (i.e., meaning cycle or lead-time reductions) and a productivity increase (i.e., throughput per asset employed)—and the elimination of disruptions to flow does not translate to the bottom line financially, then find new metrics. The chart (Figure 10.34) shows the before and after data for the new vision

Step 3: Visualize Your Target Condition

C. Analyze Data for New Process

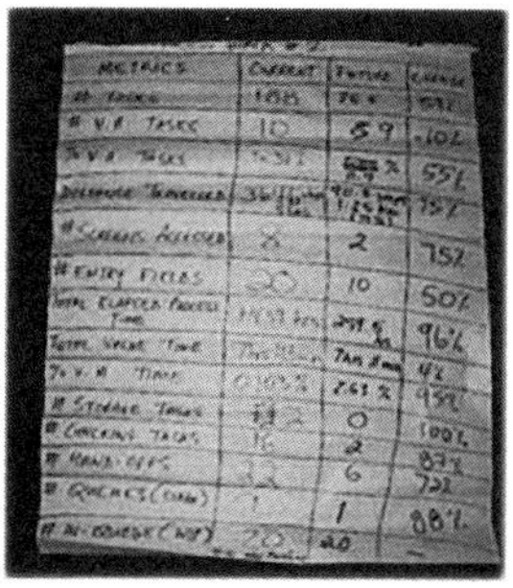

FIGURE 10.33
Flipcharting the scorecard: Comparison of current and future.

		Current	Future	Change	% Change
1	# of tasks	91.0	65.0	−26.0	−29%
2	# of VA tasks	14.0	14.0	0.0	0%
3	% of VA tasks	15%	22%	6%	40%
4	Distance traveled	250.0	100.0	−150.0	−60%
5	Total elapsed time (days)	32.0	19.0	−13.0	−41%
6	Total VA time	3.5	3.5	0.0	0%
7	% of VA time	11%	18%	7%	68%
8	# of Storage points	0.0	0.0	0.0	0%
9	# of Checking steps	27.0	21.0	−6.0	−22%
10	# of Hand-offs	31.0	24.0	−7.0	−23%
11	# of Staging steps	29.0	19.0	−10.0	−34%
12	# in Queue	15.0	10.0	−5.0	−33%

FIGURE 10.34

Completed process scorecard: Before and after measures for a design engineering process.

		Current	Future	% Change
1	# of tasks	30	14	53%
2	# of VA tasks	4	4	0%
3	% of VA tasks	13%	29%	114%
4	Distance traveled	587	337	43%
5	Total elapsed time (10 hr days)	17	0.7	96%
6	Total VA time (minutes)	138	70	49%
7	% of VA time	1.4%	16.7%	1132%
8	# of Storage points	1	1	0%
9	# of Checking steps	2	2	0%
10	# of Hands-offs	5	5	0%
11	# of Staging steps	9	0	100%
12	# in Queue	312	6	98%

FIGURE 10.35

Completed process scorecard: Before and after measures for a manufacturing process.

from a treasure hunt team looking at a design engineering process from "request to quote" through "quote to engineering release." The experiment resulted in a reduction of 41% in total cycle time in this process through the elimination of waste as identified by the hunt. That's a lot of treasure.

In Figure 10.35 the data analysis of a simple product component that resulted in an experiment and ultimate rollout of a new, continuous flow process (e.g., production cell or value stream) that reduced the "time-in-the-shop" from 17 days to *one* day. More treasure.

D: Layout and Distance for New Vision

Next, the team creates a layout that shows the flow of the new process (Figure 10.36). For example, they show the new co-location of people and equipment required to achieve the vision for the future. They calculate the distance traveled in the improved process and record the data as well as the reduction in the movement of information in and out of manual and computer systems. Simply put, this is a better route to the destination when asking the GPS to "avoid all waste end-to-end" as the preferred route characteristic. The previous route criteria were likely programmed for "reduce costs at each discrete resource." The new process is creating a more direct route to customer value, redoing and eliminating detours and multiple back and forths, and the duplication of data into multiple spreadsheets of firmware software.

E: Issues and Challenges

This is where team members should put on their black hats and offer every reason as to why the new process will *not* work. Bring on the voice of defenders of the status quo and document what they say. This is a healthy session of cleansing the system of all negative thoughts and throwing out the rationalizations, excuses, and "they won't let us" thinking. This is a reality check to review—perceived or real—barriers, concerns, risks, roadblocks, tensions and support, that are preventing buy-in. Questions to ask include:

- Who are the customers and do we understand their perspective?
- Where will buy-in be especially important for success of the new process?

Step 3: Visualize Your Target Condition

D. Design Layout and Distance

FIGURE 10.36
Flipcharting the new process flow layout.

- What are the potential roadblocks?
- With whom do we need to communicate?
- Who needs to review and approve decisions?
- Will we need any partners or collaborators?
- Will we need specific information or advice?
- Will we need special systems or equipment?
- Will we need to use special tools or templates?
- How will we evaluate success?
- What risks should we anticipate and manage?

Position a new flipchart page beside the vision statements and record the issues and challenges for each statement. Consider each of these potential impediments and discuss and discover countermeasures to each one. The objective of this exercise is to recognize that, for the most part, what are perceived as limitations to the realization of our new process, are readily removed when the costs and the benefits are compared.

F: Actions and Resources

Over a decade ago, in my book, *The Future: You Can't Get There from Here* (OTI Inc,. 2004), I addressed the same idea of trying to change the thoughtware and now, I am pleased to say, "you *can* get there from here," if you follow this process. At this point, we can identify specific actions needed to overcome the issues and challenges and make the vision a reality (Figure 10.37). Answer the Who? What? Where? When? Why? How?

Step 3: Visualize Your Target Condition

E. Record the Issues & Challenges

Each Vision Statement may have:

- Barriers
- Tensions
- Concerns
- Risks
- Competition
- Roadblocks
- Support required
- Buy-in needed

FIGURE 10.37
Challenging the team: anticipate and prepare for challenges to implementation.

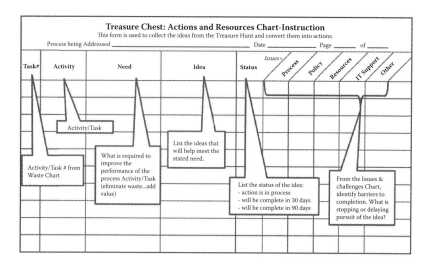

FIGURE 10.38
Treasure Chest instructions to collect opportunities to eliminate waste.

and detail the actions to be worked on and the resources required. Place a fresh flipchart page beside the issues and challenges, and record for each statement the actions to execute. Again, be sure that each action generated by covering up the Post-it notes on the Process Flow Map created from the treasure hunt is captured. Complete the Treasure Chest chart and create an idea bank of possible actions that can be converted into an experiment that can be deployed in Step 4. Using the issues and challenges data collected, determine if the actions required are a change in policy or process or alternatively, an issue of redeploying resources or converting/removing unenabling technology. Of course, it could be something else entirely, but these are the big four (Figure 10.38 and Figure 10.39).

Step 4: Experiment and Learn

The team has created a current state of affairs and a vision of the future, which forms the hypothesis to begin closing the gap between the two states. Now it is time to create, schedule, and run an experiment (Figure 10.40).

The Freedom of Experimenting

Real efficiencies only come from the freedom to experiment by the people who do the work and, to do this, the measures must be in the hands of the people who do the work. One of the problems in the vertical

Treasure Chest: Actions and Resources Chart-Example

This form is used to collect all the ideas from the Treasure Hunt and convert them into actions.

Process being Addressed _____ I.T. support Process _____ Date _____ Page _____ of _____

Task #	Activity	Need	Idea	Status	Issues				
					Process	Policy	Resources	IT Support	Other
18	Small capex approval	Fast track approval under certain $ threshold	Local pre-approval up to $ 50k	In process	X	X			
43–51	New PC	Quick response request	Laptop Kan Ban	In process	X	X		X	
21	Provide PC tools	Ability to send customers current version files	Update Office 2011	90 days				X	Need budget approval

FIGURE 10.39

Example of a Treasure Chest of ideas to eliminate waste in an IT support process.

Top: Employees are experimenting with rearranging their workstations in a better sequence, based on the learning from their treasure hunt. Bottom left: Operator is experimenting with a new layout for his equipment. Bottom right: An employee is experimenting with a new way to store his supplies.

FIGURE 10.40
The experiments begin.

structure is that decisions tend to get bigger the higher up the ladder they are made. As we move decision-making farther from the core process, up to the people occupying the office tower, and away from the people living in the street, there tends to be less and less oversight. Often there is more oversight of a $100 frontline expenditure than a $20 million decision made by a CEO. Shouldn't there be more freedom at lower levels with treasure hunting being a never-ending journey and a daily habit?

Vertically-structured organizations, specialist functions, and siloized departments—each interested in optimizing their part with policies, measures, and management systems—hide disruptions in the horizontal flow of value to the customer. As such, the value of buried treasure goes unmeasured and, yet, it is perhaps the biggest unaddressed cost of doing business. As I have said, it is the processes, more than the products or services, that will legislate our wealth-generating successes. Business processes are chock full of buried treasure that can dramatically improve the ability to fulfill customer demand. Seventy percent—that's 70%—of defecting customers would have stayed if a problem had been resolved the first time instead of requiring multiple interactions.[2] It costs 6 to 10 times as much to attract a new customer as it does to keep an existing customer.[3] A report by Accenture said that more than half of surveyed customers said they had left at least one vendor because of poor service. And again, they would have stayed if the problem had been resolved.[4] This need is increased when one considers that the typical customer tells, on average, 16 other people about a poor service experience, but only tells 9 about good ones.[5] And, it has a

Step 4: Experiment and Learn

A. Create experiment
B. Schedule experiment
C. Run experiment

FIGURE 10.41

Three steps to running an experiment. In this photo, the operator is experimenting with a new layout for his equipment.

multiplier effect, therefore, poor service is talked about again and again. This isn't an inescapable cost of doing business; it's a blatant failure to provide a process that can meet customer requirements. Discovering buried treasure unlocks deeply-ingrained problems that prevent most organizations from consistently fulfilling customer demand efficiently and effectively (Figure 10.41).

Problems are opportunities in disguise.

Augustine "Og" Mandino
Author of *The Greatest Salesman in the World*

WASTE, WASTE, WASTE ... AND MORE WASTE

Taiichi Ohno (1912–1990) was the first to codify the seven wastes he saw in mass production (see below), referring to any human activity that absorbs resources, but creates no value. These wastes, and others, are things in processes that get in the way of the work required to fulfill customer requirements. Some examples include:

- Mistakes that require rectification
- Making stuff no one wants
- Doing activities that are not really needed

- Moving people, materials, and information from one place to another without any purpose
- Waiting around for something upstream to happen

Since then, many other waste categories have been added, such as:

- Waste of not using full human creativity or potential
- Complexity
- Waste of energy
- Waste of labor
- Waste resulting from misaligned policy
- Lack of role clarity
- Meaningless measures, etc.

The amount of waste and its definitions may only be limited by the imagination; however, for purposes of an effective treasure hunt, in any type of process (i.e., logistics, transactional, relationship, knowledge transfer) from call centers to back offices and from laboratories to distribution centers, the original seven wastes given to us by Ohno, plus the one covering policy, account for over 80% of the things that cause disruptions to flow. I have listed dozens of waste categories from my over 1,600 treasure hunts, categorized as strategy, policy, and process wastes, but for now let's keep to the powerful truths of Taiichi Ohno and the Toyota Production System. For your initial treasure hunts, you should at least understand the essential classifications of activities that cause a disruption to the flow in your processes.

The Seven "Deadly" Wastes—Plus One

1. Waste of Overproduction

Definition: Producing more than is needed or producing faster than is needed (considered the most fundamental waste because it leads to most other wastes). This includes:

- Producing items earlier or in greater quantities than required by the customer
- Producing more or faster information than the customer needs and/or more information than the next process needs
- Creating reports no one reads or making more copies than needed

Characteristics:

- Inventory stockpiles
- Extra equipment/investment and manpower
- Unbalanced material flow
- Complex inventory management
- Wasted space—outside or off-premise storage
- Large lot sizes
- Hidden problems—scrap and rework

Causes:

- Incapable process
- Lack of communication
- Reward system/local optimization
- Changeover times

2. Waste of Defects

Definition: Mistakes that require rectification:

- Repair or replacement of a product or service to meet customer requirements
- Data entry errors, pricing errors, missing information, missed specifications, or lost records

Characteristics:

- Manpower to inspect or rework
- Quarantined and scrap products
- Firefighting culture (reactive, not proactive)
- Fault-finding/defensiveness
- Poor service/customer relations

Causes:

- Incapable process/excess variation
- Lack of standard work

- Lack of training/operator errors
- Incapable suppliers

3. Waste of Conveyance/Transportation

Definition: Moving materials and/or information from place to place or moving material or information in and out of storage or systems/spreadsheets/templates, etc.:

- Contrary to the concept of continuous flow production
- Transfer of information or materials from people to people, department to department, application to application

Characteristics:

- Manpower to inspect or rework
- Quarantined and scrap products
- Firefighting culture (reactive, not proactive)
- Fault-finding/defensiveness
- Poor service/customer relations

Causes:

- Incapable process/excess variation
- Lack of standard work
- Lack of training/operator errors
- Incapable suppliers

4. Waste of Over-Processing

Definition: Producing to tolerances or specifications in excess of customer requirements:

- Processing with over-capable equipment

Characteristics:

- Process bottlenecks
- Over-sized equipment
- No clear customer specifications
- Redundant approvals/excess information and reports

Causes:

- Engineering changes without process changes
- New technology used on old products
- Lack of customer input regarding requirements
- Ineffective policies and procedures
- Decision making at inappropriate levels

5. *Waste of Storage (Excess Inventory)*

Definition: Any supply in excess of levels needed to meet customer requirements:

- Excessive procurement of materials creates clutter and excessive storage / staging locations
- Information needed to fulfill the organizational requirements is not provided accurately, timely or in a format that is easy to use
- Information is inaccurate, incomplete or late
- A year's worth of production or office supplies is received at the same time
- Waiting files, e-mail queues
- Excess raw material, WIP, finished goods

Characteristics:

- Inventory stockpiles—FISH (First-In-Still-Here), not FIFO (First-In-First-Out)
- Massive rework effort when problems are encountered
- Long lead time for engineering changes
- Excess material handling and storage space
- Slow response to changes in customer demand

Causes:

- Incapable processes and suppliers
- Uncontrolled bottleneck process
- Inaccurate forecasts
- Reward system/local optimization
- Long changeover times

6. Waste of Waiting

Definition: Idle time created by a lack of synchronization (balance) within a process or between processes:

- Employees watching over automated machines, waiting for the next step to be processed
- Having no work due to lack of stock, lack of information, and machine/system downtime, etc.
- Resource (people, time, money) lost waiting for information, a meeting, a signature, a returned phone call, a copier or computer breakdown

Characteristics:

- Person waiting for machine
- Machine waiting for person (load/unload)
- Person waiting for person
- Unbalanced work
- Equipment downtime

Causes:

- Inconsistent work methods
- Long machine changeover
- Poor man/machine effectiveness
- Lack of proper machine

7. Waste of Motion

Definition: Movement of people or machines that does not add value to the product/service:

- Walking, searching for files, extra clicks or keystrokes, clearing away files on the desk, gathering information, looking through manuals and catalogs, or handling paperwork, reaching

Characteristics:

- Looking/walking to find tools
- Excess reaching or bending

- Machines/materials too far apart
- Conveyors between equipment
- "Busy" movements between process cycles

Causes:

- Equipment, office, and plant layout
- Lack of workplace organization
- Inconsistent work methods
- Large batch sizes

8. Policy Waste

Definition: Rules, procedures, strategies, and policies that are misaligned with the purpose of the process and thus cause activities that disrupt the flow of value to the customer:

- Creating incentives that lead to optimizing a part of the process, a function, or a department at the expense of the continuous flow of the entire value delivery system

Characteristics:

- Information processed and transferred in batches
- Functions aligned by department
- Sequential versus concurrent activities
- Entering information multiple times in multiple places
- Stand-alone spreadsheets and software programs
- Elongated lead times

Causes:

- Sourcing to low-cost supplier regardless of minimum batch size or geographic location
- Working on resources instead of workflow
- Measuring the target of the process versus the capability of the process
- Focusing on shareholder value versus customer value
- Fear of experimentation

Waste not, want not.

REFERENCES

1. Parkinson, M. 2012. *The power of visual communication*. Online from Billion Dollar Graphics at: http://www.billiondollargraphics.com/infographics.html.
2. Reichheld, F. F., and W. E. Sassrer, Jr. 2000. Zero defections: Quality comes to services. *Harvard Business Review*, October 1.
3. Beard, R. 2011. *COA 101: A primer for the MSP on the cost of customer acquisition. The MSP Excellence Journal*, July 1. Online at: http://blog.clientheartbeat.com/9-customer-retention-strategies-for-msps/.
4. Honts, R., and J. Hansen. 2010. *Maximizing customer retention. A strategic approach to effective churn management.* Global Consumer Research report. Dublin: Accenture, 2.
5. Reichheld and Sassrer, Zero defections.

11

The Experiment: Creating a Process-Focused Organization

Our own attitude is that we are chartered with discovering the best way of doing everything and that we must regard every process employed in the business today as purely experimental.

Henry Ford

LET THE EXPERIMENTATION BEGIN

If you are sitting in a vertically-structured organization with functions operating in silos, but are serious about becoming process-focused to drive down cost while improving the ability to deliver customer value, then an end-to-end redesign is required. Experimentation must become the modus operandi, the driving force in redesigning the operation system underlying your business model. This means the design and deployment of a series of experiments that allow the organization to learn and adapt its way through a succession of target conditions, always moving toward a future condition as envisioned in the big picture developed in the treasure hunt. In the Purpose–Measure–Action Model, action is the experiments that give the enterprise access to a whole new world of continuous performance improvement that is waiting to be uncovered. Treasure hunting and experimentation are the foundation of a legitimate continuous process improvement methodology that, done right, will be "baked" into the enterprise. Continuous performance improvement is an extremely valuable and a massive cross-organization asset.

After a treasure hunt, the experimentation begins. In Chapter 10, we defined some wastes; however, there are many other wastes we can identify and eliminate and, at the end of this chapter, I have set out a long, albeit, partial, list. One such waste is complexity, where the idea is to find simple solutions instead of complex ones. Complex solutions tend to produce more waste and are harder for people to manage. A good example is the elaborate data gathering and reporting requirements at many steps of a process. Many of the jobs done by a complex system can be simplified when the process is simplified, and, through experimentation, simple ways can be discovered to process what the customer expects, respond to customer requests/needs, and ensure suppliers deliver on time and on quality. For example, I avoid Starbucks because I don't speak the language and cannot simply order a black, hot cup of "joe." Instead, I have to learn what a "venti double shot, no whip, nonfat mocha is." Sorry, that's not serving my needs. So, I'm not a regular customer.

The experiment to install a continuous flow process is best done as a model line. A model line adheres to the principle of "an inch wide and a mile deep." As described earlier in the Chennai back office processing and in the credit card acquisition process (Chapters 1 and 6), we began with a single model line in order to see the flow of information and then ran the experiment for a short period of time (i.e., a few days or 30, 60, or 90 days). At ABC Adhesives, we took one product line and ran an experiment to dramatically improve the performance and then, based on the learning, created an enterprise-wide, process-focused organization. In the last step of the treasure hunt, we designed an end-to-end experiment. Typically, such an experiment can be executed by following what I call the "Process Redesign Thoughtware Package." The inherent methodology needs to be adjusted based on circumstances and the type of process being dealt with (i.e., logistics, transactional, relationship, knowledge-based), but the essentials are the same.

EIGHT-STEP METHODOLOGY OF PROCESS REDESIGN

These eight basic steps will work in all cases (with some limitations) and they have worked well for every organization that followed them.

> **Step 1**: Analyze product types, quantities, and process sequence. Understand the customer demand and the types and frequency of that demand. Select one type of demand for the experiment (i.e., process-focused model line).

Step 2: Locate people, workstations, and equipment in the proper sequence based on the type of demand identified.

Step 3: Design a work space with minimum distance between people, workstations, and equipment.

Step 4: Process and move one piece (i.e., smallest batches possible) at a time.

Step 5: Separate people from dedicated equipment/workstations. Allow people to float to the place where the constraint in the process currently exists.

Step 6: Train people to perform multiple jobs. The purpose is to fulfill customer demand, not optimize a specific function.

Step 7: Produce at the rate of consumption.

Step 8: Distribute work evenly.

In an effort to better understand these critical steps, I will go through each using an example of a business whose performance dramatically improved after the redesign. This illustration is based on a government agency (the Agency). Though it is a part of the public service sector, in many ways it acts like a private sector enterprise. The Agency supplies secure documents to various government sectors (e.g., passports, visas, other travel documents, assorted operating licenses, lottery tickets) and draws revenue from applicants rather than taxpayers. As such, although it is part of the civil service and associated public unions, there is a revenue incentive to improve productivity. This makes it a particularly good demonstration of the power of process thoughtware, in that it enables excellent results in throughput, time, and cost even though it is a heavily legacy-based, unionized, quasi-public service, and a transactional-based setting. It's worth noting that the Agency has been diligent in keeping up with security technology (i.e., digitally printed photos of the bearer, holographic imaging, embedded chips, etc.).

In the initial treasure hunt, we focused on one type of secure document and the process from application through issuing (Figure 11.1).

The process is:

1. The Agency receives the application form (online download) from regional offices, selected retailers, embassies/missions).
2. The examiner determines if the applicant qualifies.
3. The secure document is printed at one of two centralized print centers.
4. The document is mailed out.

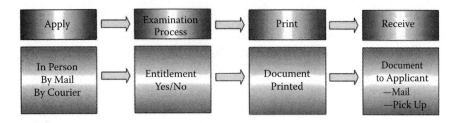

FIGURE 11.1
Current document fulfillment process: Application through issuing.

FROM BAD TO WORSE

At the start of the treasure hunt, the quoted processing time had increased to 20 days (from an earlier 10 days) with a volume of 2.5 million units per year. Like the quantification of demand in Chapter 7, this results in customer demand of one document every 15.5 seconds, assuming a 7-hour day, 220 days a year. This volume was steadily increasing for numerous reasons: post 9/11 and increased rigor of cross-border travel; trade globalization; increase in travel to China; demographics (e.g., baby boomers retiring and traveling); and more rigid risk thresholds. The Agency was coping with this volume increase and backlog by the use of overtime and by asking employees to work faster, which was resulting in multiple workarounds, increased rejection of applications, employee dissatisfaction, and decreasing involvement of employees in decision making. This is typical of a standard axiom: As pressure increases on a work process, management deploys tighter command-and-control tactics. And tighter controls cascade down, department by department, silo by silo, inch by inch, until they are fiefdoms among themselves and the customer is lost in management's bunker reinforcement activities. In a conventional organization structure, when outside pressure to perform better is applied, invariably the "silos" get thicker walls, more restrictive policies are decreed from above (president now needs to approve paperclip purchase), and measures become ever more functionalized and evaluative ("All's okay on my shift"). At this particular company, ironically, for such a regulated operation, there was very little standard work. Of course, the ultimate consequences were felt by the customer, where turnaround times stretched well beyond the quoted 10 days to an average of 60 days as there was a backlog of 15,000 applications on any given day. The treasure hunt was extremely revealing (Figure 11.2), including the remarkable fact that each application traveled 3,730 feet (0.75 kilometers) (Figure 11.3).

After some initial treasure hunts, the focus of the experiment was on the examination process (Figure 11.1). This process is shown in more detailed discrete steps in Figure 11.2. The objective of the experiment was to improve the ability to meet customer demand (i.e., throughput—convert work in process to revenue), reduce cycle time (i.e., from receipt of customer application to sending to print center), and decrease cost (i.e., productivity as expressed by units processed per FTE (full-time equivalent)).

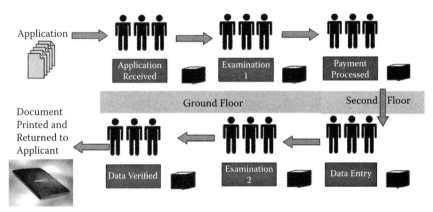

Processing Occurred on 2 Floors of Segmented Departments

FIGURE 11.2
Examination process is highly "siloized" and geographically dispersed–no flow.

Treasure Hunt Results	
Simple Application	**Treasure Hunt Observations**
Quantity of Activities	95
Quantity of Value-Adding Activities	10
% of Activities Adding Value	10.5%
Distance Traveled (feet)	3730 feet
Elapsed Time (days)	23 days
Value-Adding Time (min)	44 min
% of Time Adding Value	0.003%
Quantity of Hand-offs	21
Quantity of Stage Points	22
Number in Process	12668

FIGURE 11.3
Scorecard from the treasure hunt on the "Simple" document fulfillment process.

We began the eight steps after completing the one or more treasure hunts required to get us to a point where we were free and entitled to experiment with manageable risk.

Step 1

This step is to study what quantity of parts, information, and services are needed and the sequence of the process:

- Determine standard travel routes the products/services take.
- Group together products/services with same or similar routings.
- Identify processing times for each specific activity.
- Determine possible "families" for products/services with the same routing.
- Design a unique process flow for each "family."

In this initial step, the effort was to determine the unique volumes and flow sequence of different types of secure documents. It was determined there were essentially three types (families) as determined by the rules of time and sequence. The families were defined as: a "simple" process, a "phone call" process, and a "complex" process. Immediate rejection for obvious variances (e.g., suspected fraud) were sent out to another area of professionals.

Simple process: Simple could be processed without any additional information. The information from the treasure hunt assumed a simple application where all the required information to examine and make a disposition on the request was available in the application package.

Phone call process: Where a single phone call made to the applicant could clarify and resolve a missing piece of data within 24 hours. (Note that a message could be left, as long as the return call came within the 24 hours).

Complex process: There was information missing that would require a delay of more than 24 hours to remedy (Figure 11.4).

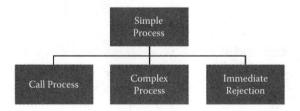

FIGURE 11.4
The new process-focused structure.

The determination for classifying families (service or product types) is based on results from a more detailed analysis, post the treasure hunt, using the Process Routing Chart, which looks at how each application traveled and how many of each there were. Figure 11.5 shows how the variety of travel routes were all processed through the same set of functions, regardless of their sequence or time to resolve. After the dedicated processes were put in place, the immediate rejections were reduced dramatically—from 33% to 11.9%—with a dedicated call process and problem-solving process (i.e., complex). This immediate and dramatic improvement in the performance of the process is because we put in a real–time dedicated problem-solving process.

Now that it was determined what possible groupings (product families with the same routing) could be aligned into similar processes, we could move on to the next step, structural alignment.

Step 2

This step includes locating people, workstations, computer terminals, and equipment in the proper sequence based on the type of demand identified.

It is always best to standardize and design the process flow for the simplest process and then move to successively more complex ones. Traditionally, the simple flow, when properly designed, will start with the ability to accommodate about 60% of the volume of total customer demand and move to a capability of accommodating about 80%, as waste is continually identified and removed through experimentation. This improvement is not based on the variety or complexity of the product or service. Rather the similarity of the process is the influencer. It determines what items of materials or information or transactions can "carpool" together each day for their journey through the process. Where there is too much variance from item to item to fit that (carpool) and location, some accommodation can be made by dropping some off earlier than others, or perhaps diverting for a short block or two. However, anything greater suggests the need for another process family. It is the time and sequence of the process that is used to determine product families. The differentiator is one of complexity, not volume. To accommodate more volume, the simple process can be duplicated and then more than one identical process stream can be set up. We looked at the simple process flow because it was the highest volume and for illustration purposes, Figure 11.6 and Figure 11.7 show the Agency's before and after—before

Process Routing Chart

Application Received	Examination #1	Call Required	Rejected	Payment Processed	Data Entry	Examination #2	Data Verified	Go to Print	Simple Process	Call Process	Complex Process	Rejected
X	X		X									X
X	X		X									X
X	X	X	X							X		
X	X			X	X		X	X	X			
X	X	X		X	X	X	X	X			X	
X	X	X	X									X
X	X	X		X	X		X	X		X		
X	X	X	X		X					X		
X	X	X			X	X				X		
X	X	X		X	X	X	X	X			X	
X	X			X	X	X	X	X			X	
Total Volumes before Process Redesign									47%	14%	7%	33%
Total Volumes after Process Redesign									58%	16%	14%	12%

FIGURE 11.5

Process Routing Chart: Identifying "families."

Typical Information Flow

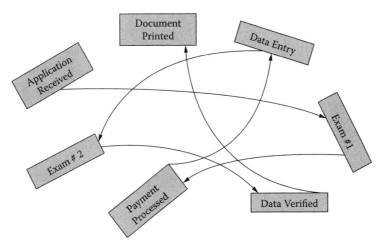

FIGURE 11.6

When there is no natural data flow, there is high likelihood of incomplete, late, or inaccurate information being passed on.

Process-Focused Design

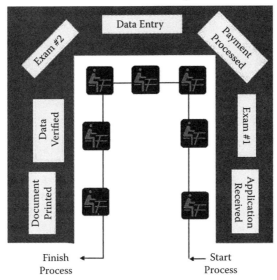

FIGURE 11.7

Creating a horizontal process flow.

people, workstations, and equipment were sequenced in a common flow, and then after.

There are multiple ways to locate everything in sequence so that the flow of value to the customer is visible and disruptions to that flow can be managed. The structure can be a straight line or linear layout arrangement with multiple machine/workstation/equipment operations, which means it is people-centered and process-flow based. Things are sequential, regardless of whether the structure is straight line or "U" shaped. The structure could be a modified circle or several processes connected. However, the structure is not an island layout with separate departments and functions living in private villages.

Set out in Figure 11.8 through Figure 11.14 are a few examples of different configurations.

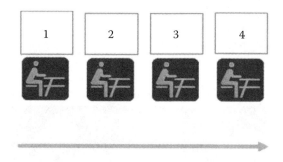

FIGURE 11.8
Design option for hand-transferred one-piece flow.

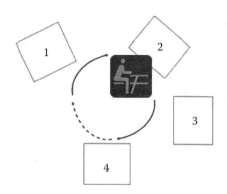

FIGURE 11.9
Design option for U-shaped one-piece flow.

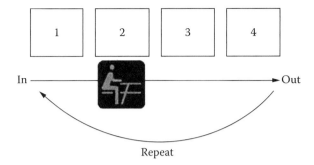

FIGURE 11.10
Design option for straight-line one-piece flow (multi-process).

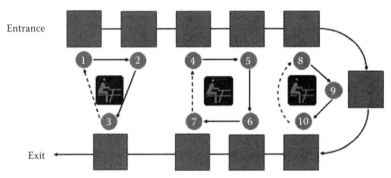

Some Advantages:
   Shortest distance for people to walk
   Work enters and leaves same place
   Increased communication (minimizes the distance between people)
   Easier to balance the work load between people - they can flex between jobs, help each other

FIGURE 11.11
Design option for "U" shaped one-piece flow. The best arrangement is often "U" shaped.

Regardless of the configuration, the sequencing of workstations, equipment, and people in a process-focused organization should be followed by Step 3, which places all activities, from end-to-end, as close together as possible.

Step 3

This step includes designing a workspace with minimum distance between people, workstations, and equipment.

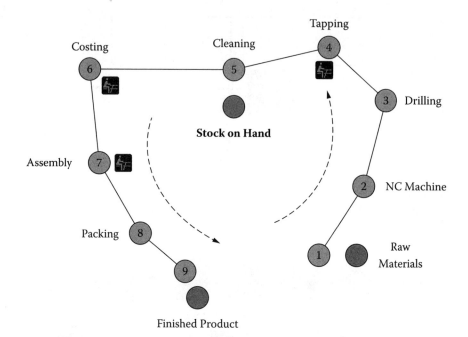

FIGURE 11.12
Design option for modified-circle one-piece flow.

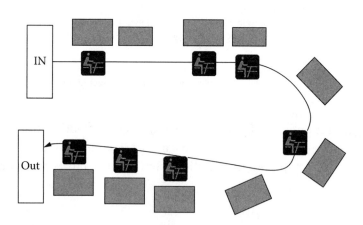

FIGURE 11.13
Design option for "U" line one-piece flow. "U" lines are basically concave.

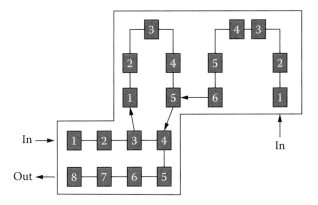

FIGURE 11.14
Design option for one-piece flow with several processes connected.

It is best to use small, dedicated equipment and workstations wherever possible and to store information and materials as close to the point of use as possible. In addition, flexibility and open space greatly enhance the ability of the process to continually learn and adapt to customers' ever-changing demand (Figure 11.15 and Figure 11.16).

As we are always running the initial experiment as a model line (a pilot), we do not need to include all the variations that the new continuous flow process can handle. We only need to sample a few variations at first and, as we constantly eliminate more waste through the experiment, additional simple process streams of value can easily be added. To give an easy image, assume a quick service restaurant (QSR) recognizes that 80% of its customers order coffee, 60% just coffee with no food, and 20% of the coffee drinkers order just black (no sugar, no milk). The initial model line design might be a process flow for just black coffee, but we soon realize it can accommodate all coffee drinkers by designing for the addition of milk and sugar, without hurting the customer demand rate. It might, for example, have a separate self-serve area for adding milk and sugar. However, it would not want to add in coffee orders that included additional requests with the coffee because the coffee demand cadence would be jeopardized. Another process-flow design would be required for coffee and perhaps items that could be retrieved in under 60 seconds (muffins, Danish, cookies), and a third process flow might be designed for customized requests (e.g., tea and a toasted sandwich).

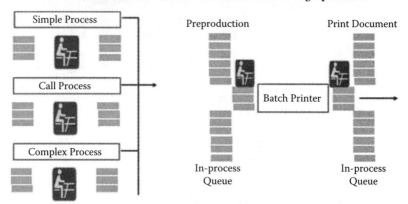

**Created Small Lot Flow through the Examination
Process, But Document Still Bottlenecked at the Printing Operation**

FIGURE 11.15
Extending the horizontal process flow from examination to printing.

**Batch printer replaced with smaller, flexible
printing pods.**

Simple Process	One-piece Unit	Printer Pod
Call Process	One-piece Unit	Printer Pod
Complex Process	One-piece Unit	Printer Pod

FIGURE 11.16
After a process redesign in the printing operation as well.

Step 4

This step is the processing and moving of one customer request/piece/
item/at a time (i.e., smallest batches possible) (Figure 11.17).

Once the new flow is designed and we have begun to eliminate "white
space," we have no need for large batches. The Agency was moving applications through the examination process, which covered two floors, and

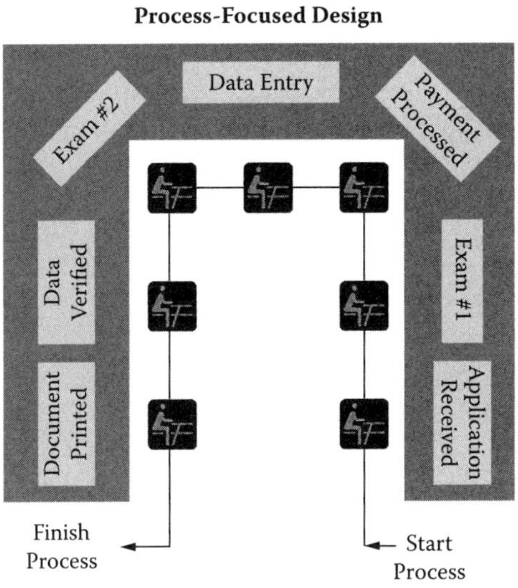

Process-Focused Design

FIGURE 11.17
Processing and moving one document at a time.

nearly a kilometer of travel (three and four flights, respectively, above the receiving dock where the applications came in). Also, the applications were moved in batches of 250 in boxes containing 50 applications and 5 boxes per shipment. Each application was in a large, clear plastic envelope containing all elements of the application (i.e., photos, application form, references, personal history, current documents, testimonials, witness documents). The idea of moving one or a few applications at a time was just not seen as feasible because of the amount of transportation, motion, and overprocessing required. In other words, the amount of waste needed to be covered up (amortized) by creating large batches of production. It would be absurd, after all, to move one application at a time, 3,700 feet. Actually, no one even knew about or recognized this amount of wasteful movement because it was well hidden in the existing functional organization. It was only revealed in the treasure hunt. In addition to the data collected, the following wastes (Figure 11.18), were collected by the wasteologists. The task was to eliminate this waste through the first steps of the experiment by moving workstations and functions as close together, in sequence, as possible and process at the pace the next operator could handle. There is no point in opening 250 applications in an hour if the examiner could only examine one every 10 minutes.

Waste Identified in Treasure Hunt	
• Too many steps in the process	• Lack of coordination and cooperation between Assistant Managers and Managers
• Too many reports in the system	• Big push for month-end processing (batch & queue)
• No consistent training across Agency	• Non-level processing due to different dates for electronic and paper file commitments
• Too many documents bottlenecking the print center	• Many instances of counting and recounting
• Too many recounting steps throughout process	• Excessive staging and queuing throughout process
• Too many different sizes of envelopes	• Assistant Manager's offices in middle of floor and very disruptive to flow
• Too many applications sitting in the process not moving	• Work desks are too small for tasks
• Too many unnecessary document scans	• Not all desks are in use
• Too much waiting between steps in the process	• Wasted envelopes
• Delays caused by bulk mailing	• Misprinted labels
• People always chasing missing documents	• Defective materials from supplier
• Too many people in "fire-fighting" mode	• High number of errors on postal codes
• Moving of carts across three floors in building	• Numerous system malfunctions
• Travel distance between sections on a floor	• No standard way for many activities, each time done differently
• Many boxes in the cell from QC to labels	• Elevator access sometimes restricted
• Long distance to loading dock	• Spoils handled by different group of people

FIGURE 11.18
Waste identified in the treasure hunt.

Step 5

This step separates people from equipment and workstations. The most value an employee can add to a process is to work at the current constraint point in that process, where the flow is being bottlenecked. The employee's job is to remove the cause that is impeding the value stream.

At this stage, as we were lowering the proverbial water line and processing fewer and fewer applications at a time, at any one point in the process, we were exposing disruptions and allocating people to where they were needed.

A member of the process who opened mail might best be deployed to do payment processing or data verification at any time in the process. Now that all were in close proximity and could see the flow of value to the customer, it allowed my making process constraints obvious, where the employee was needed at the moment, and how they could best countermeasure disruptions. People could float to the place where the constraint in the process currently existed. Once a process has been established, the output of the process pipe could always be limited by the narrowest point in that flow (i.e., bottleneck). If that constraint allows fewer applications through than the process demand requires, then all attention needs to be on opening up that constraint. In a process-focused design, the constraint becomes visible and obvious and resources can naturally flow to that point. The lesson here is that because we have a "long pole in the tent" does not mean we have a capacity limitation, it means we have a resource balancing issue. Of course, we would require resources that were capable of performing various tasks within that process. No longer can the allegiance be to the one particular duty, the new assignment becomes the fulfillment of customer demand. Cross-training is now a critical performance specification.

Step 6

This step is to train people to perform multiple jobs within the process.

The purpose is to fulfill customer demand, not optimize a specific function; therefore, each role now needs to be geared to working on the activity that best allows customer value to be delivered. Always ask: What is the best thing that can be done to enhance customer demand at this point? This is achieved by understanding what skills are needed to operate the process and then designing a matrix of people and processes (Figure 11.19).

	Identify skills people need to perform jobs in the process						
Name	Open and Triage	Exam #1	Process Payment	Data entry	Exam #2	Verify Data	Print Docs
Jack	X	X	X	X	X	X	X
Helen	X		X			X	
Bill		X			X		
Minnie	X		X	X		X	

FIGURE 11.19
Creating flexibility in the horizontal process flow through multi-skilling.

There also should be natural passing zones, where jobs can be grouped or made interchangeable as required. For example, process payment and data entry may be seen as one activity or within a passing zone.

Finally, as part of managing a continuous flow operation, it's important to simplify instructions and operations, including software applications, data entry templates, and operating conventions. Visual management (i.e., pictures and signs) is an excellent way to achieve standard work, consistency of performance, and easy cross-training. (Note: For more about Visual Management, please visit http://thoughtware.ca)

Since bottleneck tasks need additional resources, we can assume that nonbottleneck activities need less resources. Rather than have those resources continue to operate and exacerbate the constraint, it would be better to have them only produce enough of that particular job to meet customer demand. In other words, stop producing when the downstream operations in the process no longer can consume any more volume at that point.

Step 7

This step means producing at the rate of consumption.

It is much easier to pull a string than push a string. Once we had completed Steps 1 through 6, we were *entitled* to pull rather than push the string. Pulling means producing at the rate of consumption, as measured by the customer's requirements, which are at the farthest downstream point of the process and where demand is set and the upstream pull is established. Again, there is no use opening 400 applications every hour if the consumption rate is only 325 every hour. Instead, it would be better to use the cross-training capability developed in Steps 5 and 6 to reallocate that resource to a point where only 250 applications an hour can be handled (i.e., a bottleneck or constraint in the process). As mentioned in Chapter 7 (Performance on Purpose), we need to establish the demand and then design upstream through our end-to-end value delivery process. For example, if we required 2.5 million applications per annum (i.e., 325 an hour), we needed to design our flow to produce 325 every hour or 5.4 per minute. This is the cadence or pace of the process, as a quantifiable design point for the process. The documents were sent to printing at the rate printing could consume them, which should match the rate the customer is demanding them. Speed matches

No. of Hours per Day to Process the Document Applications = 7
No. of Document Applications Required per Day = 1623

$$\frac{7 \text{ hours (or 25,200 seconds)}}{1623 \text{ Documents}} \qquad \begin{array}{c} 1 \text{ Document every} \\ 15.53 \text{ seconds} \end{array}$$

Customer Demand: 1623 Documents examined every day

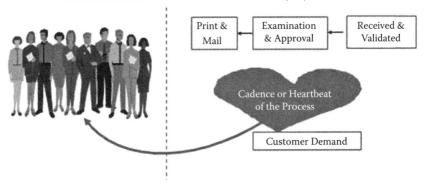

FIGURE 11.20
The purpose of the process can be defined by its demand: one (secure) document delivered to a customer every 16 seconds.

the demand rate or at least that is the equation for which the process is solving. Solving the equation of meeting customer demand comes from the ongoing experiments needed to eliminate the disruptions to flow impacting customer demand (Figure 11.20).

Step 8

The last step is distributing work evenly.

Capacity comes from the ability to continually reduce the processing batch size through the elimination of waste while increasing throughput and reducing the cycle time from end to end; thereby, driving down costs (i.e., *throughput:* more out the end of the process; *cycle time:* less time from end to end; and costs: more through with the same investment base). These are the three operating dimensions of process that drive ROCE (return on capital employed). As discussed earlier, these work in unison with one another. The key for meeting this equation is to level-load and even out the flow, like an old-time fire brigade handing off buckets of water at a constant pace and seamless flow.

Simple Passport Application	Treasure Hunt Observations	Results of the Experiment
Quantity of Activities	95	18
Quantity of Value-Adding Activities	10	10
% of Activities Adding Value	10.5%	55%
Distance Traveled (feet)	3730 feet	60
Elapsed Time (days)	23 days	2 days* (24 hours security alert posted)
Value-Adding Time (min)	44 min	14
% of Time Adding Value	0.003%	.052%
Quantity of Hand-offs	21	5
Quantity of Stage Points	22	1
Quantity of Staging	12668	<200

FIGURE 11.21
Found treasure: Experiment results.

After redesigning, the Agency as a process-focused operation, they ran an experiment for 90 days and achieved the following results:

- Throughput increased by 26%
- Cycle time reduced by 91%
- Cost per application reduced by 18.9%
- Rejected applications reduced from 33% to 11.9%

The real eye opener was the before and after comparison from the data collected in the treasure hunt (Figure 11.21).

GETTING STARTED

Based on over 1,600 treasure hunts and thousands of experiments, I have set out a partial list of the types of treasures to look for on your treasure hunt journey. These are based on the fundamental principle of respect for people and a disruption to the flow of value to the customer. It shifts the focus from the individual to the process. Most people are doing their best; the problem is always a process issue and there is a reason for everything. We can best work together through our experiments to understand the reasons for the problem, learning, and adapting as we go. We need to focus on the primacy of process, its purpose to deliver customer value, the measures of the capability of the process to meet the purpose, and actions through respect for people and experimentation. The critical starting point is always value. Value can only be defined by the customer and only meaningful when defined in specific terms (i.e., mathematical delivery cadence). However, value is created by the producer, from the customer's perspective, but for a host of reasons that value is very hard for the producer to define. This is because they lack a process perspective, process thinking, and a process mind—the new thoughtware.

Treasures

- Complex solutions tend to produce more waste and are harder for people to manage.
- Unnecessary movement and steps of people. Enter data once and use common formats.
- Producing more than the exact transactions the customer wants, when the customer wants them.
- People working at cross purposes and the effort required to correct the outcome.
- The effort used to complete an unnecessary or inappropriate assignment is waste.
- Resources lost as people wait for information, a meeting, a signature, a returned phone call, a copier or computer down, etc.
- All movement that does not add value, such as walking and waiting.
- Any nonoptimally performed work (employees may be hard at work, but there is a better way to do the job).
- Energy used for supervision or monitoring that does not produce sustainable, long-term improvements in overall performance.
- Resources expended to compensate and/or correct outcomes that deviate from expected or typical outcomes.
- The effort used to arbitrarily change a process without understanding all the consequences, and the effort required to compensate or correct the unexpected consequences of the arbitrary change.
- Value lost as a result of employing processes that satisfy short-term goals, but do not add value to customers or shareholders.
- Effort required for correction of unpredictable process outcomes due to initially unknown causes.
- Energy wasted because a job is not done the best way by all those who do it.

- Processes competing with one another.
- Resources wasted by compensating for poorly scheduled activities.
- Resources used to create and maintain informal processes that replace "official" processes or conflict with other informal processes.
- Resources invested in material or information that piles up between workstations.
- Efforts used for inspection and rework.
- Resources required to duplicate work that is rendered useless by an error.
- Effort required to change data, formats, and reports between process steps and owners.
- Resources required to repair the consequences of or compensate for the absence of key data.
- The effort required to transfer information (or material) within an organization that is not fully integrated into the process chain being used.
- Effort employed to deal with unnecessary information or the effort required to fix problems that it causes.
- Effort used to create incorrect information or deal with the consequences of it.
- All process resources that are applied to a service before they are required, all raw material that is not being used, and all material that is ready to be shipped, but is being held.
- Resources expended in midprocess that cannot yet be used by downstream process steps.
- Resources tied up in equipment and buildings that are not maximally utilized.
- All transport of material and information, except that used to deliver products and services directly to customers.
- Delays, long setups, and unplanned downtime of equipment, people, and processes.
- Poor data, poor specifications, missing information, late arrivals, and inadequate training.
- The movement of materials or information that does not add value to the product/service, such as double and triple handling of goods or data and the needless movement and reentering of information.
- Inaccurate, incomplete, or late information.
- Any kind of idleness (queue)—visible as well as invisible—including equipment, information, requests, people, and all inventories.

- Arrangement of equipment, people, workstations, and supply locations.
- Technology that is not available and appropriate.
- Technology for technology's sake.
- Rework/returns/damage, mistakes, defects.

For more than 20 years, I have challenged management in organizations around the world—in every imaginable type of business—to understand process, dig into their operations, and undertake extreme immersion to discover the buried treasure in every process and experiment. And, when they have, the results are indisputable and the improvement exceptional. This is because process is the preeminent, driving force behind performance improvement.

Let the treasure hunting abound and the experimentation begin.

12

Carrots Aren't for Everybody

The first lesson of economics is scarcity, there is never enough of anything to satisfy all those who want it ... first lesson of politics is to ignore the first lesson of economics.

Thomas Sowell

IF IT WAS EASY, EVERYONE WOULD BE DOING IT

To borrow from Thomas Sowell's insight above, the process mind knows that long-term sustainable growth is only available through process and, yet, it recognizes that this growth is regularly trumped by daily, firefighting realities driven by a short-term view that manifests itself in the dictum, "make the month." It seems that all the elements of the process mind are valid until the functional organization intervenes.

Not long ago, I was facilitating a CEO roundtable discussion and we were talking about the difficulty of fighting the organization's immune system and breaking through the bozone layer (see Chapter 4, section The Imperative Is Imperative). Frank, a CEO of a large company in Connecticut, shared what he called, the Carrot Diet. He had heard it from someone else and said he didn't know its origin, but considered the principle transcendent. [*Author's note: I have researched its origin, but can find nothing beyond anonymous.*] Frank was referring to a colleague's frustration with the lack of return on his investment in another vaunted performance improvement program. Why would a process-focused approach to performance improvement be any different? The story started with: Success in business is like the Carrot Diet.

If you master the secret of the Diet, you will be successful at what you do. Here is his story:

THE CARROT DIET

The Carrot Diet is a straightforward technique for safely losing weight. The concept is simple: eat one pound of raw carrots a half-hour before every meal or snack; not cooked, not juiced, not sticks—just whole, raw carrots. After eating one pound of carrots, you may eat anything and everything else you like. You don't need to count fat grams or worry about calories and if you want hot fudge sundaes, go for it. That's it, pretty easy, right? It requires no special menus or equipment and it works every time. And, yet, experience demonstrates that not one person in a hundred is successful with the Carrot Diet, even for a day or two (similar to the documented success rate of continuous improvement programs). People fail in their resolve because they do not know the secret of the Carrot Diet and without the secret, it does not work. Frank then led us through a tale of a carrot application gone wrong in his fellow CEO's business, where they were trying to apply the carrot approach to achieve performance improvement.

Initially, everyone rallied around and supported the initiative, the Total Company Carrot Program (TCCP). Everyone was ready and eager to eat carrots whenever called upon. The mission was clear and all the promotional material was created: carrot coffee cups, carrot notepaper cubes, and laminated carrot cards. Things seemed to be going well until the first carrots appeared on the employees' already full plates. Problems arose. On the manufacturing floor, they complained that they didn't have time to eat carrots. They said, "We know carrots are important, but do you want carrots or production? We don't have time for both." They promised to eat a few carrots when things slowed down. But, things never slowed down. The engineers began work on improvements to the carrot approach. They determined that carrots worked because of the beta-carotene. So, instead of actually eating carrots, which they agreed were more appropriate for manufacturing people, they decided they could take a beta-carotene pill each day and get the benefits of hundreds of carrots. They ate no carrots. Human Resources discovered some potential problems with the carrot approach. The labor contract never actually said workers had to chew on the job and meat-lovers on the workforce might be offended by the focus on a vegetable. So, Human Resources recommended that carrots be put on hold until these issues were researched. Wanting to set an example, they ate no carrots and were careful not to speak of the orange vegetable. To ensure Carrot Diet success, the information technology people suggested development of a carrot-consumption tracking program. That way, all levels of management would be able to plan and monitor the results of the carrot initiative. Staff members said they could design and install such a system in 15 months for about $350,000. They recommended that carrots be postponed until the system was beta-tested. Preliminary carrot calculations indicated a huge profit as a result of the initiative, but upon further analysis, the accounting department discovered carrots were not in the budget and the accounting system did not have a line item to track carrot expenditures. Worse, there wasn't a labor code to assign to carrot-eating time. Was it training or straight labor? Accounting suggested a delay in eating carrots until these questions could be addressed. The president, Frank's friend, who fully endorsed the initiative, spent countless hours in support of the TCCP. To demonstrate senior commitment, he visited every company location and gave kickoff speeches. He approved a carrot newsletter, carrot pens, and carrot golf shirts. He renamed the executive conference room the Carrot War Room and had walls covered with mission statements, plans, and statistics. Unfortunately, the president was not able to stay completely focused on TCCP because other business issues demanded his attention. New opportunities and day-to-day activities consumed much of his time, so he delegated TCCP to another executive who, unfortunately, was also very busy. As you can guess, the initiative gradually declined into failure. Despite the good intentions and everyone supporting the concept, few carrots were eaten. A year later, the only evidence of carrots at the company was the occasional laminated wallet card on an empty desk.

THE CARROT SECRET

Frank asked and answered this question: Did the company fail because the carrot approach failed? No. The company failed not because the idea was wrong, but because the execution, the deployment, was wrong; because management did not understand the secret to the carrot approach. Many people think the secret is that you have to eat carrots. This is true, you do have to eat them. However, that's not the secret. The secret is this: *There is no alternative to eating the carrots. No exceptions.* It doesn't matter how smart you are, how intuitive your insights, or how computer-literate you are. And no matter what you do, from quantum research to hand-assembled toys, you have to take carrots, snap them off, chew them up, and swallow them down. These fundamental actions must be clearly identified and measured every day if anyone expects to effectively do anything new. That's the secret: Eat your carrots every day before every meal, even if you are busy and full—especially when you are busy and full. Eating your carrots is the only way to overcome the resistance of the functional organization.

By the way, Frank learned from his friend's experience and he has successfully had his people eat their carrots. He went on to explain how the change was evident everywhere. His concluding comment was most appropriate to our discussion: "Our business is now running on a healthy diet of process thinking because of the carrot secret."

Inherent in the carrot story are a few key points about the process mind:

- Changing the way we think, like dieting, is not easy, but it can be done. And, the long-term health of the business depends on it.
- Changing to a better way of working and overcoming bozone inertia can be done, but it requires understanding, commitment, and extreme emersion at every level.
- If exceptions undermine the rule, the rule falters and fails. Many impediments to process thinking are self-inflicted by policy, which runs counter to the five principles of process thinking: (1) only do what the customer values, (2) remove all obstacles that prevent flow, (3) make problems visible, (4) use disciplined methodology to solve problems, and (5) the people doing the work know best.
- Without respect for people, no diet will work.

Strict adherence to a carrot diet is the only way to embed these principles and practices. Go treasure hunting and learn through experimentation.

One of the challenges of process thinking, or a carrot diet, is the pedagogy itself. My experience suggests there are four basic pedagogies used in trying to deliver performance improvement and the application of each depends on the need, circumstances, and appropriate fit. New thoughtware does not consider these right or wrong, rather they are appropriate or inappropriate. However, the only effective approach in creating a continuous process improvement capability to expose problems with people willing and able to resolve the problems is through a learn-and-adapt methodology (No. 4 below).

Four Basic Pedagogies to Deliver Performance Improvement:

1. **The Top-down Approach:** Thou shalt be a process-focused organization. The boss dictates from on high. Sometimes benevolent dictatorships work, but not in most cases and not for long. In the middle of a battle, when bullets are flying, someone has to dictate the action. Management's role in this approach is to articulate the "why" of purpose, break down the silos, respect the people, and manage cash and customer value.

2. **The Episodic Approach:** Major change led by major event imple-mentation. That's the TQM (Total Quality Management) model. It came out of Japan when management brought back tools like Quality Circles. They became the rage, but they were only tools and led to dis-appointment and discredit. Episodic programs like Quality Circles, when grafted onto vertical structures, don't work because they are programs, not business models. You have never seen a Quality Circle or TQM or Six Sigma plant or organization, but you will see process-focused plants and organizations. The flaw in the episodic approach can be seen in programs that are set up so people from various functions meet every Tuesday for discussions. Decisions are made and then everyone goes back to work in their traditional functions. It's not integrated into the collective thoughtware or process; it's just an event, which may work if it's a well-defined task (i.e., assessing and installing a new computer system).

3. **The Expert Approach:** Bring in a Six Sigma expert to teach standard deviation and lead people through it. Six Sigma requires an expert steeped in particular knowledge and content. Making it stick is the problem. Six Sigma can be effective on major projects (i.e., the $20-bill problems), but it is not effective on most of the problems inherent in the process (i.e., the daily pennies). It's like bringing in an elephant gun to tackle a mouse problem. Obviously, it depends on what the problem is, but the issue with Six Sigma is that it is not process-focused. Not to mention that the training requires long lead times (e.g., 20 days over a 4-month period), it's expensive and 90% of the problems it's trying to solve can be solved with the seven critical tools that Dr. Ishikawa taught (i.e., histograms, cause-effect diagrams, check-sheets, Pareto, flow charts, control charts, scatter diagrams). These simple but profound techniques can be taught in four days, or six 20-minute learning modules. Or as needed.

4. **The Learn-and-Adapt Approach:** This approach is the new thought-ware and the cornerstone of continuous improvement: experiment-ing, discovering, learning, adapting. Act. Learn. Reflect. Adapt. Then move forward. Make a change, see how it works, and how it could work better. It's continual experimentation, and the experiment is always successful because you learn more. That's new thoughtware. It's the scientific method that Western civilization has used for the past 1,000 years to solve problems. It's used for validation of reliability through trial and error.

Process thinking is grounded in the Learn-and-Adapt Approach. The other approaches are appropriate or inappropriate depending on the circumstances, but success comes from extreme emersion by the people in the process. Learn-and-adapt is difficult because people are engrossed in well-established practices and managers are not comfortable with the scientific method based on trial and error. They are comfortable with decision-making based on past experience; they are masters of business, not masters of fine arts and not good at failing and then rethinking, trying again, and improving. It is foreign to the way they think. However, when people understand that the purpose is to improve the process and they are allowed to experiment and learn, then the thinking changes and it begins to stick. And then the sky is the limit. In all my experience, when management sets an objective of, say, "increase capacity by 20% in three months," and then lets the people experiment their way to that goal, the results are always extraordinary.

Nothing illustrates this approach better than when I take people on a treasure hunt and ask them a few questions about what they saw. They easily point out that there were, for example, 42 steps of which only 3 steps added any value. I ask them what they think of 0.27% value-added. They are usually somewhere between shocked and embarrassed. I ask if they think they could get that percentage from, let's say, 0.27 to 5%? "Heck, yes, tomorrow," is the typical response. My next question is: What would you do differently? There is never a shortage of ideas. Sometimes there's a bit of finger pointing, but we quickly move to a no-blame culture because the waste and the 0.27% is the reality and nobody is at fault. I also get them thinking about how to improve things without spending money—not a nickel. How would they design a process with no waste? What would it look like? I know they know. The guys at ABC Adhesives have been doing what they do for years; they know. Soon, there is a collective conversation and a productive dialogue about a better way of doing things and, in no time, something has improved, and then they do it again—and again. It is process innovation, the catalyst of performance improvement.

TECHNOLOGY IS NOT A PANACEA

Inherent in most of this discussion about continuous process improvement is the old thoughtware that tries to solve capacity problems with technology, specifically business management software. Companies spend millions on bringing in a suite of integrated applications that a company can use to store and manage data from every stage of business, including selling, ordering, planning, scheduling, building, shipping, and costing. The claim is that the system will provide an integrated real-time view of core business processes, using common databases maintained by a database management system, to track business resources—cash, raw materials, production capacity—and the status of business commitments: orders, purchase orders, and payroll. However, multimillion-dollar enterprise-wide system software mirrors the functionalized organization it is selling to, managing multiple interdependent variables as discrete resource points, with little regard for understanding and improvement of the business process. We don't need to report on our processes, we need to eliminate the waste in them. All the information required can be extracted through a treasure hunt and its problem-solving tools and techniques. Over the past decade, IT investments have become the largest category of capital expenditure in American businesses; however, none of them are geared to the core task of creating processes that expose disruption in the flow of value to the customer and give employees the information required to fix these disruptions before they reach the customer.

These systems are essentially another fix-the-resource solution. They don't always work. As I mentioned earlier, the traditional thinking behind centralized information systems is one of building a *reliable* process, but the process-focused organization is looking not to reliability, but to building an *adaptive* process that can respond to incessant variation. These management information systems eliminate the ability of the people in the process to solve the problem. It's a classic example of trying to use technology to build in reliability when what is really needed is more adaptability and flexibility.

TECHNOLOGY CAN'T REPLACE AIR TRAFFIC CONTROLLERS

The idea of buying an enterprise-wide software management information system to schedule a distribution center or plant is not only old thoughtware, it's fundamentally impossible. As I said in Chapter 2, there is a real difference between investing in capability and capacity. A colleague of mine once shared with me a brilliant analogy of air traffic control and the folly of forecasting, scheduling, and trying to control multiple active, dependent variables with a passive, distant information system.

An air traffic controller can "sell" slots to land a plane and build what we might call capacity planning and give lead time indicators to pilots (i.e., vendors, suppliers), but they can't schedule moment-to-moment because there is too much dependency and too many variables. You might schedule a plane to land in Nashville at 9:02, but that is dependent on traffic at O'Hara in Chicago, weather, overbooking, and many other factors. An air traffic controller can do all the scheduling he/she wants, but he/she has to be ready to adapt, on a moment's notice. The same in a distribution center. You can schedule all the workflow (i.e., trucks for a week), but you know the reality will be quite different. Because there's too much interdependency in the process and every day, every hour, every minute there are variables. So, trying to build an algorithm or framework to predict dependent variables is impossible.

Think of your employees as air traffic controllers, overseeing a crucial process all day long.

The only way to deal with dependent variables is to go into the process, directly observe the process, understand it, and give the people the power to make moment-to-moment decisions as the variables occur, like any clear-thinking supervisor does with the air traffic controller. Think of your employees as air traffic controllers, overseeing a crucial process all day long. If you do, they will create a faster, better, safer process than you can imagine.

I am not saying technology will not continue to be critical to business enterprises. Virginia Rometty, the chief executive of IBM, claims that "data" constitutes a vast new natural resource, which promises to be for the twenty-first century what steam power was for the eighteenth, electricity for the nineteenth, and hydrocarbons for the twentieth.[1] We are currently overwhelmed with these data and technology is helping us sort it into decisional information. There are more than 1 trillion interconnected and intelligent objects and organisms, including 1 billion transistors for every person on the planet and about 2.7 billion of those people are currently connected to the Internet.[2] No doubt, powerful new computing systems can sort and make sense of this data in an incredibly rapid fashion. But not like humans. We need the real-time, contextual, tactile, and actionable type of data that can only be gleaned from the process by real-time, direct observation of the process through treasure hunting. We need new thoughtware as much as new software.

Some years ago, I worked with a commercial furniture company in North America who predominantly supplied large chain hotels. When they received an order for 400 rooms from, say, International Hotel Group, they proceeded to make 400 credenzas, 400 bathroom cabinets, 400 headboards, and 400 of whatever items were required. However, business began to dry up when China rose with its seemingly limitless supply of low-cost labor, an artificially low currency, and significant government incentives to attract foreign investment. The Chinese could land (i.e., manufacture, ship, and deliver) a complete set of products for the hotel at about half the price that the North American company could build them. So, the company adopted a process mind and began a three-year journey to realign the organization as a process-focused, low-batch, high-velocity, and customer-focused business. They applied the Purpose–Measure–Action model. They used process thinking to increase the capacity and drive down the price and survived by being able to diversify the business and build customized, one-off projects like courthouse furniture that was not amenable to China because it was too customized. They became nimble and cost effective. China's labor advantage is coming down and, by 2015, the Boston Consulting Group estimates that China's labor cost advantage will be down to 39%, from 55%.[3] Despite this advantage, labor accounts for only a small portion of the overall cost of manufacturing and when transportation, duties, supply chains, and industrial real estate are fully accounted for, North America becomes a competitive option. This is true if—and it's an iffy if—we actually do redesign our organizations from sluggish functional parts to sleek process flows. When the furniture company became a process-focused organization and labor rates came down in China and the costs went up in transportation, they took back the big hotel project business in North America. They learned how to build small lot sizes instead of building batches of credenzas and began building a room at a time (i.e., all the pieces needed in a room). And, when they had a whole floor ready, they shipped it, which was advantageous to the customer, the installation contractor. The contractor coordinated cranes and people on a floor-by-floor basis and didn't have to store furniture because it arrived as the floor was ready to accept it. The critical lesson in this example is that a North American company can compete and thrive regardless of the location if—and it's a big if—they adapt and redesign their operating system based on process thinking.

WHAT THE PROCESS MIND SEES—AT A GLANCE

The chart in Figure 12.1 shows, at a glance, the fundamental comparison of old and new thoughtware.

Vertical -Focused Shareholder Perspective	The Organization's Thoughtware System	Process-Focused Customer Perspective	The Process Mind
Provide Shareholder Value (*e.g., meet the month*)	Purpose is...	Fulfilling Customer Value (*e.g., fulfill customer demand*)	Profit is generated by meeting customers' needs repeatedly...shareholder value comes from meeting analysts' short-term expectations
Departments/ Functions (*e.g., sales department*)	Structure is...	Business Processes (*e.g., demand generation process*)	Products and services flow horizontally...organizations are designed vertically
Targets (*e.g., units shipped*)	Focus is...	Capability (*e.g., inventory turns*)	Targets are useless if the process is not capable
Cost Management -Unit Cost (*e.g., economies of scale*)	Financial Guidance is...	Cash flow (*e.g., economies of flow*)	Cash and inventory don't lie...the rest is creative accounting architecture
Control people (*e.g., avoid mistakes*)	Role of Management is...	Teach people (*e.g., learn and adapt*)	...to be successful...fail more
Evaluative (*e.g., after the fact judgement*)	Measure of success is...	Navigational (*e.g., real-time lead indicators*)	The purpose of a measure is to help understand and improve the process, then incite action on that process
Applied to discrete resources (*e.g., equipment utilization*)	Activities are...	Applied to the workflow (*e.g., equipment availability*)	Managing discrete resources causes costs to go up...*always*; managing workflow causes costs to go down...*always*
Separate from the work itself (*e.g., information factory-computer reports*)	Basis of decision making is...	Integrated with the Work itself (*e.g., visual management-direct observation*)	Information Factories provide after-the-fact interpretation of what happened...direct observation is the truth

FIGURE 12.1
Looking at the Thoughtware of the enterprise and how it changes when seen from a Process-Focused perspective.

THINK ABOUT IT

I have used the stories about carrot diets, air traffic controllers, hotel furniture, and all the organizations in these chapters in an attempt to bring to life the purpose of this book, which is to help you begin to see the intrinsic primacy and power of process in your organization and recognize its unparalleled potential to improve performance to, as yet unimagined, heights. I realize that the primacy of process and the understanding of its potential is caught in the conundrum of being simple and straightforward, and, yet, hard to see and difficult, primarily because it is hidden under a century of now out-dated and ineffective thoughtware. Until we introduce new thoughtware and begin to, literally, see our organizations differently, nothing much is going to change in a sustainable way. Worldwide, the evidence is unequivocal and this hypothesis has been proven. We need only begin to develop and apply the process mind.

REFERENCES

1. Sirkin, H. L., M. Zinser, and D. Hohner. 2011. *Made in America, again.* Boston: The Boston Consulting Group, 3.
2. The Year of the Smarter Enterprise, Economist Magazine. November 18, 2013/From the World in 2014 Print Edition. http://www.economist.com/news/21589108-new-model-firm-its-way-says-virginia-rometty-chief-executi-.
3. Ibid.

Index

A

ABC Adhesives, 40–43, 113–114, 151
Action, 185, *See also* Experimentation;
      Treasure hunting
  learning requires failure, 190
  leveraging power of the people, 195
  Purpose-Measure-Action model, 19,
      143, 185–186, 245
  visualizing target condition, 232–233
Air traffic controller, 276
Amazon, 33, 35–36
Amortization, 160, 199–200
Analyzing current condition, 215–225
Analyzing the current condition, *See also*
      Treasure hunt findings report
Analyzing the new process, 229–230
APICS, 153–154
Apple, xxi, 21–22, 24–25, 29–34, 44, 84,
      90, 132
Archeologist/pacer, 209–210
Assembly line manufacturing system,
      53–54
Average unit cost (AUC), 12–13

B

Balanced Scorecard, 125–130
Bank Corp, 34
Barra, Mary, 64
Batch and queue thinking, 6–13, 39, 135
  moving to continuous process flow,
      57–59
Berkshire Hathaway, 84
Best Buy, 33
BlackBerry, 22–23
Boeing, 55, 151–153, 154, 156
Bottlenecks, 239, 240, 260–262
Bozone layer, 86, 269
Buffett, Warren, 44
Business models, 31, 87–88, 97
  software development, 163

Business process outsourcing (BPO),
      4–6, 8, 33
  process-focused measures, 8–9
  process improvement results, 9–13

C

Capability, 107–108
  capacity versus, 139, 275
  measures, 18, 123, 171–172
  targets versus, 164–165
Capacity
  all about process, 139–141
  availability versus utilization
      mentality, 114
  capability versus, 139, 275
  as opportunity, not waste, 41–43
  technology and, 70, 139–140, 274–275
  throughput and cycle time, 263
Carrot Diet, 269–272
Cash flow process, 93–94
Cell phone plans, 161–162
Changeover time reduction, 160
Chennai Paradox, xx, 1–4, 13, 105
China, 85, 90–91, 139, 277
Circuit City, 33
Collaboration, 75
Complexity, 158, 246, 251
Context of information, 179
Continuous process improvement, 72–73,
      153–155, 245, *See also* Lean;
      Process thinking/process mind
  constancy of purpose, 68
  experimentation and process redesign
      methodology, 246–264,
      See also Experimentation;
      Process redesign
  fads, 67
  failures of Lean, xv–xvi, 60, 61, 66
  lack of success, xv–xvi, 48–49, 73–74,
      See also Management resistance
      to process improvement